PEREGRINE

POWER, VIOLENC

Power, Violence, Decision, writes the autho
The first is that politics is both necessary an
politics is an autonomous form of human act
explained away. The third is that political part of political action; they are action, not merely understanding or explanation.'

Politics is about decision-making and one of its motive forces is violence or fear of violence. Using source material which ranges from Marx to Kurt Vonnegut, Professor Mackenzie attempts an unprecedented synthesis of the motive forces behind decision-making.

The ambiguous myth of Prometheus, most recently used by Robert Lowell to express America's situation in the 1960s, is taken as an underlying theme. And, against a background of myth and poetry, the author skilfully points out the metaphors to which the social sciences have recourse in their attempts to tame these concepts of power, violence and decision.

W. J. M. Mackenzie was born in 1909 in Edinburgh and educated at Balliol College, Oxford, where he was a classical scholar, and Edinburgh University, where he took a law degree. At Oxford he taught classics from 1933 to 1936 and politics from 1936 to 1948, apart from the war, when he served for five years as a civil servant with the Air Staff and with the Joint Staff Mission in Washington. In 1949 he became Professor of Government at Manchester University, and in 1966 he was appointed to a chair in the Department of Politics at Glasgow University. From 1952 to 1960 he was an adviser on East African constitutional development; and since 1959 he has been an adviser on the development of English regional and local government. He was awarded the C.B.E. in 1963.

With J. W. Grove, Professor Mackenzie has written *Central Administration in Britain* (1957). He has also written *Free Elections* (1958), *British Government since 1918* (1950), *The Study of Political Science Today* (1972), *Politics and Social Science* (Penguin Books, 1967), and, with K. Robinson, he has edited *Five Elections in Africa* (1959).

W. J. M. MACKENZIE

Power, Violence, Decision

PENGUIN BOOKS

Penguin Books Ltd, Harmondsworth, Middlesex, England
Penguin Books Inc., 7110 Ambassador Road, Baltimore, Maryland 21207, U.S.A.
Penguin Books Australia Ltd, Ringwood, Victoria, Australia
Penguin Books Canada Ltd, 41 Steelcase Road West, Markham, Ontario, Canada
Penguin Books (N.Z.) Ltd, 182–190 Wairau Road, Auckland 10, New Zealand

—

First published 1975

—

—

Made and printed in Great Britain by
Cox & Wyman Ltd, London, Reading and Fakenham
Set in Monotype Plantin

—

CONTENTS

PREFACE

THIS book has three guiding principles.

The first is that politics is both necessary and dangerous.

The second is that politics is an autonomous form of human action; to be understood, not to be explained away.

The third is that political words are an integral part of political action; they are action, not merely understanding or explanation.

The last point will be made more fully in the next chapter. The first two may be summed up by saying that politics is about decision-making by or for human collectivities, and that one of its motive forces is violence or the fear of violence – perhaps in general the fear of violence rather than the act. To a great extent, politicians skate on the thin ice of the sea of violence; perhaps better, they are managers of violence and succeed only in so far as they accept Conrad's maxim:

> In the destructive element immerse ... To follow the dream, and again to follow the dream – and so – *ewig – usque ad finem*[1] ...

The ambiguities of the word 'decision' will be explored in Part IV; it is used by analogy in talking of the 'decisions' of machines and animals, but it is argued here that the basis of the analogy lies in human self-consciousness and in human social procedures, and that the word 'decision' is a word of action, not of illusion. It is easy to say this, difficult to construe; there is extraordinary unanimity in the use of 'action language' by modern theorists, across the board, Christians, Marxists, existentialists, sociologists, psychiatrists, alike.[2] But their meanings, it seems, are

1. Joseph Conrad, *Lord Jim*, p. 216 of 1928 edition.

2. The first edition of Talcott Parsons, *The Structure of Social Action*, published in 1937 (New York, McGraw-Hill), is a useful landmark, in that he was early in observing a persistent trend. Perhaps in that period we all agreed to jettison 'man's immortal soul' – and then we surreptitiously put it back again. Cf. C. R. Wallraff, writing of Jaspers' teaching in the 1930s: 'People spoke of *Existenz* rather than the "soul"': *Karl Jaspers: An Introduction to his Philosophy* (Princeton UP; 1970) p. 8.

not the same. Similarly, there is a remarkable degree of agreement that human action takes place within a framework of events explicable in terms of natural laws: 'I cannot by taking thought add one cubit to my stature'[3] – but there are knowable relationships between genetic inheritance, climate, nutrition and other factors. If it were possible to use human beings as laboratory animals (which it is not, and the reasons are ethical and political), it would not be particularly hard *within limits* to control the stature of the next generation (or groups drawn from it) by 'scientific' means.[4]

Perhaps this is only the old story of 'freedom' and 'necessity'; the old antinomy crops up in many languages and in many epochs, and no progress is made towards reconciliation or even towards an agreed statement.

As regards method, I have found myself in agreement with P. C. Lloyd, that 'social science frequently operates with sets of opposed generalizations'.[5] In fact, I have not regarded it as part of the political scientist's job to attack questions that are too big for him – the destiny of man and his universe. I am not even sure that there can be found 'top level generalizations', such that they have a scientific rather than ideological character. To be told that 'if you understood our theory you would see that it explains *everything*' makes me suspicious. I fear – am literally *frightened* by – the situation described by MacIntyre in relation to Freud's disciples, by Wallraff in relation to existentialism: 'the way in which the very use of the vocabulary commits the novice – quite unconsciously – to acceptance of a complex theoretical framework'[6]: the contrast drawn by Wallraff (p. 12) between the con-

3. *Matthew*, VI, 27.

4. 'There is a famous quotation from Engels, to the effect that men make their history themselves but in a given environment that conditions them.' Quoted, from Sartre's use of it, by David Cooper in R. D. Laing and D. G. Cooper, *Reason and Violence* (Tavistock, 1964): see also Louis Althusser's reference to Engels and Sartre at p. 127 and elsewhere in *For Marx* (English translation, Penguin Books; 1969: French original; 1965).

5. At p. 32 of his essay on 'Conflict Theory and Yoruba Kingdoms' in I. M. Lewis, ed., *History and Social Anthropology* (ASA Monograph 7: Tavistock; 1968). See below, p. 55, note 9, p. 91 note 3

6. Alasdair MacIntyre: *Against the Self-Images of the Age* (Duckworth; 1971), at p. 29.

text of English post-war philosophy and the 'hermeneutic circle' of existentialism.

But I find it persuasive if there is an open normative appeal from general theory to faith and will (*certum est quia impossible est*[7]); even more persuasive if the positivist claims merely to provide one tool (or even 'the best' tool) of analysis among others.

At any rate, this book is concerned with middle level generalizations, and indeed the words or concepts with which it deals belong to a middle ground between normative and empirical study; perhaps for that reason relatively neglected by political scientists – too factual for the philosophers, too normative for the behaviourists.

The book therefore draws on a wide range of sources, and claims no originality except in presentation. But we are all at present struggling to find an adequate political 'world-view'; and experiments in presentation may be important.

7. Quoted from Tertullian: *De Carne Christi*, ii, 5.

January 1974.

I owe many debts too diffuse to be acknowledged here, and two specific ones; one to Michael Scott, now lecturer at the Glasgow College of Technology, for his exploration of recent American work on violence; the other to my secretary, Sheila Hamilton, without whose help there would have been no book.

W.J.M.M.

Part One

Power We've reached the end of the road, the topmost stone on the rooftop of the world.

Force Beyond here, everything is downhill.

[Robert Lowell: *Prometheus Bound*
p. 3, repeated p. 66.]

CHAPTER I

INTRODUCTORY

I remember hunting for . . . what shall I call them? Causes, knots, heads of action? . . . Each thought was like a finger touching, tampering and testing, and trying to give things a little of my bias to alter and advance. [Robert Lowell, *Prometheus Bound*, p. 50.]

THIS book arises out of my previous work on *Politics and Social Science*, published in 1967, which reflected the political and intellectual situation of 1965 and 1966. It is not a sequel, continuation or recantation, and to the best of my ability I have written it so that it can stand alone.

But nothing can stand alone without context or perspective.

Data Revolution and Behavioural Movement

Politics and Social Science represented one man's response to two related phenomena in the social sciences: 'the data revolution' and the 'behavioural movement'. The former meant that for the first time there existed technological resources for the storage, processing and analysis of political, social and economic data on a very large scale. The human species, so far as we can label and quantify its members, can be stored in the memory of a computer or inter-connected series of computers, and these data can be analysed in answer to all sorts of likely or unlikely questions about correlations and about populations.

The latter, the phrase 'behavioural movement', developed far beyond the imagination of the sponsors who launched it in the late 1940s, and historical retrospect will show that it was not stable nor coherent in character for very long. However, the emphasis throughout was on 'numeracy' as the key to 'science'; the standards set were those of quantitative psychology, at a not very advanced level. The movement in general was never clear about the further implications of the word 'behavioural'. Certainly, it recognized the scientific primacy of what could be counted;

probably it had no general view about what could appropriately be counted – certainly it had no sophistication about observer and observed, objective and subjective, communication as distinct from 'verbal behaviour'. In a word, it had not acquired the logic and techniques which make true behaviourists, such as Skinner and Eysenck, very hard to answer on their own ground; which are indeed largely right, *on their own ground.* Unlike Thoreau's *Walden*, Skinner's political Utopia, *Walden Two*, has not yet been treated adequately as a book relevant to the history of political thought.[1]

Retrospectively, I can see what happened to my argument. A logical first step would have been to take numerate politics at its highest levels, for instance in the work of Angus Campbell, Donald Stokes, and David Butler; to scrutinize this from the point of view of laboratory and survey work focused on more specific problems, with subjects less liable to distort the experiment by feed-back: and on that basis to assess what had been done, what might be done, by a strict and careful application of methods pioneered by laboratory psychologists. The best of their work can face the test of replication; replication (by and large) is beyond our resources in politics, and we do not even face the test, let alone pass it, except at the level of very small, very local propositions.

So what?

That job has still to be done, but it needs someone more rigorously trained than I have been in behavioural method and quantitative techniques, someone whose main interest lies in fields where these tactics have been successful. I have not these qualifications, and half-consciously I evaded the crux of the matter and assumed three things that I could not demonstrate; first, that there were as yet no signs of 'cumulative science' at the level of controlled study of specific problems; secondly, that the range and character of the data and the problems of 'macro-politics' would discourage a prudent 'numerate' from tackling them;[2] thirdly, that (to put it crudely) the cash resources for a

1. But Sir Karl Popper has picked up this point recently, *Objective Knowledge, An Evolutionary Approach* (OUP; 1972) at p. 222, footnote 34.

2. Science as *The Art of the Soluble*; essays by P. B. Medawar (Methuen; 1967).

large-scale long-term operation would not be available, so that one could hope at the most for an accumulation of disconnected correlations related to problems arising by accident – for instance, did the opinion polls go wrong over the British election of June 1970 and if so why?

Passing that kind of science by, I put my money on two other approaches to science, of which I find it easier to get a technical grasp; and which have a secure place in the text-books about scientific thought.

The Social Biology of Man

One of these is through the biological sciences, which have provided relatively recently a textbook case of scientific development into a new field. The stages have been (and some of them are still with us):

(1) The encyclopedist: in this case the direct observer, whether gamekeeper or parson (Gilbert White or Kilvert), or indeed Kalahari Bushman, or Amazon Indian, each in relation to his living environment.

(2) The taxonomist; and the Bushman or Amazon Indian got that far. But their taxonomies (says Lévi-Strauss) diverged from ours in directions which suited *them* better; and it is not very clear why Western taxonomy developed as it did from Aristotle through to Cuvier and Linnaeus, evading so many interesting side-tracks on its way.

(3) Perhaps geology broke the spell: taxonomy is now seen as 'The Succession of Life through Geological Time';[3] once the fixity of species had gone, there arose the question *Why* do things change?

(4) And so to a general theory of evolution, which has many controversies but is as solidly based as any science on general theory, direct observation, and experiment.

(5) Finally, and in my life time, observation, experiment and theory have advanced beyond 'explanation' of the individual animal to explanation of the social existence of the species in its habitat. When you see a robin in the garden now, you should not

3. A British Museum publication: sixth edn; 1964.

see only a little brown bird with a red breast and a peculiarly impudent and confiding manner: you should see also this robin in relation to other robins, in their annual cycle of mating, birth and death, and in relation to the resources of the environment and to competitors for them.

Hence ethology and ecology, best-sellers of the last decade; it is characteristic of the hazards of political science that these have now fed back strongly into human politics about the environment.

I had not anticipated this. I had meant to say simply that if you want to study man 'scientifically' the obvious thing to do is to start with human biology. If you want to start social inquiry with a Model of Man (H. A. Simon's title[4]) it would be sensible to explain to students what is known about human physiology at the individual level. Perhaps most of it is rather obvious, and some of it is rather uncertain and obscure; nevertheless, the physical anthropology of *homo sapiens* sets bounds to his political systems.

If one asks how strict these bounds may be, one is at once involved in problems of social biology and in the analogies and differences between human and animal ethology. It is obvious that the biological success of the human species is due largely to the plasticity of its social institutions: but to what is *that* due? and has it limits comparable to physiological limits?[5]

In this area it seems clear to me that the study of social man exists as science, with secure claims to objectivity, discovery and cumulative knowledge. At present, the field seems to break into linguistics, brain physiology, non-verbal communication, patterns of behaviour in small groups of varying duration; I may be wrong, but at any rate here are scientific frontiers, and advances are made.

As we move up the scale of size and complexity things get more difficult. Much has been and can be done in the study of more or less simple, more or less isolated societies. But they are dying, as modern man invades the New Guinea Highlands, the Amazon basin, the great deserts, the Arctic fringe.

4. *Models of Man: Social and Rational* (New York, Wiley; 1957).

5. 'Somewhere along the evolutionary line, man, developing this habit of thinking of symbols, had provided himself with more alternatives than he could manage, more systems of alternatives than he could manage.' (Brian W. Aldiss, *Greybeard*, Panther Books; 1968, p. 93).

Something has been achieved in the study of organizations, the problems of 'human engineering' in situations artificially bounded by specified purpose, dominant authority, selective recruitment. H. A. Simon includes this sort of 'engineering' among *The Sciences of the Artificial*,[6] and undoubtedly he is right to bring the analogy of engineering and applied science generally into discussion of the 'human sciences'.

Undoubtedly human social entities have been and can be 'engineered'. But it is not in fact easy to create even a relatively enclosed social entity within 'the global village'; and the study of power in modern communities has got stuck for the present, in that every 'micro' community so far studied is infected by the political, social, economic environment of a great community and feeds back into that environment. Social workers sent into small communities develop new loyalties; research workers consciously or unconsciously shape research towards the policy debates of the encapsulating great community.

So let us look at the total environment? Indeed we do; but at that level there collapse the claims of politics and sociology to advance like natural sciences, and economics does not do much better.

Heuristic Theory

Instinctively, reaching that level, I made a leap from science as observation and experiment to science as a dependant on theory which precedes observation and experiment; heuristic theory, the conceptual pre-conditions of inquiry, a framework which organizes research and cannot be displaced by it. I put my money on general systems theory, partly because of the electronically defined model of an energy-information system, which seems exact enough to be susceptible of measurement on its own ground, general enough to be fruitful in propositions about inter-connection – and these are what matter most in politics.

Much the same claims are made by Raymond Boudon for 'structuralism',[7] as are made by Von Bertalanffy for 'general

6. (MIT Press; 1969.)

7. R. Boudon (trans. Michalina Vaughan): *The Uses of Structuralism* (Heinemann; 1971).

systems theory';[8] each has its adherents, dedicated people, and this is not the place to argue whether or not the two conceptual frameworks correspond homologically (but see p. 58). The point relevant to the present context is that a 'scientific' approach does not confine us to piece-meal statistical inquiry, such as is prescribed by the behaviourists, nor to the slow development of a social biology of man as social animal. It permits, indeed encourages, the emergence of a general framework or paradigm of the universe of scientific inquiry.

These points are here made more explicitly than in *Politics and Social Science*, and indeed with more confidence. Recent controversies over the history of science point to this kind of analysis (not necessarily in this form); so do recent advances at the frontiers of what we can securely call scientific knowledge about 'social man'. But these cool judgments have not proved very relevant to the questions asked urgently by men about politics in the years since 1965.

An attempt at model-building by retrospect is very risky, even if one carefully and logically samples contemporary material. But let us at least postulate that after Hiroshima the name of science was one of appalling power. It divided the consciences of nuclear scientists; it impressed mankind for the first time with the danger of total self-destruction; it offered the promise of peace, and endless plenty, through science and its application.

Political science was a very small adherent on the margin of the scientific paradigm and its wagon-train.

The Limits of Science, the Power of Images

But now the paradigm has changed, and once again political science tags along as camp-follower. Or it would do so, if it could form for itself a clear notion of the available camps and their character. In a sense, I feel myself less alien in this territory than in that of the 'big machines': partly because, though the world is different now, yet there is a smell or flavour, or texture of the 1930s about it; partly because the intellectual style of such politics

8. Ludwig von Bertalanffy: *General Systems Theory* (New York, Braziller; 1968).

is that in which I was educated, a style of symbol and metaphor, saints and devils, myth and allegory. Gut-reaction politics, rather than scientific politics; it is very dangerous, very nasty, but traditional.

Three fairly precise remarks:

(1) It is possible to express the difference by saying that in social science political study sought objectivity. It did not deny subjectivity but sought for a standing ground outside it. But subjectivity cannot be thus expelled: not personally, in that the student feels with what he observes; not scientifically, in that men talk to him, they tell him what they think, feel and fear, by their words, expressions, gestures, modulations. One can describe objectively in terms of 'verbal behaviour', 'non-verbal communication'. But nevertheless there is a content, a meaning, which passes between man and man.

(2) Secondly, that content is not wholly nor even largely conceptual. Concepts can be teased out from it, as is done with infinite care by the best of the linguistic philosophers, those with trained ears for several languages. But men talk not concepts but words; not words only but images; not with voice only but with all the resources of tone, gesture and symbolic solidarity.

Perhaps this seems painfully banal, and indeed the field has been trampled almost to destruction by its own specialists, the literary and aesthetic analysts. Yet who can persuade social scientists to read seriously *The Road to Xanadu*,[9] *The Romantic Agony*,[10] the works of Leavis, Empson's *Seven Types of Ambiguity*,[11] the infinitely tedious commentaries on symbolist poetry, on Dada, on the images of Baroque art, the character of music as communication?[12] The case is not really hopeless; Coleridge, Nietzsche, even Wagner are creeping into the curriculum.

(3) Perhaps de Gaulle, if he had troubled (and he was himself

9. J. Livingston Lowes: *The Road to Xanadu: a study in the ways of the imagination* (Boston, Houghton Mifflin; 1927).

10. Mario Praz (trans. A. Davidson): *The Romantic Agony* (OUP; 1933).

11. (Chatto & Windus; 1930).

12. 'Invert all three axioms of conceptual reasoning, and you have the axioms of musical thought – at any rate, inasmuch as it aims at communication.' Hans Keller on 'Billy Budd': *The Listener*, 28 September 1972, p. 419.

intensely aware of politics as style and image), would have dramatized this change of focus as a challenge by France to America. Which would be rubbish – except in so far as it became the tool of a politician of genius. There is a difference; the literature of political imagination in America has been a throw-back from academic to populist in style. The best of American blacks write brilliant prose (not so Herbert Marcuse) and create style and beauty. But their style is to evade categories of style: to 'be themselves' in style, and that is about the hardest of all tricks of style to master. That is Soul.[13] Whereas the politics of revolt in France has been grounded in the aesthetic controversies of the academics, even under the slogan of 'L'imagination au pouvoir'.

It is this convergence and contrast in the use of images which awakes interest. Is the substance of politics to be found in symbols and images? Or are these the by-product of technology, of gigantic industrial structures, capitalist and socialist?[14]

13. Tony Palmer's article 'Have you got Soul?' (*Observer* colour supplement, October 1972).

14. As Roland Barthes would have it; *Mythologies* (Paris, Éditions du Seuil; 1957).

CHAPTER 2

TACTICAL

Who knows anything about God, except that his ways are dark and very seldom pleasant? [Robert Lowell, *Prometheus Bound*, p. 7.]

FIRST problem, is the book's title rightly chosen? To me, in my variant of English, power, violence, decision, thus juxtaposed, are words which together suggest the size and danger of real politics, from which academic politics dare not become detached. They interlock so as to indicate the boundaries and structure of a context, and this interweaving or entanglement is hard (for me at least) to explain by the well-tried academic rules about beginning at the beginning, proceeding to the middle and going on to the end. Indeed, what has to be explained is that (as in the mazes of Celtic decoration) one can begin at any point and proceed through any other point, with an inexhaustible choice of bifurcations and recapitulations.

Perhaps this problem can then be disintegrated into two. Do these three words convey to readers, as to me, the sense of what is serious in politics? Are readers prepared to consider as helpful to understanding the image of entangled aesthetic structure rather than that of scientific textbooks? The difference is not that between confusion and order, but that between two kinds of order. That of scientific exposition is bounded by the compulsions of sequence in time and logic. It is unilinear in three dimensions, through a series of lectures, a series of theorems, chosen to carry conviction and to impose learning. Peter Medawar has written of the scientific article as a kind of hoax;[1] an ordered public statement of what did not happen in the process of discovery. In one sense such a hoax is necessary to make science public property; a structure of propositions testable by logical consistency and by

1. Is the Scientific Paper a Fraud? (*Listener*; 12 September 1963), referred to on p. 151 of *The Art of the Soluble* (Methuen; 1967): 'the studied hypocrisy expected of a contribution to a learned journal' (*Induction and Intuition in Scientific Thought*, Methuen; 1969, p. 32).

experiments which can in principle (and often in practice) be recapitulated.

Scientific Discovery and Exposition

But the hoax of the scientific article (and *a fortiori* that of the scientific textbook) is one step, a perfectly proper one, in a process of exploration and community building. An individual explores a problem not in a linear but in a multi-dimensional way.[2] Much has been written, in a way rather baffling to non-scientists, about the process of mathematical discovery, in which the brain (a lot of rather mushy-looking cell tissue) works its way quietly and privately towards patterns of unification. And then the conscious man 'makes public' the 'discovery'; the scientific article or textbook may fail, but in so far as it succeeds it proceeds from an individual to a community of those who understand and can use the theorem or explanation.

Clearly the philosophy and sociology of science have in recent years been in a state of excitement and confusion, and there is no longer an agreed intellectual orthodoxy about what happens in science, about the science of science. The layman has really no hope of understanding the shape of controversy over sub-nuclear particles, because he has not been 'socialized into' the community of those who communicate through the relevant mathematical language. Even James D. Watson, on *The Double Helix*,[3] the elucidation of the mechanism of heredity, is pretty elusive about his role as scientific model-builder, though he is brilliant as dramatic artist in illustrating the dynamics of one sector of the scientific community.

But there have been recently three well-documented cases of

2. 'Péguy's rejection of the logic of linear statement (1972) in *Victor-Marie Comte Hugo*' (Steiner, p. 169). Carlyle makes the same point about history: 'All narrative is, by its nature, of only one dimension; only travels forward towards one, or towards successive points: Narrative is *linear*, Action is *solid*. Alas for our "chains", or chainlets of "causes and effects" . . .' Essay 'On History', at p. 55 of *Thomas Carlyle, Selected Writings*, A. Shelston, ed. (Penguin Books; 1971).

3. (Weidenfeld & Nicolson; 1968) See also 'The Double Helix Revisited' in *The Listener*, 14 December 1972, p. 819.

scientific discovery readily accessible to different kinds of non-scientific reader. One of them I used in *Politics and Social Science*,[4] the process of growth from field naturalist to social biology. Luckily, books about birds and beasts sell well; there is no single narrative of discovery, but any good public library can provide ample documentation. For me (and I am not expert) this begins conceptually with 'the ancestor', Eliot Howard, and his book on *Territory in Bird Life*, published in 1920;[5] and then it can be followed through the next stages in the work of Konrad Lorenz, Nikko Tinbergen, David Lack, W. H. Thorpe and others, who might be thought as a loosely-jointed community of professional scientists, and also as the leaders of an immense army of concerned amateurs.[6]

A second example, available to any language scholar, is that of the decipherment of 'Minoan Linear B' by Michael Ventris and John Chadwick, recorded very lucidly in the latter's book.[7] There exist a relatively limited number of texts in the script, found in circumstances which suggest that they are mainly inventories. There are about eighty-nine distinct characters, and that in itself offers a clue as to what kind of script it must be; not Chinese in type (too few), not alphabetic (too many), therefore perhaps a syllabary. But there is no Rosetta stone, that is to say there is no bilingual inscription, giving the sense in parallel in another language and another script.

The massive guess made by Ventris and Chadwick was that the language was Greek: a guess contrary to all previous knowledge about the date at which invaders from the North had first moved into the Eastern Mediterranean – it put the Greeks at least 500 years farther back in history. But it broke the code by establishing

4. (Penguin Books; 1967.)

5. (John Murray.)

6. As a single strand of detective science, using these resources fully, I commend G. V. T. Matthews, *Bird Navigation* (Second edn, Cambridge UP; 1968).

7. *The Decipherment of Linear B* (Cambridge UP, 2nd edn; 1967). See also Sterling Dow and John Chadwick, *The Linear Scripts and the Tablets as Historical Documents* (Cambridge UP; 1971). Anyone attracted by this game might try also J. E. S. Thompson, *Maya Hieroglyphs without Tears* (British Museum; 1972)

a connection between signs and objects through words; and it broke well-grounded academic opposition by its coherence, its consistency and above all by its applicability to new material. Not without bitterness, a community of scholars was re-educated.

A third case, which has perhaps caused raised eyebrows rather than personal attacks, is that of the megalithic astronomical observatories; almost simultaneously, Professor Hawkins[8] decoded Stonehenge, Professor Thom[9] detected lunar observatories in Scottish megalithic constructions of a rather later date. The thing has been rather muddled by calling these monuments computers; call them 'calendars', and there emerge a host of parallels in great preliterate cultures elsewhere, in particular Iran, Egypt and Central America.[10] Forget Druids, and realize the intellectual capacity of man when organized in scientific communities linked by a common understanding of logic and observations.

These three cases illustrate my personal paradigm of science: the individual mind or minds (no need to bother in this context whether you call it 'mind' or 'brain'), the public communication, the building and growth of the community of that science. It is possible that 'Popperites' and 'Kuhnites' (unfair shorthand, I know) might agree thus far; there would then be confused disagreement about the intellectual and social character of each of these scientific communities and of the community including all scientific communities.

But with the best will in the world, and such knowledge and

8. G. S. Hawkins, *Stonehenge Decoded* (Fontana Books; 1970).

9. A. Thom, *Megalithic Sites in Britain* (OUP; 1967): *Megalithic Lunar Observatories* (OUP; 1971). Both these scholars took part in a joint Royal Society/British Academy seminar on 'The Place of Astronomy in the Ancient World' held on 7 and 8 December 1972. So far, only brief summaries of the papers are available.

10. A guess. Calendars became big business at a time of growing investment of big resources in agriculture. Farming is a matter of leads and lags: one has to get the seed in the ground, the embryo in the womb, x months before the season of maximum growth. The first Greek work on agriculture, Hesiod's poem of about 700 BC, is called *Works and Days*: it was not irrelevant for Edmund Spenser to write The Shepherd's *Calendar*, or for Benjamin Franklin to print and sell Poor Richard's *Almanack*. Prometheus too 'taught men the rising and the setting of the stars' (Lowell; 1970, p. 21).

ingenuity as I can muster, I have not found that words and observations click together so that I have a worthwhile 'scientific article' to offer. Nor do I find it very interesting to search for the errors of those who thought they had heard it click. For one thing, I respect them too much: in Oakeshott's words, I am 'one who would do better if only he knew how'.[11] For another, it is infinitely tedious to read the examination answers of students repeating half-remembered refutations of the great systems of great men; and I can't believe that the students enjoy it much, either. Great scholastics are fine, it is the tribe of little ones who become a pest, now as in the decline of the mediaeval world. Then sets in the regress of books about books about . . ., which has indeed cursed even poetry itself since Pound, Eliot and Joyce.

Mythological Explanation

The option which I am offering, to put it in shorthand, is that of mythological explanation and contextual definition. This is perfectly respectable, even old-fashioned; the trouble is not to think of it but to do it.

In both cases one has to explain the method by example; and of course the standard example of mythological explanation is that of the structure of psychoanalysis expounded by Freud through the Oedipus myth.[12] Whether he was right or wrong is another question; but certainly the myth had power, perhaps like a 'powerful' scientific theory – or perhaps not.[13]

Reading Lévi-Strauss, one feels as if the smallest and hungriest bands had stores of myths far richer than ours. This is perhaps an illusion arising from his method, which ranges across mythological systems, but never studies one such system in depth within its boundaries of cultural communication. There is indeed

11. In 'Political Education' (1951), p. 111 of *Rationalism in Politics and Other Essays* (Methuen; 1962).

12. On Freud's social context and 'para-scientific methodology', see (for instance) Steiner (1972), pp. 83–5.

13. Jacques Monod sees them as radically different: *Le hasard et la nécessité* (Paris, Éditions du Seuil; 1970, p. 183).

the vast mythological cycle of Jesus Christ, his saints and martyrs, but it seems to have gone dead in our imagination, eroded perhaps by too much scholarship in doctrine and history.[14] But perhaps myths do not vanish; perhaps as they fall asleep in one culture they awake refreshed in another.

Oh Christianity, Christianity,
That has grown kinder now, as in the political world
The colonial system grows kinder before it vanishes, are you vanishing?
Is it not time for you to vanish?[15]

Explanation by myth was certainly one of the strands of the romantic movement – one has only to mutter 'Faust' to give the clue. Wagner perhaps exhausted the possibilities of the Ring of Power; he scarcely began to explore those of the Grail. And perhaps Nietzsche was the first consciously to bring back Greek myth into the explanation of politics.

'Prometheus', which I choose here as the myth of power, violence and decision, played rather a small part in the cycle of Greek myths, viewed historically; a few lines in Hesiod; three plays by Aeschylus, of which two are lost; some tantalizing sarcasms in Aristophanes; an eccentric application by Plato.[16] The last had few to follow it: but it says two interesting things. Firstly, in a debate about political education Protagoras explicitly makes the offer – 'shall I make the case by telling a myth or by stating an argument?' Secondly, Protagoras reserves politics (and justice) to Zeus. His Prometheus establishes man technologically, but cannot give him what is equally necessary for survival, the capacity to live politically; the power to decide justly without violence.

But the main trend of the myth has been different; that not even God has the power to decide justly without violence.

14. Compare Alistair Kee, 'Christianity without religion', *The Listener*; 14 December 1972, p. 838 and F. W. Dillistone: *Traditional Symbols and the Contemporary World* (Epworth: 1972).

15. Stevie Smith, 'How do you see?' in *Scorpion and other Poems* (Longmans; 1972). Roland Barthes finds a great store of bourgeois myths: *Mythologies* (1957; English translation of a selection by Annette Lavers, Cape; 1972). But in his theory, such myths do not enrich language, they 'steal' it (p. 217).

16. *Protagoras*, 320d.

The scraps of Prometheus myth in the Hesiodic poems (where he first appears about 700 BC in a post-heroic age) are puzzling. He is of the fraternity of the Titans, the warriors of the old generation of gods, who were thrown like fallen angels into Tartarus[17] or punished in monstrous ways, as was Atlas who must hold up the sky, Typho who is pinned under the volcano Etna.[18] For Prometheus, there was invented the monstrous punishment of the torturing eagle on the pinnacle of the Caucasus. But the tale shifts at that point to a version in which Prometheus is no hero, rather a divine thief, the trickster or twister known in myths all over the world:[19] 'of finely drawn plans', 'of devious intellect'.[20] In this lesser folk tale he gives fire to men, teaches men to cheat the gods at sacrifice: and Zeus's response is against men not against Prometheus, is ironical not dreadful. He gives them woman: or in another story, the gorgeous Pandora with her box of evils – and Hope (a good or an evil?) at the bottom of the box. Almost certainly it was Aeschylus, 200 years later,[21] who gave unity to the myth, establishing a new variant of his favourite theme that violence will beget violence till there is superhuman reconciliation. This was the history of the house of Atreus, of which all three plays survive; murder of daughter, murder of husband, murder of mother; the Furies; the idea of Apollo and Athena, the new generation of gods, the new

17. Clearly Milton used *Theogony*, lines 720ff.

18. Lowell, p. 18. There is some measure of agreement that Aeschylus knew Sicily well and refers here to an eruption of Etna sometime in the years 479–84 BC. There is an exciting guess that the Prometheus trilogy was first performed shortly after that time, in the city of Etna, founded by Aeschylus's patron, Hieron of Syracuse: and that the third play of the trilogy was not *Prometheus Unbound*, but *The Women of Etna*, from which a few lines survive. (Hugh Lloyd-Jones, *The Justice of Zeus*, California UP; 1971, pp. 98–103).

19. See for instance the references in Mary Douglas: *Purity and Danger* (Routledge; 1966); the Trickster in the Tärot pack (Paul Huson: *The Devil's Picturebook*. Sphere Books; 1972, p. 124) and the Red Indian Trickster and fire-bringer Mänäbush (Mircea Eliade, *The Quest: History and Meaning in Religion* (Chicago UP; 1969) at pp. 141–2).

20. *ποικιλόβουλὸζ* (*Theog.* 1.521), *αγκυλομἠτὴζ* (*Theog.* 1.546).

21. For a Marxist view of Aeschylus's Prometheus by a man who was a good Greek scholar, though a naïve Marxist, see George Thomson, *Aeschylus and Athens: A Study in the Social Origins of Drama* (Lawrence & Wishart; 1941), and his edition of *Aeschylus: Prometheus Bound* (Cambridge; 1932).

law which admits, indeed requires, compensation and final peace. In the *Prometheus*, it is the history of the gods themselves; the evil Kronos who devoured his children (Goya's image of the god as a black hole in space); the one son who escaped; the new weapon, the new lord; Prometheus technologist of victory, who became the first rebel,[22] giving fire, technology and hope to the oppressed; the exercise of Power and Violence (personified as Zeus's ministers in the opening scene), which is omnipotent yet powerless, since the new power already lies in the grasp of necessity. The lost play of Aeschylus, *Prometheus Unbound*, worked reconciliation, in a way now difficult to reconstruct or even to understand; Shelley's dream-like poem solved the problem by abolishing it. But it persists.

The myth took new force in the Middle Ages, and Simone Weil built upon its Christian features. Perhaps (some have thought) Milton's Satan is a child of this myth, and of that of Job also. Mary Shelley (at eighteen) rendered it as *Frankenstein or The Modern Prometheus*, in the extraordinary burst of creativity chronicled by Christopher Small in *Ariel like a Harpy*.[23] Shelley gave it one revolutionary twist, that of a single blow of violence, which would create peace on earth for ever. Marx gave it another, which paid its due to the intellectual and dialectical (and unending?) schema of Aeschylus. 'Prometheus is the foremost saint and martyr in the philosopher's calendar': 'like Prometheus who stole fire from heaven and began to build houses and settle on the earth, so philosophy once it has evolved so as to impinge on the world, it turns itself against the world that it finds. So now Hegelian philosophy.'[24]

22. Cf. Albert Camus: *The Rebel* (first published 1951 as *L'Homme révolté*; trans. Antony Bower, Penguin Books; 1971) Prometheus is there humbled rather than glorified (p. 41, p. 46), as prototype of Sade and Borel.

23. *Shelley, Mary and Frankenstein* (Gollancz; 1972). Her tale has been endlessly re-played, in vulgar versions; a recognition of its power as myth, like that of Dr Jekyll and Mr Hyde? (Simone de Beauvoir, *Must we burn Sade?* p. 14 of NEL edition; 1972). Count Dracula too? (Gabriel Ronay, *The Dracula Myth*, W. H. Allen; 1972).

24. David McLellan (trans. and ed.): *Karl Marx: Early Texts* (Blackwell; 1971), at pp. 14 and 19.

Finally, Robert Lowell re-shaped the play in prose to express the dilemma of the Ivy League intellectuals in the 1960s. 'Prometheus in rebelling is justly fighting for intelligence and justice, or justly fighting against necessity, or he is *un*justly fighting, because he is fighting necessity, what is'.[25]

It will be clear that this is 'mythological explanation' of an American political hell, as Sartre's *Huis Clos* and *Les Mouches* expound a French one.

Contextual Definition

Contextual definition is more difficult. Clearly it is better, in the present context, to exemplify myth than to define it. But to decline to define 'definition'? Perverse: but to define 'definition' is to attack central problems of philosophy, and in that I am not likely to be successful.

First, therefore, some examples of distinguishable types of definition; I hope that each example is central in character and that the philosophical troubles over distinctions, overlaps and peripheries can be circumvented.[26]

(1) Ostensive

(*a*) 'That is John over there, the one with red hair.'

(*b*) 'That is a horse: and that: and that: . . .'

(2) Stipulative: Let the line A–B be designated X.

(3) Word-thing:

(*a*) 'Justice is the interest of the stronger'.

(*b*) '*Horse* (equus caballus). The horse is an important and valuable member of the Mammalia. For its zoological history the article Equidae should be consulted' . . . and so on for 13 columns [*Encyclopedia Britannica*, 1961 edn, Vol. 11, p. 754].

(*c*) '*Horn, Cape*, a steep rocky headland on Horn Island, at the southernmost extremity of South America, lies

25. Robert Lowell, Preface, p. vi.

26. I rest, precariously, on Richard Robinson's book: *Definition* (OUP; 1954); it is learned, lucid and careful, but even a layman is aware that it does not go very deep.

55°59′S, 67°12′W. in Tierra del Fuego (q.v.) archipelago, Magallanes province, Chile' [ibid., p. 749).

(4) Operational; and this has elements in common both with (3) and with (5). 'Heat is what we measure by the following instruments which have been found by experience to give readings consistent with one another and consistent through time.' 'Intelligence is what we measure by the following tests which . . .' – and so on. 'Measurement,' writes Brian Ellis, 'is the link between mathematics and science . . . Yet strangely it has attracted little attention.' His book illustrates how formidable are the conceptual difficulties.[27]

(5) Lexicographical: an average entry in an average dictionary. For instance:

Fossi-logy.	1776 [Incorrectly f. FOSSIL sb. + -LOGY.] That branch of science which treats of fossils; palaeontology; also, a treatise on this –1812. So †Fossi·logist, one who studies f. vars. Fossilo·logy (*rare*), Fossilo·lo'gical a., Fossilo·logist.
Foster-brother.	[OE. fóster-brózor, f. FOSTER sb.[1]] A male child nursed at the same breast as, or reared with, another of different parentage.
Foundry.	(fau.ndri). 1601. [a. F. fond(e)rie, f. fondre; see FOUND v.[3]] 1. The art of business of casting metal; *concr.* castings. 2. An establishment in which founding of metal or glass is carried on. Also *fig.* 1645.[28]

(6) And then contextual, the practice of the New English Dictionary (begun nearly a century ago), or of the great dictionaries of Latin and Greek. These do give 'meanings': but the more important thing is that they classify 'contexts' and then illustrate each 'use in context' by direct quotation. This kind of dictionary is a composition of great art; it is also good reading for any compulsive word-watcher or word-ecologist. One line of thought which it opens up is that derived from Wittgenstein, that the meaning of a word *is* (consists in, is identical with, has

27. Brian Ellis: *Basic Concepts of Measurement* (Cambridge UP; 1966).

28. Taken from *The Shorter Oxford English Dictionary* (OUP, third edn; 1972).

no existence apart from) its use. Language (even if merely framed in one's own mind, and to that extent solipsist) is wholly contained within contexts of human interaction, and cannot get outside these. Another line of thought, equally familiar since the explorations of Richards and his pupil Empson,[29] is that a word can be enriched by the interplay of contexts, so that 'true poetry' ('jewels five words long, That on the stretched fore-finger of all Time Sparkle for ever'[30]) resides not only in sounds and meanings but in over-tones or harmonics: to contrast two Shakespeare lines, 'the multitudinous seas incarnadine', 'she should have died hereafter'. Or in Aeschylus 'the numberless laughter of the sea waves'. A 'big' poem (even a short one) must contain more than that, but this interplay of contexts can be seen as one dimension of language deployed as art. To put the matter more formally, 'When a context has affected us in the past the recurrence of merely a part of the context will cause us to react in the same way in which we reacted before. A sigh is always a stimulus similar to some part of an original stimulus and sufficient to call up an excitation similar to that caused by the original stimulus.'[31]

And yet there lies in wait for the richness of entangled contexts the censure of impropriety. 'You ought not to use that word in that context' – and this too we have to learn socially, and perhaps to defy.[32]

Here is an example which baffles me, drawn from a descriptive article in *The Listener*.[33] The article by a woman, describes a Women's Lib meeting in London.

29. In particular, William Empson, *Seven Types of Ambiguity* (Chatto & Windus; 1949).

30. Tennyson, *The Princess*, ii, 1.355.

31. Murray Edelman, *The Symbolic Uses of Politics* (Urbana, University of Illinois Press; 1964, p. 106). H. D. Duncan: *Language and Literature in Society* (1953: New York, Bedminster Press; 1961) also has valuable references for instance to Malinowski (p. 82) and to Kenneth Burke (p. 230, fn. 21). E. A. Carswell and R. Rommetveit, ed.: *Social Contexts of Messages* (Academic Press; 1971) deals with relevant research in psycholinguistics.

32. 'He had discovered that long human words rarely changed their meanings but short words were slippery, changing without pattern. Short human words were like trying to lift water with a knife.' (Robert Heinlein, *Stranger in a Strange Land*, 1961; NEL; 1971, p. 138).

33. Caroline Blackwood (3 June 1971).

In the last ten years or so there has been quite a fuss over four-letter words and their use in society. The list is wonderfully rich, and by no means limited to sex words; there are other basics, such as snot, clap, fart, turd, which belonged to the same social context. This was (I think) oral – one should not write them down; and masculine, but not to be used in all masculine contexts. Certainly not to the vicar or the school-master, 'outsiders' in natural conversation; perhaps pseudo-rough rather than earthy, the Rugby players in the communal bath[34] rather than the farm-worker. But certainly male; in my innocent youth, I think we assumed that women had a right to four letter words (and related songs) which were their own, not ours. How tragic, if we were wrong.

Now the proprieties are unclear. The words can be printed, but only in posh papers; the BBC is very shifty about it (though it can afford a bit of nudity nowadays); transcribed into a police-man's notebook they are certainly evidence for the offence of insulting behaviour likely to cause a breach of the peace; and there has been no flagging that I can see in the old music-hall trade of systematic ambiguity in the use of metaphorical synonyms, in mixed company. But we are all in a muddle, and Women's Lib too.

The story, very briefly, is of a well-attended, well-organized women's meeting, with a platform party of old-fashioned radicals, respectable in style, practical in securing action. To them, enter the new radical, Jane Arden, shouting incessantly from the back of the hall 'shit, shit, shit', 'prick, prick, prick'. A conscious effort, clearly, to move words from one context into another, male into female, improper into proper, and so to explode conventions. There is a direct analogy in the history of the word 'mother fucker' in political contexts, at first explosive, then eroded into conventionality.[35]

But unconsciously? Two things, at least. Firstly, a pretentious

34. See David Storey's *This Sporting Life* (Penguin Books; 1968), and his latest play, *The Changing Room* (Cape; 1972).

35. A point clearly made in David Cooper, *The Death of the Family* (Penguin Books; 1972), at p. 84. See also 'Language as Missile and Shield': H. O. Lasswell, N. Leites et al., *The Language of Politics* (New York, Stewart, 1949; MIT, 1965).

assertion of 'radical chic',[36] of a style in words, dress, hair, make-up, dance, walk, gesture, which is consistent, artificial, transitory, but yet compulsive, as fashion is. But (secondly) what seems to a male ear to be solecism in the choice of words; in this context, certainly 'balls', 'cock', even 'cunt', but scarcely 'shit' and 'prick'.[37] That is to say, there are proprieties even in the use of improper words. If you are to make political use of masculine words out of context, do please use the words properly, or you will fail to communicate with men. But she was trying to communicate with women?

In fact, the story seems ambiguous, like all the best parables. To cap it, here is a quotation from science fiction:

> As has already been established, the superior Myrinian culture, the so-called Confluence of Headwaters, is somewhere in the region of eleven million (Earth) years old, and its language, Confluence, has been established even longer. The etymological team of the Seventh Research Fleet was privileged to sit at the feet of two gentlemen of the Oeldrid Stance Academy. They found that Confluence is a language-cum-posture, and that meanings of words can be radically modified or altered entirely by the stance assumed by the speaker. There is, therefore, no possibility of ever compiling a one-to-one dictionary of English-Confluence, Confluence-English words.
>
> Nevertheless, the list of Confluent words that follows disregards the stances involved, which number almost nine thousand and are all named, and merely offers a few definitions, some of which must be regarded as tentative...

And the first definition –

> AB WE TEL MIN The sensation that one neither agrees nor disagrees with what is being said to one, but that one simply wishes to depart from the presence of the speaker.[38]

36. Tom Wolfe, *Radical Chic or Mau-Mauing the Flak Catchers* (Bantam Books; 1972).

37. '"Prick" is power' writes Kate Millett, commenting on Henry Miller (*Sexual Politics* (Hart-Davis; 1971), p. 307). But others might write '"Cunt" is power': whereas love = mutual power.

38. Bryan W. Aldiss, 'Confluence', pp. 177–84 in Judith Merril, ed., *The Best of Sci-Fi 12* (Mayflower Books; 1970).

In fact, we all talk Myrinian[39] unawares, but imperfectly and therefore with breaks in communication. These matter as much in politics as in private life. And here I cannot resist inserting most of a poem by D. J. Enright, which says it all.

> I continue to weep, I go on weeping
> Into my gin, my rather weak gin –
>
> I see a country where the people will vote
> Vote for a government that admits the word Fuck
>
> I see another where the people will vote
> Vote for a government that excludes the word Fuck
>
> 'But why do you weep, weep into your gin
> On account of a word, of merely a word?'
>
> To permit the people to use the word Fuck
> To forbid the people to use the word Fuck
>
> For reasons arrived at, explained and agreed
> For reasons arrived at, explained and agreed –
>
> Which is why I am weeping, weep into my gin
> That we live in a word-world, world only of words
>
> And what, as the sober man said is my portion
> But gin and despair, dissipation and tears?[40]

The Contexts of Power, Violence, Decision

To return to orthodox analysis. The NED is badly out of date in detail, and its Supplements do not help much as regards observation of the changing profiles and contexts of established words even in the usage of the United Kingdom. American and other changing forms of English it cannot even attempt to measure; and

39. 'Living beings, above elementary units, dispose of a large, manifold range of articulation: postures, gestures, colorations, tonalities, secretions, facial mien', George Steiner, 'The Language Animal' at p. 58 of his book *Extra-Territorial: Papers on Literature and the Language Revolution* (Faber; 1972).

40. D. J. Enright: 'Daughters of Earth', in *Daughters of Earth* (Chatto & Windus; 1972).

of course it tells us nothing at all about usage in other languages, however closely akin. No assumptions should be made even about the use of the French words 'le pouvoir', 'la violence', 'la décision'.

One can use the relevant NED articles in two ways; first, as maps of usage, secondly as indicators of the 'cohabitation' of words.

Take first the word *power*; the lay-out of the NED article, first published in 1909, makes a broad distinction between power as a quality, power as person, power in various technical and metaphorical senses, such as horse-power or electric power.

The notion of a power as a person is surely secondary? It admits a wide range; a chieftain has 'his power', which is something like a 'posse', a band who can be destroyed; there are the Great Powers and Super-Powers; a man may be 'a power in the land', there are 'the powers that be' – 'For there is no power but of God: the powers that be are ordained of God' [*Romans* xiii, i].

Power as quality has a broad span of meaning; the NED reports it under six heads. Of these the simplest is that of 'being able to do' something, and the most complex is the one we want for this discussion: 'possession of control or command over others; dominion; rule; government, domination, sway, command; control, influence, authority'. This is the family of words in which we are involved; elsewhere in the article one can trace a few of the images of the same family; power 'of life and death', 'of pit and gallows', 'of the keys', 'of the sword'.

In terms of usage power seems to be a 'big' word; it has some seven columns to itself, whereas 'violence' and 'violent' only have five and a half columns together, 'decision' and 'decide' only one column together. But this evidence is not worth much statistically.

The basic definition of *violence* (1928) is as follows: 'The exercise of physical force so as to inflict injury on, or cause damage to, persons or property; action or conduct characterized by this; treatment or usage tending to cause bodily injury or forcibly interfering with personal freedom.'

Rather too dry a definition? Too much concerned with objective violence as act, rather than with subjective violence as affect?

Probably this complaint is adequately met by drawing on the family of words which we meet in the article. 'Violence and rapacity' are contrasted with 'tranquillity and repose'; one meets such words as outrage, wresting, perversion, unauthorized, reckless, injurious, severe, destructive, great force, vehemence, intensity, ardour, passion, fury.

And the adjective attaches itself to such nouns as the sun, heat, poison, blood, pain, disease, passions, death, with a pleasant shift of metaphor to violent sound, violent colour, even 'a violent smell of sulphur'.

Finally two quotations apt for political study. 'Charles the fifth ... was wont to say that the King of Spaine ruled over Asses, doing nothing without blowes and violence' (1617). 'In a Common-wealth once Instituted, or acquired, Promises proceeding from fear of death, or violence, are no Covenants'. (1651, Hobbes; Leviathan II. xx, p. 104 of Everyman edn, 1914.]

There is no great divergence of usage between the verb '*decide*' and the noun '*decision*', except that the latter can be used in a secondary sense 'as a quality': 'Determination, firmness decidedness of character', as can the verbal adjective 'decided'.

Three things are emphasized in defining both noun and verb: first, 'to determine (a question, controversy or cause) by giving the victory to one side or the other'; secondly, 'The final and definite result of examining a question: a conclusion, judgement (especially in law)'; thirdly, 'the making up of one's mind on any point or on a course of action; a resolution, determination'.

The 1897 volume gives only one quotation to illustrate the collective decisions of assemblies, states or peoples, which present the greatest difficulties for political science. Clearly it does not exclude the existence of collective decisions from the worlds of usage and of practice: but the tone of the article is perhaps a little too Hobbesian to be quite fair to notions about 'democratic decision-making' as embodied in speech and writing some seventy-five years later. It is clear from the 1971 Supplement that there has been a real change of usage in seventy-five years, and that 'decision-making' and 'decision-makers' are now established in political usage, perhaps with a slight flavour of the jargon of 'management games'. It is also striking that there is now a whole family of words related to mathematical decision theory which may or may not be relevant to problems of decision as human action.[41]

Here, finally, are three quotations from the 1897 volume to give an indication of context:

And either end in peace – which God so frame! –
Or to the place of difference call the swords
Which must decide it. [1597, Shakespeare, 2 Henry IV, IV: 182.]

To compel men to obey his Decisions. [1651, Hobbes, *Leviathan*, III, xlii 311.]

... for likest Gods they seemd,
Stood they or mov'd, in stature, motion, arms
Fit to decide the Empire of great Heav'n. [1667, Milton, *Paradise Lost*, VI, 303.]

Much more could be said if one were to seek to disentangle shades of meaning, in the spirit of the late J. L. Austin. The measures here suggested are very crude; the political world changes, and its words with it. They do however suggest one final question.

Power and Violence are words of purely 'gut-reaction' politics: Decision has other contexts too, for instance those of authority, law, freedom, consent, justice. Is there another kind of politics, to which Shelley points in *Prometheus Unbound*? or one kind only, bi-polar between good and evil, victory and defeat?

A little more will be said about this in Part IV, which deals with Decision. But it is not the subject of this book.

—

Note on the Prometheus Myth

C'est le propre des grandes créations du passé de répondre toujours par quelque côté aux tendances diverses, aux préoccupations successives de l'avenir dans le domaine religieux ou moral, et le caractère du Prométhée d'Eschyle était assez riche pour qu'on ait pu trouver en lui un représentant on un symbole des croyances et des aspirations qui, au cours des siècles, ont tour à tour prédominé dans le coeur humain.

[Louis Séchan: *Le Mythe de Prométhée*.]

41. See Chapter 17, p. 222 below.

My original plan was to link Aeschylus – Plato – the Shelleys – Marx – Lowell, and I have stuck fairly close to this. But as I went on I discovered many variants and a more complex history.

The strongest tradition was that the Titan, Prometheus, was son of the older Titan Iapetus and of Earth herself, the oldest being of all, born of Chaos, and (in another version) wedded to Heaven.

Prometheus's wife was (in Lowell's version) Alcyone,[42] daughter of Ocean: one of their sons was Deucalion. Deucalion was a man or a hero, not a god; the Greek Noah, who survived a flood which destroyed the first race of men, and with his wife created a new race of men and women by casting behind them stones, 'the bones of their mother', Earth.

Prometheus and Deucalion were merged, and Prometheus was given a new role; moulder of men, breather of life (the fire stolen from heaven). There is testimony that this version was current just after the time of Plato and Aristotle, and one is tempted to imagine a lost play or dialogue by someone who was as creative as Aeschylus in his use of myth.

This was the version (Prometheus Plasticator) which lived through the late classical world and was given a new twist in Christian theology. Olga Raggio's splendid article in 'The Myth of Prometheus'[43] traces it through Catullus, Horace, Propertius and Ovid in the 'Golden Age', apparently misses the two ironic dialogues of Lucian[44] in the second century AD, but explores fairly fully the role of Prometheus in Neo-Platonic mystical theory, a role more important in the long run.[45]

The early middle ages produced a new syncretism; Prometheus muddled with a son of Japhet son of Noah, Prometheus as benign magician and astrologer, Prometheus as a Lord of Rings. Legend seems to have been gradually re-moulded as allegory, for which

42. 'Kingfisher girl', symbol of undisturbed tranquillity; 'a dot of blue . . . lost in the distance'.

43. 'Its survival and metamorphoses up to the eighteenth century': *Journal of the Warburg and Courtauld Institutes* 21 (1958), p. 44.

44. Lucian, *Works*, C. Jacobitz, ed., Vol. I, pp. 8 and 62 (Leipzig Teubner, 1905).

45. She refers to Plotinus, *Enneads*, VI, 3, 14.

Dr Raggio presents fascinating pictorial examples: Prometheus moulded form and gave life (his fire) to men and to animals, God added soul or spirit to men. What is more, he became patron of painters and other shapers of men.[46]

This is probably what Shakespeare meant by the 'right Promethean fire'.[47] Hesiod was available in translation by 1471, Aeschylus by 1518; Erasmus picked up anew the Aeschylean image of intellect and its self-torture: and the bound Titan came back into graphic symbolism in that period.

I may have missed seventeenth and eighteenth century material: Prometheus takes the centre of the stage again in the neo-classical period. 'Keats, Hölderlin, Foscolo, figures of defeated Titans. The gods rewarded their worship by visiting them with tuberculosis and dementia. They were the race of Prometheus.'[48]

This is perhaps right in spirit, not quite right in detail. The first new Prometheus I know is that of Goethe in the *Oxford Book of German Verse*;[49] Goethe in his youth (about 1771–5) portrays a vigorous, rather insolent young Titan, not foreshadowing tragedy. There was a Beethoven ballet *Creatures of Prometheus*, now lost, performed in Vienna in 1801. But I still think that images were fused decisively, and re-diffused, in that extraordinary group at Diodati in the wet summer of 1816 – the Shelleys, Byron and the baby William, whom the Shelleys had 'made'. Byron has a share in the heritage: the Prometheus which he wrote that summer was second-rate, but he had better Promethean heroes, as in *Manfred*. But it was the Shelleys who blended and renewed the ancient and medieval traditions, Prometheus Plasticator and Prometheus Bound, and we have lived on their inheritance.

It is true that Coleridge managed to say something different in

46. Villani, *On the famous citizens of Florence* (1381–2) quoted by John Larner, *Culture and Society in Italy, 1290–1420* (Batsford; 1971).

47. *Love's Labour's Lost* IV. 3, 1.348: and *Othello* as quoted on Chapter 14, p. 176 below. I can find only one reference to Prometheus on the Caucasus, and this is in *Titus Andronicus* (Act II. 1, line 17), a much disputed play.

48. Mario Praz: *On Neoclassicism* (trans. Angus Davidson, Thames & Hudson; 1969, p. 226).

49. Third edn, OUP; 1967: No. 97, p. 109, and Small (1972), pp. 52 and 191.

the introduction of a typical Coleridge non-project: 'On the Prometheus of Aeschylus: an Essay, preparatory to a series of disquisitions respecting the Egyptian, in connection with the sacerdotal theology, and in contrast with the mysteries of ancient Greece. Read at the Royal Society of Literature, May 18, 1825':[50] thirty-seven pages, and really rubbish (I think) but for one or two blazing sentences: One of these, on Prometheus and the Birth of Tragedy, I have quoted in a footnote on p. 187. This clarifies Nietzsche: the other, which seems to me to be equally convincing, very lucidly propounds dialectic, the concept that links old Aeschylus to young Marx.[51]

It is striking that in a sense both Nietzsche and Rimbaud, like young Marx, dedicated themselves to Prometheus. *The Birth of Tragedy* is full of references to Aeschylus and to Prometheus; and it is striking that in a preface of December 1871 presenting the book to Wagner, Nietzsche refers to 'the Prometheus Unbound' on the title page. It is equally striking that in May 1871, Rimbaud at sixteen, in a long letter about the future of poetry, writes of '*le poète vraiment voleur de feu*'.

Marx, Nietzsche and Rimbaud, a triangle of Prometheans: but the Titan then lost his fire, and I know of no creative use of the myth since that time, except that by Robert Lowell.[52] On the other hand, it is still very widely known and quoted. To take only two examples, George Thomson in *Aeschylus and Athens* (1941) adopts Prometheus as 'the patron saint of the proletariat' (he does not give his source for this); Barbara Ward and Réne Dubos in *Only One Earth*,[53] extend the metaphor of 'Promethean fire' to describe nuclear energy as fire fetched from heaven, alien, hostile and destructive, unless mastered by adaptive man: fire demands intellect. And Nigel Harris (rather unexpectedly, for a good Marxist) identifies Prometheus with capitalism – 'The

50. H. N. Coleridge, ed.: *The Literary Remains of Samuel Taylor Coleridge* (London, William Pickering; 1835), Vol. 2., p. 323.

51. 1836 edn, Vol. 2, pp. 342–3.

52. Penguin Books; 1972.

53. *Competition and the Corporate Society: British Conservatives, the State and Industry, 1945–1964* (Methuen; 1972).

capitalist Prometheus in the backward countries was a weakling, no match for the State or the foreigner.'[54] And Hitler claimed that the Aryans were Prometheus, to mankind.[55]

54. Denis Donoghue's T. S. Eliot Memorial Lectures (two of which were published in *The Times Literary Supplement*, 3 and 10 November, 1972) came too late for use in the text. He adds some recent references and uses the myth creatively himself, in critical analysis of Milton, Lawrence, and T. S. Eliot. I cannot resist one quotation –

> 'Power gives its manifestations irrefutable authority, detaching them from ethical scrutiny as if they were acts of fate: it moves the actions into a theatre of spectacle, force and destiny, where the question of right and wrong is overwhelmed by the inescapable presence of power.'

(TLS, 3 Nov. 1972, p. 1340, Col. 5).

55. Mein Kampf: Vol 1 Chap. II, *Volk und Rasse.*

Part Two

POWER

Power is a great thing, you know. To be able to move and control great affairs – not the characters and situations on a stage, Mr Foster; but the real – that is the greatest of all pleasures. You feel it in the stomach . . . Here, I feel it now. [Eric Ambler: *Judgment on Deltchev* (Fontana Books; 1966, p. 177).]

All passions have two meanings, Juliette: one, which is very unjust to the victim; the other, which is singularly just to the person who exercises it. And this fundamental antagonism cannot be transcended because it is the truth itself.
[Sade, as quoted by Simone de Beauvoir (1962), p. 49.]

Mine eyes have seen the glory of the coming of the Lord:
He is trampling out the vintage where the grapes of wrath are stored;
He hath loosed the fatal lightning of His terrible swift sword;
His truth is marching on . . .
. . . So the world shall be His footstool, and the soul of time His slave;
Our God is marching on!
[Julia Ward Howe (1819–1910) *et al.*, *The Church Hymnary* (rev. edn, OUP 1927).]

CHAPTER 3

THE STUDY OF POWER

I imagined that each new thought was another upward step on my circling road. To no purpose perhaps. No step reached a landing, no piece of knowledge ever quite turned into wisdom. [Robert Lowell, *Prometheus Bound*, p. 52.]

Proverbs and Images

REFLECTIONS on politics have always included reflections on power, generally as the dark side of the story: dark in various respects.

First, power is contrasted with authority. One owes obedience to authority as a duty; to power only as a necessity. But is not authority debtor to power, for its origin and for its defence?

Secondly, it is contrasted with ideal politics as factual politics; beautiful theories slain by an ugly little fact.[1] Politics as *Who gets what when how?*[2], the politics of greed and selfishness – and who is not in the last resort greedy and selfish? What distinguishes Napoleon from Chaka Zulu or Al Capone except that he killed more men more quickly?

Thirdly, power is a talisman fatal to him who seizes it. It is at once an illusion and a killer; few except the mentally sick find pleasure in its exercise, in the end it is haunted by the rites of Nemi:

These trees in whose dim shadow
The ghostly priest doth reign,
The priest who slew the slayer
And shall himself be slain.[3]

The revolution devours its children.

1. Attributed to T. H. Huxley by Sheldon Wolin, *American Political Science Review* 63 (1969), p. 1082.

2. H. D. Lasswell (1936: Glencoe, Free Press; 1951).

3. Macaulay, *Lays of Ancient Rome*. Frazer used this as epigraph for the first chapter of the first volume of *The Golden Bough: The Magic Art and the Evolution of Kings* (third edn, Macmillan; 1913).

'You are new gods newly come to power and you think the citadel you have seized is exempt from troubles. But twice I have seen lords of power cast down from that citadel; and I shall see next the fall of the present lord, the swiftest and most shameful.'[4]

There is of course an under-tow against the main force of this tide of gnomic wisdom. It will pass for honesty if a politician is so bold as to say 'I am in politics for power; and I find pleasure in exercising power', and it is reckoned a sound point if the tough-minded retort on the tender-minded that the latter have no grasp of the reality of politics. But the tender-minded in turn deny the premise; 'Remember, my sons, that there exists only "good", pure and simple: there is no such thing as "so that good may come" '.[5]

The implications of the word are therefore complex; in the present argument I emphasize those which are dark, dangerous, astringent, colours and shapes like those of Francis Bacon's art. The Prometheus legend has its parallels in Hebrew and northern mythology; and it is striking that the first great historians, Herodotus and Thucydides, built their histories of Asia and Greece in the fifth century on the same model, the former observing the insolence and fall of Persia, the latter the insolence and fall of Athens, the early sunrise of new power, its darkening twilight.

We are apt to treat 'Plato's Thrasymachus' as if he were a real person, a naïve theorist of scientism, defining justice as power, and power as the interest of the stronger. Perhaps there were such people in Athenian politics fifty years before Plato wrote *The Republic*: and if so Thucydides had already dealt justly with them in the Melian Dialogue and other 'speeches' in which he shapes and sharpens the myth of Athenian history in his own lifetime.[6] But 'Thrasymachus' is a mere ghost, used to put on

4. Aeschylus, *Prometheus Bound*, pp. 955–959, my literal translation.

5. Ignazio Silone: *L'Avventura d'un Povero Cristiano* (Milano, Mondadori; 1968), p. 199 (my crude translation. I owe the quotation to an Honours thesis, Glasgow 1972, by Father C. J. Ryan). The reference is to *Romans* III. 8.

6. For Thucydides see in particular F. M. Cornford: *Thucydides Mythhistoricus* (first published 1907); 'The Unconscious Element in Literature and Philosophy' in *The Unwritten Philosophy and other essays* (Cambridge

record three points about politics that were perfectly clear to any reflective person at the end of the fifth century BC.

In modern language, these were, briefly –

(1) That a 'strength' theory of politics would not do, because there is in the end always something stronger than the strong, either by coalition or by a new break-in.

(2) That a 'command' theory of politics would not do, because a command implies an obedience; two wills or more are involved, in continuing relation, and in so far as they are human wills (not those of beasts) they interact.

(3) That no one 'knows' his own 'interest' in any final sense – and the powerful man guesses no better than the peasant.

I wrote that these theories 'would not do', in the colloquial sense that you could not expect anyone to defend them for long, in face of logical and historical argument. Undoubtedly, such argument would entangle fact and value, and I am not clear that Thucydides and Plato ever saw and accepted the distinction. The discourse would be of this form: 'You can see what happened to Kronos and the Titans, to Xerxes, to Kleon and Alkibiades, gods and men who tried to act out these principles. And if you try to state the principles rigorously you will find that logical confusion is involved. And if you met anyone who acted like that in daily life you would certainly agree with me that he was foolish and wicked, perhaps mad.' Substitute Hitler throughout the statement, and it will stand intact: a muddled statement, but absolutely convincing to the generation of the 1930s, as in the first quarter of the fourth century BC.

It may also convince the generation of the 1960s.

UP; 1950) p. 1; Adam Parry, 'Thucydides' Historical Perspective', at p. 47 of Adam Parry, ed., *Yale Classical Studies* XXII (Cambridge UP; 1972); and A. Geoffrey Woodhead, *Thucydides on the Nature of Power* (Martin Classical Lectures Vol. 24: Harvard UP; 1970), which uses recent literature very well. More generally – Mario Attilio Levi: *Political Power in the Ancient World* (in Italian, 1955: in English trans. Jane Costello, Weidenfeld & Nicolson; 1965), and (particularly on Thrasymachus, pp. 270–8) A. W. H. Adkins, *Merit and Responsibility. A Study in Greek Values* (OUP; 1960).

Behavioural Analysis

There is no need to recapitulate here what has been written by so many of us (and we now read it endlessly in examination answers) about the 'community power debate'[7] in the USA in the 1950s and 1960s; the notion that the structure of power in the United States could be discovered empirically by detailed study of cities and local communities. We know and repeat the well-worn criticisms; perhaps not emphasizing enough the high intellectual quality of the exercise, within the framework and limits of American academic language. It is not clear that the current debate about violence has sustained these standards.

To put it briefly, all contestants in that earlier debate agreed to reject Thrasymachus, Hitler, Stalin. On both sides the principles stated were at least respectable, logically and ethically; what went wrong, on both sides, was the failure of scientism, the failure to operationalize 'power' satisfactorily, and to pass from 'insights' (and these were good) to the sort of science that can be built cumulatively through 'scientific articles' and the replication of experiment.

The legacy of that debate can be summarized in two catch phrases; 'power is relational', 'power is situational'. The statements look alike, but their status is not quite similar.

The former is 'heuristic'. It amounts to saying: 'It has proved useless to treat power as if it were a "thing" a sword held in the hand, a loaded gun; these *and no more*. This has failed, in practice and in comprehension. Let us try another tack: let us assume that we shall understand better (and succeed better in practice) if we treat power as a form of interaction between people. We accept that there are other forms of such interaction. But we do emphasize, *interaction* and *people*.'

What's wrong with that? Nothing, except that it is not clear that you can 'prove' it, since you can't define (in any sense) *interaction* and *people* except by making unverified assumptions about the nature of man.

The latter statement, 'power is situational' operates differently and at a local level. Suppose we begin to understand something in

7. See *Politics and Social Science* (1967), Chapter 14.

general about power relations, then what can we say about cases? In particular, what can we say about power in the USA? No scholar would expect to find a simple answer in so complex a case: but there may be a choice of models, and a procedure for choosing the better or the best model.

The models offered are, on the one hand, oligarchic; that centres of power in the state are mutually reinforcing, that the USA is best understood as a single power system: on the other hand, plural, that the USA is best understood, technologically, socially and politically, as a collection rather than a system, composed of a jumble of arenas or communities, each with its own politics and its own power structure. In Dahl's language, the second model is that of polyarchy, the first is that of oligarchy.

Various points about this:

(1) The models do not necessarily confuse fact and value; it would be quite sensible to say 'the USA *is* an oligarchy: it *ought to be* a polyarchy – I'll try to work in that direction.' – or to reverse the statement.

(2) The models are not mutually exclusive; sceptical rather than dogmatic political scientists now tend to use both models in seeking understanding of political situations. But probably one model takes the lead in any exposition, consciously or unconsciously: and there thus creep in commitments as regards their relative importance, which entangle the enquirer in political alignments.

(3) The oligarchy/polyarchy argument sought to be an idiographic and historical one about the American case. But even if the argument had remained at that level, it would inevitably have been used as a building block in larger studies; and in fact there has been a shift, step by step, from argument about the USA to argument about power in 'the global village'. At that level, it is hard even for the most pragmatical historian to control the contending pulls of rhetoric, ideology, ethics, and political alignment.

System as Metaphor

The next part of the argument is concerned with 'power as relational'; and it has two themes. First, to seek to understand relationships is to seek to explain them as a system. The word 'system' has already crept into the text [on p. 53]; it is almost impossible to keep it out of any contemporary discussion, and yet it is a word which has to be handled warily. There has been a great deal of writing about 'the systems concept'; here are a few quotations –

Wholes need no detailed description. Anything is a whole which operates in quasi-independence of its environment. A rock is a whole, and so is a mammal, an apple, a committee. Wholes are not a level of analysis but that from which analysis starts. [J. Feibleman and J. W. Friend.]

The physico-chemical picture of the living organism is only half the truth. The missing half concerns the nature of the organizational relationships that make the behaviour of obviously living systems uniquely different from that of obviously non-living systems and give it a teleological quality not found elsewhere. [G. Sommerhoff.]

Now if an organism is confronted with the problem of behaving approximately rationally, or adaptively, in a particular environment, the kinds of simplifications that are suitable may depend not only on the characteristics – sensory, neural, and other – of the organism, but equally upon the structure of the environment . . . We are not interested in describing some physically objective world in its totality, but only those aspects of the totality that have relevance as the 'life space' of the organism considered. Hence, what we call the 'environment' will depend upon the 'needs', 'drives', or 'goals' of the organism, and upon its perceptual apparatus. [H. A. Simon.]

The analysis of the characteristics of enterprises as systems would appear to have strategic significance for furthering our understanding of a great number of specific industrial problems . . . They have found their main business to be in the analysis of a specific bureaucracy as a complex social system, concerned less with the individual differences of the actors than with the situationally shaped roles they perform. [F. E. Emery and E. L. Trust.][8]

These illustrate some of the difficulties one would have to face in trying to frame a logic of systems analysis: problems which are important but in the present context secondary. Would it be

8. All four from F. E. Emery, ed., *Systems Thinking* (Penguin Books; 1969), pp. 31, 147, 215, 281.

agreed that at least we have a heuristic device, rather than an axiom or an empirical truth? We reconnoitre a puzzling situation on the basis 'let's assume there is a system here', as one goes to a thing that looks like a crossword saying 'these look like clues – surely there must be answers?' But spoof crosswords are not unknown.

The second point is that in using 'systems' heuristically one often tries the trick of switching contexts: one tries out different 'system analogies', Newtonian, biological, electronic, and seeks for a 'fit', and in the process one may or may not evolve either a more specific kind of system model or a more generalized model.

It is argued that this is what has happened in the quest for 'power as relational', and this part of the book is planned as follows, following the clue of 'system as metaphor'.

I make a first distinction between equilibrium systems and conflict systems, a useful distinction specified recently by P. C. Lloyd.[9] Equilibrium systems adopt as metaphors and models some very successful sciences, in particular Newtonian physics, biology, ecology, cybernetics. These are systems within which human will and action are located simply as natural phenomena, analogous to relations within the science postulated as analogy. Conflict systems seek to treat will, choice, decision, action as real and as unique to man; but they seek explanation, postulate system, and therefore do not (indeed, cannot) take the object of their study as random and without order. They find *systems* of conflict.

Systems are classified in many other ways,[10] one of these is as stable as against unstable. At first sight, this coincides with the distinction between equilibrium and conflict: but equilibrium may be unstable, conflict may be regarded as cyclical or endlessly repetitive.

9. See Preface, p. 10, note 5; and his views of the subjective appeal of functional and conflict models in *Classes, Crises and Coups* (MacGibbon & Kee; London, 1971), p. 16. See also Cynthia Russett: *The Concept of Equilibrium in American Social Thought* (Yale UP; 1966).

10. See for instance James G. Miller, *Behavioral Science*, 10 (1965), p. 193; open – closed: abstracted – concrete: abstracted – conceptual: living – non-living.

My general argument in this Part of the book is that if we are to choose a systems approach to the problem of understanding power we are led to choose a system which postulates both conflict of will and unstable equilibrium. I suspect that some conflict theories are also equilibrium theories; and some equilibrium theories try to be less static, more dynamic, by building in elements of conflict. But the distinction will perhaps serve, as a model of models.

I have divided equilibrium models into three:

(1) Functional: the science is biology, the analogy is that of a living thing.

(2) Transactional: the sciences are economics and ecology; the analogy is that of exchange within an environment, and with an environment.

(3) General systems: the science is cybernetics, the analogy is that of automatic control devices, an analogy now used extensively in various other branches of science.

Conflict theories I also divide into three (though with less confidence).

(4) Functional: the science is that of evolutionary biology, the analogy is that of an animal population with its genetic inheritance.

This began as a crude adaptation of Darwinism, and ran downhill into foolish generalizations about races and war. Perhaps one should find another title for its sophisticated and 'clean' revival.

(5) Games theory. This also is difficult to place, as it is in the relevant sense a theory of cooperation and conflict, within a system of rule-governed behaviour. It belongs here largely because of its relevance to the strategy of conflict at many levels.

It rests specifically on the mathematical work of the late John von Neumann: the analogy (I suppose) is poker.[11] But Russians may prefer the analogy of chess.[12]

(6) Dialectical theories; distinguished from all the others in that

11. I have not included here a separate chapter on Games Theory because I dealt with this directly and at some length in *Politics and Social Science* (pp. 119–37), and I have nothing new to say apart from what is to be found in Botvinnik's splendid book. There is therefore only a brief recapitulation in Chapter 7, at p. 92.

12. M. M. Botvinnik: *Computers, chess and long-range planning* (trans. A. Brown, Longman; 1971).

they insist on the reality of conflict without reconciliation. By violence the conflicting parties are destroyed; or the victor survives but is transformed, the loser vanishes from history. This is no place for an extended discussion of Hegel, Marx and their successors. But I think it fair to claim that this is the oldest of these theories or traditions, generated from logic and history before natural sciences had drawn so far ahead in terms of model-building and measurement.

The trend of the argument is that only the sixth, dialectical theory, takes seriously the present theme of power, violence, and decision. The other models provide for 'happenings', but not for actions, decisions or victories. In fact, logic and history may still be a better source of political analogies than those to be found in the natural sciences; but dialectical theorists have been rather slow to assess and plunder these new sources. To put it more directly: Marxism has for long been turned inwards, is at last being dragged out reluctantly into the twentieth century, in which it must react swiftly to new events (such as Paris, May 1968), to new data (such as those of global ecology), and to new science-based tools and analogies.

'Marxism'? Certainly the Promethean Marx first imposed this pattern of argument on Western thought. But there are now many Marxisms not one, and in addition there are theories of social change employing similar concepts but refusing to be called Marxist because they repudiate other elements in Marxist thought.

The Argument

This is intended to constitute a continuous argument, not a work of reference; and each section is kept as short as possible.

If the argument can be sustained it will lead from the last Chapter of Part II, power as victory in real and destructive conflict, to the theme of Violence in Part III. Power has been thoroughly discussed by students of politics, violence scarcely at all. Part III tries to draw on other treatments of violence both in the arts and in social science, and to relate them to the issue of violence in politics. Such a survey is necessarily superficial; I hope that charity can be extended to it in criticism, provided that it seems to make some contribution to the understanding of politics.

At this point I meet the difficulties of linear exposition, in that our notions of power and violence entail notions of decision, which cannot be handled until Part IV. It may be that some would prefer the word 'choice' to the word 'decision'; I use the latter simply because I am more concerned with political and administrative theories of decision in and for an organized human entity than with the ethics of individual choice.

These two branches of discussion may in the end prove to be inseparable: certainly a similar point arises in each case, that both in decision and in choice there is a polarity between decision as instantaneous act or commitment, decision as logical culmination of a train of reasoning. The former is affiliated in theory and image with our sense of power and violence; the latter with our sense of clear bright intellect and rational consensus.

Does this mean that one pole of decision is bad, the other good? For many reasons, no: the line of argument which I follow is that the most brilliant contemporary attempts to maximize the rationality of individual and collective decisions have met both logical and practical limits. In H. A. Simon's phrase, man can operate only with 'bounded rationality'. The bounds may be pressed outwards by systematic thought and organization, and the last chapter in the book is concerned with contemporary efforts to gain rational control of the human future. '*Mind*' is by no means '*at the End of its Tether*' (H. G. Wells's book of 1945): and, as Sophocles reminds us in the heart of the *Antigone*, a tragedy of decision, 'man is a very clever fellow . . . who has discovered for himself the emotional temper required for life in cities.'[13]

Nevertheless, we are continually thrown back from the limits of rationality in decision, the 'flaming walls of the world', in Lucretius's phrase; thrown back into the option of no decision or of decision by commitment, power and violence.

Note. Are 'structures' the same as 'systems'? Clearly the question does not make much sense as it stands, yet we are

13. Lines 347 and 355.

challenged to ask it because 'the system concept' seems to be predominant in physical, biological and social analysis at present, except in the fields of linguistic structure, literary criticism and the comparative study of myth and symbol.

Probably French *structure* is not exactly English 'structure', and French *système* is not exactly English 'system'. Much of the talk is about the structuralist schools of Barthes and Lévi-Strauss, but the general notion of 'deep structures' can be recognized as the present phase of a long course of development in 'structural studies' of symbolic communication, and has nothing especially French about it, though there is a commonplace to the effect that the French, obsessed with the perfection of their language, 'are a nation of grammarians'.[14]

Have we perhaps two distinct but analogous sets of heuristic tools; 'system' borrowed from the natural sciences, 'structure' borrowed from the sciences of symbolic communication?

Raymond Boudon has been translated as saying that the concepts usually associated with structure are 'system', 'coherence', 'whole', 'dependence of the parts on the whole', 'set of relationships', 'whole irreducible to the sum of the parts', etc.[15] Compare some of the specifications of 'systems' given on p. 54 above. Boudon here illustrates the close analogy rather than the distinction: but the rest of his book, it seems to me, could be used to

14. Notice how Sartre takes bad grammar as an example of 'projective activity' – 'Everything that can be said about projection has been said. I wish merely to relate an anecdote. A very good friend of mine had lived abroad for a long time, and his speech had become studded with Anglicisms. When he returned to France after the Liberation, we were delighted to see each other again, but shortly thereafter disagreements of a personal and political nature arose between us. We met frequently, but our relations were strained. One day, the discussion grew heated. He objected, courteously, but with a good deal of annoyance, to my opinions (which had been his own before the war) and my conduct. As he grew more excited, his French became less correct, and on three occasions the same Anglicism crept into his speech. The third time, he looked at me irritably, and asked brusquely: "Why do you keep making that exasperating mistake?"' J.-P. Sartre: *Saint Genet: actor and martyr* (1952; trans. B. Frechtman, London, W. H. Allen, 1964), p. 29, fn.

15. *The Uses of Structuralism*, trans. Michalina Vaughan (in French, Editions Gallimard, Paris, 1968: this edition, London, Heinemann, 1971).

sharpen the distinction. A *structure* in the Lévi-Strauss sense has the associations named above: but surely it would be arbitrary (though not impossible) to sweep it into the 'general systems' net as an energy/information system? Historically, and also in the light of the most recent work, it is a 'structure' of 'grammar' which finds, or prescribes, or both, rules for symbolic communication between men? And 'structure' in this sense seems apt also to specify a style, perhaps even a culture.

CHAPTER 4

THE BIOLOGICAL METAPHOR

Before man could reason, he was an animal, perhaps the slowest and least graceful, a skull with less inside it than the shell[1] of a turtle. [Robert Lowell, *Prometheus Bound*, p. 21.]

IF we are to consider power as relational, society as system, then we are led next to the metaphor of a society as a living being; a piece of poetry which underlies the now tedious controversy about functionalism.[2]

The Word 'Function' in Mathematics

The word function has at least two distinct senses, one mathematical, the other biological. The first is of the form $X = f(Y)$; in other words, you can get X from Y by performing the operation f. This can be trivial ($X = 2Y$) or it can be very complex, if X and Y are patterns and the rules for transformation (or 'mapping') involve a sequence of steps. In the scientific use of mathematics the process is fundamental; in the social sciences such strict formalization has rarely proved fruitful, but the concept of a 'transform' is nevertheless powerful as metaphor.

For instance, Wollheim, in his recent book on Freud writes on the latter's use of 'the functional hypothesis'.[3] This is true and is of extreme importance in the theory, but it is in this instance, in the middle period of Freud, a mathematical metaphor, not a biological one. An 'idea in the mind' may undergo unexpected transformations between pre-conscious, conscious and unconscious mind; one way of expressing the method of psycho-

1. So in the printed text. But surely it should read 'skull'?

2. The literature is vast: two important articles may serve as introduction. Kingsley Davis: 'The Myth of Functional Analysis as a Special Method in Sociology and Anthropology', *American Sociological Review* 24 (1959), p. 757; M. H. Lessnoff: 'Functionalism and explanation in social science', *Sociological Review*, 17, New Series, pp. 323–40, November 1969.

3. R. Wollheim, *Freud* (Fontana Books; 1971), p. 167.

analysis is to say that it seeks to understand 'transforms' or 'ideas', of the shape $X = f(Y)$.

This metaphor has a later history: in Jung as 'transforms' between collective and individual unconscious, as well as within each; in Lévi-Strauss often with an added musical metaphor, that of the transformations between theme and variations. But this approach has diverged historically from that of the biological metaphor, and perhaps it is best to keep the two apart, though they have interacted in people's minds through the word 'function'.

The Biological Metaphor

The history of the biological metaphor has had three stages. Firstly, there is the poetical analogy between human society and a man's body, which itself has two 'lessons': firstly the body has specialized organs, secondly the living body is more than the sum of its organs. There is no doubt that the rhetoric is usually that of order and subordination; the reverse of Christian radicalism ('if thine eye offend thee, pluck it out . . .') of which the sense is that the salvation of the individual soul makes claims higher than those of public order.[4]

One can find the analogy everywhere in the literature of politics: a classic case is that of Menenius Agrippa's speech in *Coriolanus* –

> There was a time when all the body's members
> Rebell'd against the belly; thus accused it:—
> That only like a gulf it did remain
> I' the midst o' the body, idle and unactive,
> Still cupboarding the viand, never bearing
> Like labour with the rest; where th'other instruments
> Did see and hear, devise, instruct, walk, feel,
> And, mutually participate, did minister
> Unto the appetite and affection common
> of the whole body.[5]

It is characteristic of Hobbes's perverse originality that he

4. 'To make man and not society master.' (Bronowski, p. 191.)
5. Act I, Sc. 1. It comes straight from Plutarch.

seems to adopt the image of the state as the body: but in fact asserts not a biological but a mechanistic doctrine, one of political engineering not of political procreation.

Secondly, there is the gradual development in biology of a strict terminology of structure, process, function, environment, fitness. That scientific language is unchallenged on its own ground; sociologists are now embarrassed to write bluntly about (say) the functions of incest prohibition, biological textbooks are still squarely based on such topics as (say) the functions of the liver. Indeed, the teaching of biology still seems to follow the rule that phenotype rehearses the history of genotype:[6] first, the dissecting table and the anatomical map of structure, secondly, structure in operation as process, thirdly the functional explanation of dead parts in relation to living process. Then understanding was widened to include animal in environment, and then species in environment, finally the (still not uncontroversial) questions of the interaction and mutual adaptation of many species and environments. The history of biology as an exact science has been as long and stern as those of physics and chemistry; and it has had the same tendency to expel abstract entities and to substitute for them the understanding of system. During the last fifty years the concept of an abstract entity called 'life' has been gradually eroded, and replaced by the concept of emergent qualities, the system which is more than the sum of its parts. The concept is by no means free from difficulty, but it has served specific practical purposes in scientific discovery.

Thirdly, there has been the attempt by social science to renew the old metaphor by giving it scientific rather than rhetorical content: and this includes much of the history of sociology since Spencer and Durkheim. 'Social Darwinism' became a by-word as misuse of scientific analogy to argue a political case, and a repugnant one at that: but one should not under-rate the explanatory power of functionalism imaginatively handled by patient observers. The 'British school' of social anthropology was never a simple unity: but it is natural to refer (as 'type-cases' of functional analysis) to Radcliffe-Brown's study of the Andaman Islanders and Malinowski's studies of the Trobrianders, studies

6. 'The unchanging secret face of the genotype.' (Bronowski, p. 185.)

which they perhaps rationalized too much in their conceptual works.[7]

The potential for a comparable analysis of politics was latent in Bagehot and in Graham Wallas, but no school developed, and in the 1930's and 1940's it was with a sense of pleasure and discovery that one came on serious studies of small-scale societies treated as models of the functional interaction of all aspects of a social system in its environment. It is probably fair (though not complete) to say, as the behavioural school did in the 1950s, that we inherited from the generation of the 1880s, that of Dicey and Bryce, nothing but institutional analysis and anecdotal illustration; but the critics did not make it plain that by the 1930s it was possible in Britain to look elsewhere for serious analysis; to the tradition of Marxism and to the tradition of social anthropology. Marxism since Lenin had proved very weak in empirical observation of reality; in that respect, the two approaches, macro and micro, proved to be complementary rather than in conflict, at least in my generation's first steps towards more serious understanding.

It is interesting, but perhaps a coincidence, that in the same period both Freud and Talcott Parsons offered functional explanations. In his early and middle periods Freud was, according to Wollheim's account, more concerned with the origin and pattern of transformations than with the structure of the mind. But in his last phase, in the 1920s and 1930s, he felt the need to describe the mind as a system, perhaps because he was no longer able to practise as therapist and was forced to stand back from the pressure of clinical decisions to take stock of the 'thing' he had been dealing with, to get a conceptual grip for purposes of exposition rather than a manipulative grip for purposes of therapy. 'The further application comes about when a constructive or constitutive role is extended to these mechanisms, and they are assigned a crucial function in the building up of the ego'.[8] It is probable that he never settled finally for one chosen model: but he seems to

7. Bronislaw Malinowski: *A Scientific Theory of Culture and Other Essays* (North Carolina UP; 1944); A. R. Radcliffe-Brown: *Structure and Function in Primitive Society* (Cohen & West; 1952).

8. Wollheim (1971), p. 200.

have been using the concept of 'functional system' heuristically.

In the same period, Talcott Parsons in *The Structure of Social Action* (the first edition published in 1937) was seeking a syncretism of Durkheim, Freud, Weber and the tradition of political economy, and he settled for an action framework and for functional analysis. Hence there came later the A-G-I-L paradigm which plagued young theorists in the 1950s:

Adaptation	⟷	*The Economy*
Goal Attainment	⟷	*The Polity*
Integration	⟷	*The Public* 'Communities', Associations
Latency	⟷	(Pattern maintenance) *Households*, Schools.[9]

And hence endless transformations, variations and quasi-empirical constructs.

Decline and Fall

But functionalism in its prime carried the seeds of decay, and in 1959 Kingsley Davis, as President of the American Sociological Association, in effect called on the dead to bury their dead.

> Several lines of analysis show that functionalism is not a special method within sociology or social anthropology . . . (p. 757)
> . . . structural-functional analysis *is* sociological analysis . . . (p. 771)
> . . . Now, however, the movement that was once an asset has turned into a liability . . . (p. 771)
> . . . It seems wise to abandon the myth for the sake of increased clarity and efficiency. (p. 757)[10]

The consequence has been that one can scarcely use the word now in a sociological context without wincing, and genuflection, and inverted commas. Why?

There is the quite irrelevant reason that Parsons in the cosmos of American sociology came to stand for Ivy League dominance,

9. This formulation comes straight from S. M. Lipset and Stein Rokkan, ed.,: *Party Systems and Voter Alignments: Cross-National Perspectives* (New York, Free Press; 1967, p. 7).

10. See p. 61 above, footnote 2.

WASP complacency, pedantic academicism. This was sound enough as politics or gut-reaction: but what arguments?

First, there are difficulties about defining function in the context of human choice and action. Characteristically, one puts the functional question, 'what is that bit for?', to or about a piece of machinery. Indeed, one must ask such questions if one is to understand or to repair an engine. Preferably, one has a handbook or an instructor; but without them one can still set to work to puzzle it out, especially if one has a notion of what the engine as a whole 'is for', and especially if one has had a chance to see it 'working'.

A machine postulates a designer; at the end of the eighteenth century it was still possible for Paley[11] to work the analogy that as a watch postulates a designer so the world and its creatures postulate God. Without God, it was harder; 'What immortal hand or eye / Dare frame thy fearful symmetry?' What is a swallow *for*? But biology after Darwin found a way round, in terms of biological success in an environment and the invisible hand of natural selection. And these concepts have been consolidated by direct observation of heredity, the gene-pool, the underlying physical facts of the genetic code.

But try this kind of functionalism on human society, and there is a dilemma. Either human society is a part of nature, a product of gene pool and success in environment, like baboon society; or human society is an artefact, postulating a designer. As a matter of common sense, the dilemma has to be overcome, by the stupid elementary process of embracing both horns together. Each view is to some extent true. But to what extent? And here the concept of function is heuristically useless, as it degenerates, when we tried to pin it down, into the nonsense of a purpose without a purposer.

Logically, it was useful as scaffolding; but for what theory?

Secondly, the analogy collapses if one presses it in a descriptive sense. Human society is not an animal, except as a piece of rhetoric. There are points of similarity, in terms of systems of sustenance,

11. William Paley (1743–1805): almost proverbial as the last apologist for cool and rational Christianity, before romantic and evangelical 'enthusiasm' broke in.

systems of coordination, systems of succession: but these are very general postulates indeed – use them to ask specific questions by comparison, and one finds that one passes at once from similarity of physiological mechanism between man and animal, to absolute contrast in respect of the mechanism of social structure. The realization that part of the animal inheritance is social has thrown a flimsy bridge across the gap. But it remains that evolution (or sudden mutation) in creating human society created something radically new, which has to be understood in its own terms, since analogies are soon exhausted.

Thirdly, and this is the point essential to the present argument, functional explanation does not explain power, but explains it away. The analogy means that the performance of each function (as with the salt level in the blood) is kept within its due limits by mechanisms which register deviation and bring back the deviant to the permitted range within a specifiable span of time – or the whole system dies. Queen ant, queen wasp, queen termite, 'queen bee' each is 'functionally necessary' to the maintenance of a social system, but none of them has power, except by an ancient, scientifically trivial analogy with mankind. In human society, all sorts of institutions may be 'functionally equivalent': a chief emerging from a rebellion, a council of elders formed from an age-set, a stateless society. But each is held within its pattern by internal balance and by interplay with the environment; no-one has 'power' except within the limits of structure and function.

Hence an obvious opening for two-pronged attack, descriptive and normative. Firstly, the world is not like that; a central characteristic of human social structure is its plasticity and adaptivity, and it is precisely this which marks it off from physiological structures. The mechanism of change is the crux, not the mechanism of stability (granted, that the latter is relevant to the former).

Secondly, carelessly used, functionalism slips back into the historic rhetoric from which it first came. The metaphor of automatic adjustment becomes once more the rhetoric of laissez-faire, the status quo, conservatism, tradition, 'leave it to those who know best', the rhetoric of the *optimates* in *Coriolanus*.

To deny that power as choice exists provides the best possible screen for those who choose.

'The hypocrite [Blake's angel] is the crux and symbol of choice.'

> 'I asked a thief to steal me a peach:
> He turned up his eyes.
> I ask'd a lithe lady to lie her down:
> Holy & meek she cries:
> As soon as I went an angel came:
> He wink't at the thief
> And smil'd at the dame,
> And without one word spoke
> Had a peach from the tree,
> And 'twixt earnest & joke
> Enjoy'd the Lady.'[12]

12. Bronowski, p. 166.

CHAPTER 5

THE WORLD AS MARKET

> This world [that of Zeus, in the days when he worked with Prometheus] was more delicate, and reasonable, and worthy of our minds, though perhaps as confused and dangerous as ever a few miles down. [Robert Lowell, *Prometheus Bound*, p. 15.]

THE word this time is 'transactional': the symbol is Mayor Daley of Chicago;[1] the admired science is economics.

Economics

In one sense, economics is the most advanced of the social sciences, in that it has been based for 200 years on a conceptual nexus which can be made as definitionally coherent as Euclidean geometry (of which it was indeed a part). This nexus has followed later transformations of mathematics undamaged, and has been fruitful (as has geometry) in deductive models which prove to be of value in coming to terms with the real world.

Detractors will say that economics has only had limited success in quantifying its symbols: and that the economics of institutions (except in Marx's hands, and perhaps in those of Schumpeter) has never yet got beyond the formalism and anecdotage for which the older generation of political scientists were attacked, perhaps unfairly. Granted that there is truth in this; yet in political analysis the market model has the same strength as the biological model, and the same weakness. Things are not decided, they happen.

This can be set out on two levels, which interlock; that of individual transactions and that of summation of preferences by the market.[2]

1. Martin Meyerson and E. C. Banfield: *Policy, Planning and the Public Interest: The Case of Public Housing in Chicago* (New York, Free Press; 1955). E. C. Banfield: *Political Influence: A New Theory of Urban Politics* (New York, Free Press; 1961). Also Norman Mailer: *Miami and the Siege of Chicago* (Paladin Books; 1972).

2. The basic economic diagrams are set out with an explanation for non-economists at pp. 173 and 175 of P. M. Blau: *Exchange and Power in Social*

A enters a market with a purchase in mind and with a view as to what he or she can 'afford' to pay. The definition of 'end' and the definition of 'resources' are hard problems: but can be assumed away (temporarily) in formal analysis. The purchase may be that of a list of commodities more or less substitutable one for another, or it may be for a single rather complex commodity, say apples. What is the best combination of quantity and quality available at a particular price?

A market, for the purpose of this elementary argument is by definition 'free', that is to say there are a number of independent sellers of apples, who have not conspired to 'rig the market'. Each of these sellers has a reflex image of a buyer's 'indifference curve', what quantity and quality he can 'afford' to sell at what price, so as to survive as a trader, with sufficient profit to buy new stock and keep himself and his family alive. The market is deemed to be fully open and visible to buyer and seller: their meeting-point represents the best that each can do in the market.

Similarly, for the market as a whole there is a general curve of demand, a general curve of supply, and these at their intersection fix the market price, the best available bargain for buyers and sellers alike. And so on, to the basic propositions of free market economics, descriptive and normative; this is a statement about how a market works (if it really is 'a market' as defined), it is a claim that (subject to the same stipulation) no institution can do better than a market in giving each man the best value. On Lord Robbin's famous definition, 'Economics is the science which studies human behaviour as a relationship between ends and scarce means which have alternative uses'.[3]

This is not the place (and I am not qualified) either to follow out the possible sophistications of the elementary model or to state its limitations fully. But it is necessary to note, for the argument that follows, four basic issues:

Life (New York, Wiley; 1964). See also (for instance) the explanations of indifference curve, marginal rate of substitution, supply and demand curves, elasticities, in Walter Birmingham: *Economics: An Introduction* (Allen & Unwin, second edn; 1962), Ch. 3.

3. *The Nature and Significance of Economic Science* (second edn, Macmillan; 1935, p. 16).

(1) The market is a system of relationships, and clearly it 'chooses' or 'decides' only in a metaphorical sense. Indeed part of the attraction of market economics is that it does not attribute responsibility for the allocation of scarce resources to any identifiable individual. Power (in that sense) vanishes from the system; not unnaturally, even socialist planners may be glad to take refuge in simulated markets as a means of evading responsibility for decisions which may mean trouble.

(2) Secondly, what is the individual preference which is maximized? Economics is not psychology: it does not ask questions about 'what does a man *really* want', 'how does he *actually* choose'. It is important to be clear that this is a strength, not a weakness, in the discipline. Perhaps it is precisely this that makes it a *discipline*, in a sense of that word stronger than is possible for any other social science; there are built into it specific rules which exclude a range of very difficult questions, and 'the discipline' claims to make progress in understanding largely because it narrows and sharpens the issues.

But this simplification rests on a paradox or circularity. In this discipline, all one knows about a man's preferences is what one learns from his transactions. Given the definition of market, then transactions are for each agent the best position available; the curve of a man's 'revealed preferences' is plotted from his transactions.

Once again 'the chooser' has disappeared; this is positive economics, not normative nor subjective.

These vanishing tricks are part of the price of postulating a system in equilibrium; at that price one buys a tool which is good and useful in its context.

(3) Thirdly, do markets as defined 'exist'? Certainly not, but neither does a Euclidean straight line; and there are some nasty problems about what any number (say 793,671 or $\sqrt{-1}$ – or what you will) really 'is'. As I have written earlier, it is relevant that the institutional study of economic institutions is relatively weak; but that is not a logical criticism of economic theory.

(4) But (finally) traders do not come naked into market. Rational behaviour (as defined) in a market (as defined) gives the best answer as to how to play the hand. But the hands are dealt

extrinsically, and the perfect market is in that sense free but unequal. The market does not re-distribute between haves and have-nots: there is nothing to be said about justice, merely about optimal use of scarce resources. In the older theory the poor could relatively do as well as the rich. Later theory adds waiting time and market information as resources which have costs; and it can be argued that the rich man can wait longer and buy better information than the poor man, and that if he trades rationally in time and information the gap between rich and poor will grow wider.

But appropriation and exploitation (like power) are not words in the market vocabulary.

Ecology

The advantages and disadvantages of applying the analogy can be seen least emotionally if one takes the ecological point of view, that each living thing survives by exchange with its environment. Nothing is secured for nothing within the ecological system of a meadow or pond, and in the process of reaching equilibrium or climax some forms of life will be impoverished and die out. The spread of a pine-wood (even a natural one) will change the vegetation beneath it as the trees grow, and it will also create opportunities for different kinds of birds and animals. The equations of interchange and maximization ('climax') have much in common with those of political economy: but we are more clearly aware of the mix-up of languages if we talk of the pine forest 'expropriating' birch trees or 'favouring' goldcrests and pine-martens.[4]

All this is rather amateurish and elementary: but it is necessary to make clear that to criticize 'transactionalism' in sociology and politics is not to attack the source of the metaphor but its application.

4. There are good visual presentations of this in *Energy and Power* ('A *Scientific American* book': San Francisco, Freeman; 1971); grass to forest over 150 years in S.E. USA (p. 50), the patterns of gardens and forest in New Guinea (p. 68). For an interesting interplay of exchange theory ('trophallaxis'), functional theory and (to some extent) learning theory in the study of ant society, see T. C. Schneisra, *Army Ants: A Study in Social Organization*, (San Francisco, Freeman; 1971) chapter 6.

Transactional Theory

The sequences of thought seem to have been rather different in sociology and in political science. The latter perhaps used transactional models earlier, in its early reaction against the formal study of institutions: was never so deeply affected by functionalism as was sociology; and followed its own line of thought in reverting to transactional theories in the 1940s and 1950s. In doing this, it explored both big and small systems; sociology, in its sharper reaction against functionalism, came to market analogies later, and in relation to small systems first.

But the two trends have come together, and there is no sharp disciplinary frontier that I can see between Banfield on *Political Influence*, Blau on *Exchange and Power in Social Life*, both emerging from Chicago, in 1961 and 1964 respectively. Nor indeed can one allocate specifically to a discipline F. G. Bailey on *Stratagems and Spoils*, published in the UK in 1969. Not that these three books, and other books which may be called transactional,[5] are by any means at one in doctrine.

Add to this group those economists who have persuaded themselves that economic theory is the key to politics, and one has an embarrassingly wide range of transactional statements from which to make a presentation. It may be cheating a little: but it will be convenient to take 'formal theories of voting' along with 'economic theories of social choice' in Chap. 16. The reader is however given notice here that there is no logical break between theories of the optimization of welfare as defined by social choice and theories of the vote as a currency in transactions in a political market.

The theory of markets has given transactional theory a spurious air of quantitative precision; and indeed the theory was generated partly because commodities and money prices may yield quantities usable for prediction in the short run (and this is well worth having). But in the long run the definition of a commodity and the stability of money are both subject to variation, so that even

5. For instance G. C. Homans, *Social Behaviour: Its Elementary Forms* (Routledge & Kegan Paul; 1961) and A. W. Gouldner, *The Coming Crisis of Western Sociology* (Heinemann; 1971), p. 395.

medium term predictions are valid only within rather banal limits. In addition, there are all sorts of problems that arise from 'the law of anticipated reactions', which means merely that human beings see things coming (or think they do), guess at the probable reactions of others, and are involved in a maze of mutual adjustments (such as rigging the market, or trading in futures) which are easy to understand but not easy to quantify.

In fact, the idea of exchange has proved to be illuminating in many fields not even conceptually quantifiable. Perhaps one is rather near a market if one takes the account of 'jobs' and 'squaring' from Cornford, whose little book has been a classic on 'the inner circle'[6] of English government for two generations now:[7]

> Squaring can be carried on at lunch; but it is better that we should meet casually. The proper course to pursue is to walk, between 2 and 4 p.m., up and down the King's Parade, and more particularly that part of it which lies between the Colleges of Pembroke and Caius. When we have succeeded in meeting accidentally, it is etiquette to talk about indifferent matters for ten minutes and then part. After walking five paces in the opposite direction you should call me back, and begin with the words, 'Oh, by the way, if you should happen . . .' The nature of Your Job must then be vaguely indicated, without mentioning names; and it should be treated by both parties as a matter of very small importance. You should hint that I am a very influential person, and that the whole thing is a secret between us. Then we shall part as before, and I shall call you back and introduce the subject of My Job, in the same formulae. By observing this procedure we shall emphasize the fact that there is *no connection whatever* between my supporting your Job and your supporting mine. This absence of connection is the essential feature of Squaring.

It is quite a logical step from this to the exchange of symbolic satisfactions[8] (such as decorations and honorary degrees). But the

6. See the essay by the late Ely Devons, 'Government on the Inner Circle', in *Papers on Planning and Economic Management* (Manchester UP; 1970, p. 140).

7. See chapter IX of F. M. Cornford: *Microcosmographia Academica* (Cambridge, Bowes; 1908).

8. In general see H. Blumer, *Symbolic Interaction, Perspective and Method* (New Jersey, Prentice-Hall; 1969).

exchange of women? Not as breeders or field-hands (no need to exchange) but as symbols of social relationships between groups called 'exogamous'? Lévi-Strauss would assimilate exchange of symbols to exchange of messages; and messages are formulated in codes which can be interpreted or 'transformed'. And so from exchange we arrive at information theory (the next chapter) and so at general linguistics (language as exchange of messages) and at deep structures.

I find it impossible to say, at present, whether these theories are substantively distinct, or are merely a series of transforms, as in projective geometry or in D'Arcy Thomson's famous diagrammatic 'transforms' of the outer profiles of fish.[9] The point to be made here is simply that transactional theory can break loose from economics and run into every domain of the social sciences, generally looking for insight rather than quantification.

The insights it seeks are in contrast with those of functional theory. The latter looks to the whole as supreme, the former looks to the individuals as constituting a system which does not transcend their interactions.

The Political Market

Back to Mayor Daley, in July 1972, excluded from the Democratic Party Convention in which he had been for twenty years a major power (the word 'power' chosen advisedly).[10] How far will transactional theory go to 'explain' Mayor Daley?

'Service and favours, the staples of the precinct captain and the ward boss'. 'Everybody needs favours'.[11] The world of Mayor Daley seems still to be precisely that of 'Mr Dooley' (writing humorously)[12] and the 'muck-rakers' (writing seriously) round about the turn of the century;[13] a world lubricated by

9. D'Arcy Thomson: *Growth and Form* (abridged edition, Cambridge UP; 1961), Chapter IX.

10. In 1968, 'the second most powerful Democrat in the nation' (i.e. after the President alone); Royko (1972), p. 162.

11. ibid. p. 65, 67.

12. Elmer Ellis: *Mr Dooley's America: A Life of Finley Peter Dunne* (New York, Knopf; 1941).

13. See for instance Lincoln Steffens: *The Shame of the Cities* (New York, Heinemann; 1904) and *Autobiography* (New York, Harrap; 1931).

'honest graft'. The first academic formulation was that of A. F. Bentley (yet another Chicago journalist) who published *The Process of Government* in 1908,[14] and has been the patron saint of all who have since then sought to understand politics as an interplay of interests. The conceptualization of politics as a 'Brownian motion' of molecules jostling at random lay fallow from Bentley's time until David Truman's development of it in 1951, as *The Governmental Process*;[15] perhaps because politics did not feel like that in the days of 'the Thirty Years' World War', the Russian Revolution, and the rise of totalitarian dictators (a transactional system may be unlovely, but it is in antithesis to totality, to Orwell's *1984*). But in the 1950s politics in the UK and the USA began at last to smell more like the old political market, and Truman's book served very well to re-open discussion.

To my mind, the discussion made it clear that the idea of market without structure had little explanatory force in political study; to market theory one had to add at least a minimum of 'institutional economics'. Once again, Chicago provided the laboratory, and much of the original work was done by 'the Chicago School' under the guidance of Professor Charles Merriam, whose son Robert Merriam ran against Daley for the office of mayor in 1955. This discussion comes later to Merriam's own book on *Political Power* (1934)[16] which goes beyond transactional theory: the latter is very well represented in *The American Party System*[17], and in Gossmell's *Machine Politics: Chicago Model*, published in 1937.[18]

Market Structure

Chicago politics has (it seems) changed so little that no new discoveries, merely new anecdotes, were added by Banfield's work in the 1950s. But his theoretical work offered a great advance, precisely in that it was a theory of market *structure*. In his

14. Reissued by the Principia Press, Bloomington, Indiana, in 1949.
15. New York, Knopf.
16. New York, McGraw-Hill.
17. New York, Macmillan 1922.
18. Chicago UP.

market, there are rich traders and poor traders, and there is distinction of roles.

The essential point is that this is a market in which transactions are mediated by a currency called 'political influence', which has some of the characteristics of money. In particular, it is transferable between different contexts, and to some extent it can be stock-piled. But it is rather like cash in a period of inflation, in that its value is eroded quite rapidly if it is not used in transactions showing an adequate return.[19] It can in fact be exchanged for money, but this is reckoned by professionals to be unwise, at least in a situation of open electoral politics. In Mayor Daley's Chicago,

> To be a success in the insurance field, a ward boss needs only two things: an office with his name on it and somebody in the office who knows how to write policies. All stores and businesses need insurance. Why not force the premium on the friendly ward boss? [p. 67].

But as for Richard Joseph Daley, the man aiming for the top,

> His virtue remained as intact as his hypocrisy [p. 90].

Of course influence is not money: it cannot be stashed away in Swiss Banks (as by a precariously poised *caudillo*), on the other hand it does not attract tax. Money in action is largely a matter of credit; so is influence, but it is easier to quantify the limits of credit than those of influence. And so on. The analogy is not perfect, but it is well worth playing, and serves to indicate the character of a particular kind of politics, possibly of an element of all politics from the level of the family (R. D. Laing seeks the origins of schizophrenia in families in which there is no 'honest graft', no tacit bargains consistently honoured)[20] to that of the super-powers.

But there are two lines of criticism which may be important:

First, it is indeed one of the attractions of the model that it has a good deal to say about the working structure of the political market. The role essential to its working is that of intermediary or middle-man: the analogy is that of a fully developed financial and commodity market, such as that of the City of London. The

19. Blau (1964), p. xv; '*Status as Expendable Capital.* Status is expended in use but can be expanded by investing it at risk.'

20. *The Politics of the Family and Other Essays* (Tavistock; 1971).

Stock Exchange is one aspect of the market, with its professionally recognized dealers: but there are also all sorts of special markets, from that for uncut diamonds to that for cargo space, and each has its own professionals, who make small margins on the quick turnover of large deals, and who are in turn interlinked, partly by big institutions, partly by gifted and lucky individuals who have found their own niche as special intermediaries.

This analogy will serve very well for the politics of a plural society: much better than does Bentley's unstructured view of pressure politics. And it can be interpreted ecologically, as a natural system in which in the end each profitable niche is filled by a biological process of competition and selection. But the analogy in fact carries one further, to a view of the market or the polity in which institutions are of central importance. Writers on the City (ever since Bagehot's *Lombard Street* – 1873) have insisted on its institutional rigidities and idiosyncrasies, on its social character, its codes of behaviour, its respect for authority; and this is equally true of the Chicago Machine, and of any other known political machine.

For some reason, 'role' is still an OK word with sociologists, though 'function' is out of fashion. The analogies used in this chapter and the previous one are not consistent: but does it matter, since neither can in any case be applied strictly? Why not treat the polity both as market and as system of roles?

Market and Context

The other difficulty is about the scope of the model thus built. Granted that a political system needs the roles of intermediaries: but are these sufficient? One wonders a little even in the context of Chicago: Mayor Daley got there as intermediary, has he not survived by authority, violence, and power, gradually hardening as he has grown older?

F. G. Bailey's scheme was built in a different context, that of Indian village politics and its integration into the politics of a province and of All-India. He and his colleagues (primarily drawn from social anthropology) have applied it to a wide range of cases in Britain and in Mediterranean countries, in an illuminating way. What I have drawn from it in particular, in a recent study of the interlocking of public and private institutions in the UK and the USA,[21] has been the concept of political arenas or communities and that of a pyramid of political levels linked by intermediaries.

A weakness of the pressure group scheme of things was that it never shook off the notion that there is always a government, that government has a stock of goodies, and that people in general have no political role but to demand things from government by threats and promises. Probably most people in the UK and USA still use that model, along with the inconsistent model of majoritarian democracy; with results which can be dangerously misleading if attempts are made to apply them to events in either country. If one looks at interactions in (for instance) British government it is less misleading to think of the farming 'arena' than of the farming 'pressure group'. This is a case in which I have had a good deal of experience since the 1930s, and I have also supervised two very relevant dissertations, M. J. F. Goldsmith on the internal politics of the milk 'arena' in the 1930s, Peter Walters on the grass-root politics of farming in the county of Cheshire, 'seed-plot'[22] of farmer politicians since the 1920s. What one finds in each 'arena', by commodity and by area, is not a disciplined organization but a polity or sub-polity, structured by roles, technologies, markets of influence, and personalities. It is a marvel of political capacity that the internal stresses generally are handled well, and come to make sense, in terms of equilibrium and of adaptivity: but this does not add up to a desk-thumping entity which might be called 'the farmers' lobby'. This is what Beaverbrook did not understand (but it was early days then) when he put the *Daily Express* behind the Agricultural Party in the late 1920s.

Similarly with the arenas or communities of the Health

21. 'Seed-plot* of gentility' (J. M. Lee (1963) p. 8.)

22. M. J. F. Goldsmith, The Genesis of the Milk Marketing Board and its Work, 1933–9, University of Manchester M.A.(Econ.) thesis; 1963. Also P. L. H. Walters, Farming politics in Cheshire: a study of the Cheshire County branch of the National Farmers' Union, University of Manchester, Ph.D. thesis; 1970, and J. M. Lee, *Social Leaders and Public Persons* (OUP; 1963).

Services; of the local authority associations; of organized football; of professional music, dance and theatre; of managers and workers in steel; and so on. Some of these are well-defined and recognize themselves; some are inchoate (for instance, the community of transport, or that of environmentalists), some might be defined objectively (for instance, that of old age pensioners, that of housewives as purchasers), but have not yet been built politically because of very severe structural difficulties.

The second point which can be developed from Bailey's scheme of Indian politics is that, as a caste community with its internal strife and adjustments cuts through Indian politics from Delhi to the village, so a British vocational community or arena cuts through British government (to take the health case) from the House of Commons and its 'specialist members', and the general and professional officials of the Ministry, through various top consultative bodies, down through associations and structures to the Regional Health Authorities, the Area Health Authorities, the Districts and the Family Practitioner Committees.[23] All these are innovations in institutional structure, introduced only after twenty-five years of 'politicking'; the same political 'persons' will be there in new 'jobs', but their 'roles' may not change till a new generation takes over.

In this 'vertical mosaic'[24] or network one can recognize that stalwart British character, the public person, first clearly specified in J. M. Lee's book *Social Leaders and Public Persons*.[25] A student can quickly learn to recognize the species in *Who's Who*, and it would include myself. But the academic member is marginal on most committees; politically essential (like the 'statutory woman'), yet not a full member of the political community of bargainers and intermediaries. Indeed the role is perhaps that of 'outsider', as described by Ronnie Frankenberg in *Village on the Border*[26] rather than that of 'intermediary'. He is

23. Dept. of Health and Social Security, *Management Arrangements for the Reorganized National Health Service* (HMSO; 1972).

24. A stimulating image owed to I. Porter, *The Vertical Mosaic: an Analysis of Social Class and Power in Canada* (Toronto UP; 1965).

25. (OUP; 1963).

26. (Cohen & West; 1957).

the licensed jester, occasionally appointed Bishop of Unrule. And so on. The point is that given the conceptual tools of arena, pyramid, intermediary one can specify some things quite exactly and seriously about the working of British government as a continuing series of decisions, indecisions and non-decisions. One can also get led off into a train of speculations about who it is who fills which role, and why; and this may be a target for wit rather than social science.

CHAPTER 6

ENERGY AND INFORMATION

Around some bend, under some moving stone, behind some thought, if it were ever the right thought, I will find my key. No, not just another of Nature's million petty clues, but a key, *my key*, *the* key, the one that must be there, because it can't be there. [Robert Lowell, *Prometheus Bound*, p. 53.]

The Political System

IN a sense, this Chapter is about David Easton, President of the American Political Science Association in 1969, author of *The Political System* in 1953, of *A Systems Analysis of Political Life* in 1965, and of other work on 'systems'.[1] The drift of the argument is that in his first book Easton did something very important, in that he broke the old 'institutions plus anecdotes' syndrome without seeking refuge in the formulae of 'behaviourism', which have tended to fragment political study in the search for hard data and the testing of specific propositions. One can engage in much debate with *The Political System* and yet maintain that its general argument was right, then and now.

But while Easton wrote, the idea of 'systems' was being reshaped in (as Shakespeare's stage directions put it) 'another part of the battlefield'. There emerged from various fundamental theorems put forward by Claude Shannon and Norbert Wiener in the 1940s a political formulation of cybernetics in the latter's book, *The Human Use of Human Beings*, published in 1950.[2] The book was perhaps not a good one; a man of genius who lacked a tactile sense of politics. But in many respects it opened a new chapter, in that it brought a new set of scientific concepts (with them, many concerned scientists) within the range of political 'modelling'; and that these concepts claim a very high level of generality, and do indeed operate throughout the scientific community, without distinction of East or West, communist or

1. The collection which he edited as *Varieties of Political Theory* (1966) is particularly valuable as an introduction.

2. Cambridge, Mass., Houghton Mifflin.

capitalist, Chinese and the rest. It is not in doubt that these are scientific concepts of great power, and that they were unfamiliar to Easton when he first sought 'a systems approach'. A personal opinion is that in his later work he never wholly 'domesticated' them, and that for a political introduction the student should now go to Karl Deutsch's text-book on *Politics and Government*, published in 1970.[3] But the point here is to indicate what the political student has to face if he is to incorporate this new language in his own; not to assess what has been achieved so far.

In a word, this is the most general form of equilibrium system yet proposed.

General Systems Theory

The problem may be set by quoting a check-list (which is in random order) of 'key terms and concepts' introduced in Chapter 7 of Deutsch's book.[4]

Key Terms and Concepts:

self-government	lead
independent	disequilibrium
sovereign	goal-seeking system
autonomy	goal
receptors	purpose
effectors	decision point
self-steering	decision area
feedback cycle	memory
amplifying feedback	self
escalation	political self
negative feedback	identity
goal state	autonomous
homeostatic process	dissociative
load	combinatorial
lag	will
gain	consciousness
	sovereignty

3. *How People decide their Fate* (Boston, Houghton Mifflin; 1970). Deutsch was President of the American Political Science Association in 1970.

4. pp. 160–61.

What is disturbing about this list is that it includes old-fashioned political words such as 'autonomy', 'self-government', sovereignty'; a new set of words, such as 'feed-back cycle', 'homeostatic process', 'lead' 'lag' 'load' 'gain'; and then other words which can be used in either language, such as 'goal', 'decision-point' and 'memory'.

Essentially, this is an attempt to talk politics in computer language; particularly that of computers harnessed to steering devices, as in space-craft and guided missiles. But it can have a hallucinatory effect, as in these sentences:

Selfhood and Autonomy. In this sense, memory is the source of selfhood and identity. To have a self means to have a memory, together with facilities for intake, output, and decision, and the feedback circuits linking them.

An ethnic or cultural group of people can be said to acquire a 'self' when it acquires a common memory and a common set of channels of social communication that links them into a self-steering system.

In terms of action, memory is the source of our autonomy. To be autonomous means to be able to apply information from the past to a decision in the present. Without memory, without an effective past, there can be no autonomy. Not every feedback system, therefore, that already is self-steering will necessarily have full autonomy. To have full autonomy a system must have a memory; it must have stored information from the past which can be recalled and fed back into the decisions of the present. If a system has such a memory, if it is truly autonomous, then even the most exhaustive knowledge of its environment will not predict with complete accuracy what it will do next, since it might act in terms of its memories as well as in terms of its current intake.

The important point about the human memory is that it is dissociative and combinatorial.

It is impossible to fix the human mind in an individual or in a group, by controlling that individual's or group's environment, for there is an ineradicable element of combinatorial freedom in the human mind and in human society.[5]

Indeed, what it is all about is perhaps most clearly set out for laymen in science fiction. 'Mind is the control of brain by

5. ibid., pp. 152–4.

memory – why should that be hard to understand?' said one of John Wyndham's Martians as early as 1935.[6] And John Wyndham has another hallucinatory story, first published in 1954,[7] about the robot, Hester, programmed to be a kindly nurse, which exercised the autonomy given it in that role by re-making an anxious, neurotic woman (the narrator's wife) as a robot, duly programmed and quite free from neurosis.

Can one dig back to a simpler and more general context, within which these statements make sense? The Society for General Systems Research has been trying since 1954 'to investigate the isomorphy of concepts, laws, and models in various fields, and to help in useful transfers from one field to another'.[8] But in reading its Yearbooks one hits the usual dilemma; that the common language of scientists is built out of mathematical symbols and operations, and that the point may be lost if one seeks a translation into words, old or new. Probably it is better in this situation to try to use words loosely but pictorially, rather than to seek a precision of which they are incapable.

The project, in its most ambitious mood, is no less than to re-state the laws of nature, including Lord Snow's favourite, the second law of thermodynamics, the one about entropy.[9]

The Unity of the Universe, as Stuff and Form

Indeed, the story (as told to children) starts like one of the pre-Socratic philosophers. 'All that there is is made out of two "things" ("substances"? "concepts"? "rules of measurement"?). These are mass/energy and information. Mass/energy (the two are, subject to certain laws, interchangeable) comes in "quanta", and these are both building blocks and driving force. Information is that which dispels uncertainty; what is random is unstructured; structure is information.' It is impossible

6. Writing as 'John Beynon': *Stowaway to Mars* (1935, reprinted in Coronet Books; 1972), p. 174.

7. 'Compassion Circuit' reprinted in Kingsley Amis and Robert Conquest, ed., *Spectrum 4* (Pan Books; 1965).

8. From an SGSR leaflet, 1969.

9. See the article by Myron Tribus and E. C. McIrvine on 'Energy and Information' in *Energy and Power* (1971).

to resist the image of God moving on the face of the waters, to order chaos. Prometheus the technologist imposes order even on fire; what he gives to man is fire ordered intellectually so that it can be manipulated.[10]

One is reminded also of the Greek 'pre-Socratic' philosophers, Democritus, Euripides, Pythagoras, Heraclitus and the others, who had by 500 BC played each his own variation on the themes of 'stuff' and 'form'. These were for Nietzsche prototypes of Zarathustra, prototypes also of the Greek tragic heroes, Prometheus among them. 'Every philosophic system is a metaphor, a work of art.' 'A philosophy is inseparable from a philosopher.'[11] General systems theory is still gnawing at the problem of 'stuff' and 'form': is this Nietzschean romanticism?

One can detect traces of the ancient cosmological grandeur of protoscience in current model-building about the very big and the very small, universe and sub-nuclear particles, galaxies, quasars and quarks. But the vogue for 'energy/information systems' started from quite precise discoveries, conceptual and technical; mathematical formulations related to the theoretical limits of capacity in communication channels; the design of computers based on binary devices ('on-off switches') operating with steadily increasing speed in steadily decreasing bulk. It is perhaps rather more than metaphor to say that nerve cells are 'on-off switches' and that the brain is a system of switches, some of which serve as storage devices or 'memories'. At any rate, the analogy has had some success as research tool, both from the side of mathematics (John von Neumann, *The Computer and the Brain*[12]) and from that of physiology (J. Z. Young, *The Memory System of the Brain*[13]). I stress the word 'some'; the scientists always pause to say that 'at present' there is 'still' a very large gap in capacity between computers and brains. The former are very fast; but in comparison they are very big and clumsy, and very limited. A great deal of

10. 'Mike is like the first man to discover fire. Fire was there all along – after he showed them how, anybody could use it . . . Mike is our Prometheus.' Robert Heinlein, op. cit., p. 356.

11. Nietzsche: *La Naissance de la philosophie à l'époque de la tragédie grecque* (Geneviève Bianquis, trans. & ed., Paris, Gallimard; 1938) p. 10.

12. Yale UP; 1958.

13. OUP; 1966.

SciFi has been written to 'model' the character of the gap and the implications of postulating a bridge.

Information can be regarded as messages; it constitutes order, and only order can convey meaning as distinct from jumble ('noise'). Languages are systems of order; so is any well-developed musical system; so are myths; so is social structure, which is ordered by language, myth and symbols, though not only by these.

So also is the genetic 'code', which conveys 'messages' to cells about the kind of animal they are to build.

In principle, the same 'message' (what is a 'message'?) can be stated in many different 'codes', and there are formulae for translation – if one can discover them. Thus information theory becomes tool and metaphor for structural analysis in the 'humanities'. The 'transforms' are sometimes set to jump gaps too big for them, and appear to fall down. But the Great Chain holds, mythologically, linking structure of gene, structure of universe, structure of brain, structure of myth.

Hence there exist systems of orderly interaction; and nothing but such systems can exist intelligibly. Some useful propositions emerge easily and helpfully. These are systems of inter-relation; they are also patterns of differentiation. They are, as it were, condensation of clouds in the sky, of mass/energy in galaxies and in stars. They are defined by boundaries: but these boundaries are not walls but zones. At the centre, there is dense interaction within the system: at the boundaries this thins off into an indeterminate zone, or even into an 'inter-stellar space'. which is not quite as empty as was once thought. The spatial image works for the earth as bio-system, or for the political entities which existed before state boundaries were invented. But the concept of boundary need not be spatial: it will operate (for instance) in terms of interactions between scientific disciplines, interactions in world markets, interactions in the development of themes in art and music.

It is also easy to absorb the concepts of encapsulated systems, systems hierarchical, interlocking, and so on. It is rather harder to understand what is meant by a 'black box' and to use the concept correctly. The image is quite plain. One has a 'machine' (say a television set or an insect or a living cell). Once we have had it in action for a bit, observed it, experimented with it, we have a notion that it has inputs (disconnect power or aerial and the signal vanishes); that it has outputs – the picture and the sound, or locomotion, or search behaviour of what seems to be a directed kind. In the case of the TV set there are knobs which we find to be regulators of the relations between inputs and outputs. Similarly, in training a dog one seeks to find and develop potentialities for controlling outputs through inputs – voice, gesture, touch, bribe.

Thus in one sense we 'understand' the TV set or the dog, in that we can manipulate that sub-system so that it serves our turn, becomes a manageable component in the larger systems in which we are ourselves operating. But in another sense we don't understand it at all. Our knowledge of 'the controls' may lead us to make guesses as to what is 'inside the black box': but for most purposes we do just as well if we imagine there is a little man with a magic lantern inside the box, as if we have a useless smattering of electronics. Crises will arise which compel us to worry about what there is in there: but it won't do much good to take the back off the set (or to chop open the dog's skull) unless you at least begin to have an inkling of 'the principles' involved at that new level.

Conceptually, this is perhaps the old view that sciences operate at different levels; that the chemist needs only a little physics, the physiologist only a little chemistry, the psychologist only a little physiology, the social scientist (the student of man as social creature) only a little psychology. This is of course rather a simple-minded view; a good case can be made the other way, to the effect that new breakthroughs are made precisely when the exceptional man does decide to open the box and poke about in it, at first very clumsily.

But 'black box' is also related to 'emergent qualities' and to the battle against 'reductionism'. Does 'general systems theory' solve 'the problem of life' by generalizing it? Certainly an energy/information system is *by definition* more than the sum of its parts. Certainly, the systems principle has been of enormous importance heuristically in giving release from temptations to vitalism and other such ghostly doctrines; if there is a gap between the sum of the parts and the performance of the whole the answer is not, cannot be, to invent an entity to bridge the gap. It must be to look again at the equations defining inter-relations within the system and to make sure that they are complete. But in complex systems (such as the brain) they never can be *complete:* what one can hope is that they be 'complete so far as relevant'. On that basis, one needs not only systems theory, but also a process of defining relevance and a process of approximation to the unattainable completeness.

Perhaps therefore general systems theory is in the end a specification about methods of inquiry, not a pre-Socratic specification about what the universe is made of (p. 86).[14] But on either basis, I approach the whole thing with awe and scepticism, as I should the world of a major religion. This could be the biggest thing imaginable, a common world-view, of great range and richness, for all men who seek to ask questions, to demand explanations, to understand. Undoubtedly, it contains elements of what used to be called 'cold cod's-wallop'. But it has a greatness of ambition which helps one to take men seriously as intellectual beings.

This is the best general equilibrium theory there is. Its possibilities are still growing; politically, in relation to mankind as system and the world as system, they are largely possibilities for good. To the point of violence, in defence of good against evil? Yes, I think so: but this in itself marks their Promethean character. A theory of order may demand violence in defence of order.

14. As Monod (1970) notes, rather contemptuously; p. 94.

CHAPTER 7

SYSTEMS OF CONFLICT

As long as the rule and order of the world remain, you will foresee only what you now see: Force: this rock unchanging, yourself unchanging. [Robert Lowell, *Prometheus Bound*, p. 4.]

IT is not a surprising conclusion that equilibrium models in spite of their diversity and range do not accommodate the concept of power as it has been used here. These theories start from the problem of continuity; their 'problematic' (as the neo-Marxists would put it[1]) is about the capacity of a human grouping to persist, retaining a distinguishable identity from one generation to another.[2]

Conflict as Endogenous and Systemic

An equilibrium theory (and a systems theory does it particularly well) can cope adequately with the problems of change, in so far as change is triggered by a force outside the system. But a struggle for power is an endogenous force, if one sees power in the context of violence and decision. 'Something' inside the system *decides* and *imposes* change. There is no conjuring trick that can find endogenous change in a system unless it has been built into the system at the outset.

Three preliminary points.

First, can these two types of theory co-exist?

Equilibrium models and conflict theory seem mutually opposed; the one stressing integration and consensus, the other conflict and incompatibilities. But social science frequently operates with sets of opposed generalizations. The two approaches are complementary.

1. This is put in an important though difficult way in Althusser, *For Marx* (1969) at pp. 66–7, including footnote 30.

2. Von Bertalanffy, in his book, *Problems of Life* (Watts; 1952), uses as his theme Goethe's metaphor of the water-fall, and his poem '*Dauer im Wechsel*' '[Duration in Change'].

Conflict theory stresses force and coercion in the maintenance of stability rather than ideological consensus. Fresh questions provide new answers – not necessarily more correct than earlier ones but conveying broader insight.[3]

This is well enough if one is prepared to regard these simply as tools of analysis, in the hands of a detached sociologist, not as statements about the real world.

About the real world they cannot both be true; nor can a sociologist accept both if he or she takes seriously a commitment to Praxis. This need not necessarily be Marxist; many non-Marxists would accept Mao's simple formulation:

If you want knowledge, you must take part in the practice of changing reality. If you want to know the taste of a pear, you must change the pear by eating it yourself.[4]

The difference between tool of analysis and guide to action is important.

Secondly, the word 'conflict' in this context has to be used carefully and without metaphor. It means conflict between persons, a battle or fight (not necessarily to the death). One may talk of 'conflicting interests' between men, meaning not actual conflict but a possible ground of conflict; and biologists write freely and without much risk of misunderstanding about 'conflicts' between species of animals or plants. But these are metaphors, and one really must not jump about (as Tennyson is perhaps apt to do) between 'Nature red in tooth and claw' and 'the nations' airy navies grappling in the central blue'.[5]

Thirdly, there is the question of a possible distinction between conflict and contradiction, which involves a further distinction between rebellion and revolution.

Conflicts, as distinct from other forms of interaction, always involve power, and it is difficult to appraise the relative power of the contenders before a conflict has settled the issue.[6]

3. P. C. Lloyd, at pp. 32–3 of 'Conflict Theory and Yoruba Kingdoms' (1968).

4. Mao Tse-Tung: 'On Practice': in *Selected Works*, Vol. I (Peking Foreign Languages Press; 1965), p. 300.

5. The first is *In Memoriam*, lvi, line 15, the second *Locksley Hall*, 1.123.

6. Lewis A. Coser: *The Functions of Social Conflict* (Routledge & Kegan Paul; 1956), p. 134.

I think it can be accepted that the concepts of conflict, will and power are mutually involved. Coser's test of power is of the form that 'A wants C, B wants C, they fight, who wins?'

Conflicts, as in Coser's scheme of things, may be brought within an equilibrium system; the definition of a contradiction excludes this. Or perhaps one should say that if one adopts a homeostatic schema then there is contradiction if conflict is not contained within safe limits but builds up exponentially until the system 'explodes'. But some would wish to postulate a more profound distinction, which is not so easy to grasp: that there is a qualitative difference between personal or group conflicts and structural contradictions; and that only the latter will give rise to creative revolutions.

Keeping these points in mind, I find it simplest to build this chapter round a basic distinction between conflict theory and revolutionary theory. But the distinction is by no means absolute; and these two do not exhaust the possibilities. I have referred already to the vogue of Social Darwinism, a myth founded on a metaphor, one of the nastier elements in the complex of Nazi and Fascist ideologies. I have also referred in Chapter 3, to the rise and generalization of games theory, which seems to have served good causes and bad ones indifferently. It is a theory of conflict, concerned with strategies for maximizing gains, minimizing losses, and in that sense it can serve (where quantities can be specified) to increase the effectiveness of military and business resources in the pursuit of power. But it is not a dialectical theory of conflict, in that there is built into the theory the distinction between zero-sum game (adversaries contend for shares of fixed and limited prize-money) and non-zero-sum game, in which the game may go, depending on the interaction of the players, towards an increase in available resources or a decrease. The latter case is hard to express mathematically and to quantify: but it has become a useful metaphor in the conduct of international relations, even in the spirit of the Sermon on the Mount – 'Agree with thine adversary quickly, whiles thou art in the way with him; lest . . . thou be cast into prison. Verily I say unto thee, thou shalt by no means come out thence, till thou hast paid the uttermost farthing.'[7]

7. *Matthew* V; 25, 26.

This has been the language of American foreign policy in the age of Dr Kissinger, not in that of L.B.J.; which is not to say that Nixon, Brezhnev and Mao have been motivated by games theory any more than by the Sermon on the Mount.

Honoris causa, one should mention also those whom James Burnham labelled *The Machiavellians*.[8] Machiavelli himself is too great for such a label; the others to whom Burnham gives the name are Mosca, Sorel, Michels and Pareto, and they have this in common, that they see politics as an endless and cyclical pursuit of power.[9] But only Pareto can claim grandeur, in that he strove for a unified and systematic social science, in which there should be an interplay of economics, politics and sociology. The scheme was too big to be quite consistently worked out (though I find it more coherent than that of Max Weber) but to it belong the general concepts of system and equilibrium, as well as more specific concepts (such as Pareto optimality and Pareto curves in economics) which have been appropriated by particular disciplines in ignorance of the grand system to which they belong.[10]

Conflict, Violence, Non-violence

Another difficulty is that only a narrow line can be drawn between theories of built-in social conflict and theories of violence. Social conflict implies violence but instrumentally – violence to secure victory. Violence theories – to be approached in Part III – insist on violence not instrumentally, but as a component of man and society for which there is no victory; an inheritance to be lived with and enjoyed, or at least to be endured as natural. The line may be artificial – it is for the reader to judge. But for the purposes of this argument the main line of Marxism is taken to be that of *instrumental* violence; with deviations to right and left,

8. (Putnam; 1943).

9. 'The strong have always done what they are able to do, and the weak what they must' (Lowell, op. cit., p. 62).

10. The works themselves are very hard to handle, and I depend greatly on S. E. Finer: *Vilfredo Pareto: Sociological Writings* (Pall Mall; 1966). See in particular the last Chapter of Professor Finer's Introduction, and the section of translated passages on Circulation of Élites; Spoliation (p. 155).

into an equilibrium of self-adjustment, into a violence theory of spontaneity.

There are corresponding ambiguities in the theory of non-violence, a word now used to refer not to a negative or null condition of passivity, but to an active alternative to 'violence', as politically defined in a given context. Non-violence too can be either instrumental (using deadly social compulsions) or expressive; the contrast between Satyagraha in Gandhi's hands, and the gentlest of our Jesus freaks.

But this is another subject, with an important bibliography of its own.[11]

Conflict as Functional

Conflict however mild implies dissent and confrontation; of two, one will emerge better off, one worse off.[12] The game is zero-sum: though not necessarily 'winner take all'.

But function implies coherent process within an organized whole. Each part is dependent on the whole. 'The whole is more than the sum of the parts.' It would be a solecism to talk of the brain in conflict with the legs over the supply of resources from the heart; or of the heart bereft of its desire by defeat in conflict with the stomach. Or rather, such metaphors might be used with a first twist to describe some horrible disease, and with a second twist to comment on 'disease' in society. In so far as one can speak at all of games-players within a biological system, the system is for them a non-zero-sum game; there need be no losers.

At this point enter Georg Simmel;[13] a rather isolated German

11. This can be built up from Adam Roberts, ed., *Civilian Resistance as a National Defence* (Penguin Books; 1969); April Carter, David Hoggett and Adam Roberts, ed., *Non-Violent Action: a selected bibliography* (rev. and enlarged ed., Housmans; 1970); H. A. Bedau, ed.: *Civil Disobedience: Theory and Practice* (New York, Pegasus; 1969); L. J. Macfarlane: *Political Disobedience* (Macmillan; 1971); Jacques Ellul: *Contre Les Violents* (Paris, Le Centurion; 1972).

12. 'A conflict exists when two people wish to carry out acts which are mutually inconsistent', Nicholson (1970), p. 2.

13. A useful book is the translation by Kurt Wolff and Reinhard Bendix of Simmel's *Conflict* and *The Web of Group-Affiliations* with a foreword by E. C. Hughes (New York, Free Press; 1955).

academic sociologist, partly Jewish, long denied the professorial chair which he deserved, a man of insights, rather than system. His paradoxes about conflict date from the early part of this century, and constitute an approach far more sophisticated than that of Social Darwinism, and not unrelated to the imaginative work of his contemporaries (Dostoyevsky, for instance) on suffering and violence. Simmel was neither individualist (but they were then rare in Germany – the crop ripened later in Vienna), nor functionalist, nor Marxist. He was a friend of Max Weber but quite unlike him, easier to bracket with some novelists of his time than with its systematic and polemical sociologists.

Hence this insight, among others, which was found helpful later; that integration is not our sole or highest criterion of the excellence of person or social group. It was after his time that the ideals of the integrated man, of the frictionless social group, declined into self-parody. The fashion changed, and such ideals came to seem silly, even malignant; Simmel was translated and became in the 1950s one of the minor classics in the examination syllabus.

The chief expositor of Simmel's views has been L. A. Coser, whose book on *The Functions of Social Conflict* was published in 1956.[14] This is a very modest and level-headed book, but Coser is explicit about his reaction against contemporary functionalism in America, in so far as it implied the excellence of harmony, quietism, and stability. Indeed, he is one of the first to note the political implications of the quest for 'integration' within the individual, for 'good human relations' at the work-place. Perhaps he should have gone further and discarded the functional metaphor entirely; instead, he sustains the metaphor but in so doing renders it inept. He wants to say that social conflict is sometimes good, sometimes bad; instead, he says that it is 'functional' or 'dysfunctional' – and in so doing (probably he was not the first) he makes a first move outside the logical framework of functionalism. Perhaps this was inevitable: and this linguistic point is merely a symptom that (as Kingsley Davis wrote in

14. See also his *Continuities in the Study of Social Conflict* (New York, Free Press, 1967).

1959[15]) the doctrine is in one sense dead, in another sense a commonplace.[16] But Coser begins to say things which foreshadow a sharper doctrine of social conflict. 'To make oneself understood and to get others to listen is not unconnected with the possession of *power* to give *force* to one's argument' (p. 134, my italics); and he notes (fn. 47 on p. 180) that political scientists were at that time 'more attentive to conflict in the political sphere than other social scientists'. In the 1960s the position seems to have been reversed; sociologists moved towards conflict theory, political scientists towards functionalism, and also towards transactional and cybernetic theories.

Most readers will think swiftly of the various ways in which conflict might be considered a 'good thing', and will note for themselves the difficulty of finding a workable line of distinction between 'good' and 'bad' conflict; unless of course one abdicates the right to prejudge conflicts and rates them as good or bad only by hindsight. So it would be out of place to summarize Simmel and Coser; one need note only that Coser's 'good society' (he goes on using the word 'functional') has a freer atmosphere of debate, a harsher flavour, a greater readiness to solve the insoluble by test of battle than was then usual in the sociological establishment.

Rebellions

'Well,' says Buck, 'a feud is this way. A man has a quarrel with another man, and kills him; then that other man's brother kills him; then the other brothers, on both sides, goes for one another; then the cousins chip in – and by-an-by everybody's killed off, and there ain't no more feud. But it's kind of slow, and takes a long time'. [Mark Twain, *The Adventures of Huckleberry Finn.*]

Twisting the screw a notch tighter, we come to theories of conflict which is cyclical, not cataclysmic: rebellion, not revolution.

Such theories are not saying that 'conflicts are functional' but that in most societies there are patterns of conflict, and also that institutional devices exist for checking conflict before it becomes

15. Above, p. 65.
16. Nicholson, op. cit., p. 24.

destructive. There are real knives, real blood, a settlement of power by cashing threats of violence; trial by combat settles power – and perhaps also authority, because there are social institutions which recognize the victor, and also restrain him; violence ends for the time being, but politics is conducted on the basis that trial by battle will come again. To reverse Clausewitz, politics is a continuation of war by other means.

In some ways the simplest case is that of the feud; simple, in that it still seems to us quite a natural arrangement in a society which has no police, but the feud proves to be complex and variable in incidence when studied in detail. The problem is primarily that Buck got it wrong: a feuding system (as distinct from no system, simply confused violence) is generally shown by close study to have a built-in moderator of some kind, which mobilizes the resources of the wider community to check the killing before it engulfs society.

One type of control stressed by social anthropologists is that of 'cross-cutting cleavages'. The rules of marriage and succession are such that a feud cannot extend far beyond the original opponents without bringing in on each side persons with strong common interests (through marriage or property) which cut across the lines of the feud and create linkages for communication and mediation. The feud is (as it were) brought to a halt gradually by a very fine network of social connections. There is a gentle but strong 'negative feed-back'; rather than 'positive feed-back' tending to explosive escalation.

Another device (compatible with the first) is that of a separate social class or status of mediator; the 'leopard-skin chief' among the Nuer,[17] the Saint among the Swat Pathans.[18] Such a person may or may not wield political power in his own right: for his role as conciliator it is necessary only that he should be someone 'special', who is a member of the society and knows it well, yet is not himself bound by the rules of the feud, neither in the case which comes to him for conciliation nor in any other.

So far as concerns the institution of the feud in Europe, the

17. E. E. Evans-Pritchard: *Nuer Religion* (OUP; 1956).

18. F. Barth: *Political Leadership among the Swat Pathans* (Athlone Press; 1959), Ch. 8.

prime source is still to be found in the best of the Icelandic sagas, in particular that of *Burnt Njal*, which shows an extremely sophisticated understanding of the interactions between law, feud and personality. I know of nothing comparable on Highland feuds or Corsican feuds, both proverbial: and the work on Albanian feuds (still alive in Maoist Albania?) is a little disappointing.[19]

For a previous generation the type case was that of Aeschylus's other great trilogy, which survives complete, and has deeply influenced both Eliot and Sartre. Perhaps this is feud heightened by the implication of incest. Father has daughter slain; mother and her lover kill father; son and daughter kill them both. But the smell of blood is never thus wiped off. The Furies hunt, snuffling and whining, on the trail of Orestes, and cannot be bought off except by higher authority and new birth. In this case, the theme is that of the superior purity of reason embodied in new gods, Apollo and Athena, as against the old gods of blood and death. Prometheus had been for the old gods against the new – 'that innumerable jumble of upstarts, all screaming with one voice, all howling for power'.[20] But Aeschylus, his creator, was playing for even higher stakes: for 'the peace in the feud', as Max Gluckman calls it,[21] and for the place of Athens as mediator in Greek politics alongside the traditional mediator, Apollo's shrine at Delphi. Peace in the feud implies a new hegemony, religious, intellectual, political.[22]

These devices are compatible with a third tradition, that of the traditional law, the men of law, and their 'dooms' backed by the assent of the community. The classical case is that of Iceland in the saga period; one recorded case among many is that of Gunnar, the man of honour, reacting against the judgement of exile imposed on him at the great annual Thing. He rejected the sentence in a burst of affection for his homestead ('fair is the lythe: I will

19. Ian Whitaker, 'Tribal Structure and National Politics in Albania, 1910–1950', in I. M. Lewis, ed., (1968). Margaret Hasluck, 'The Albanian Blood Feud', in P. Bohannan, ed.: *Law & Warfare: Studies in the Anthropology of Conflict* (New York, Natural History Press; 1967), p. 381.

20. Lowell, op. cit., p. 20, 21.

21. *Custom and Conflict in Africa* (Balckwell; 1955), Chapter I.

22. Mario Atilio Levy (1965).

not go') and the bad men were then entitled to mass against the good man and slay him, without guilt. Njal himself, the mediator, was at last the victim, and it was he who said 'with law shall our land be built up and settled, and with lawlessness wasted and spoiled'.[23]

Pragmatic, legalistic, yet violent; the great Victorian historians of law saw this pattern as common to the barbarian cultures of Northern Europe, and they sketched the development of English law as a blend of the Norman sense of government with older Anglo-Saxon habits of feud and compensation.

Following that clue, one comes to the traditions of kingship and its succession rules. Max Gluckman has perhaps put the case in its most general form in his analysis of the rites of the king in Swaziland.[24] The people need the king, the people hate the king. The antinomy runs through their lives from day to day: once a year it is brought into the open in dances and songs which express people against king – but not people against kingship. The present king is reminded that he lives precariously, that he is dispensable; but the office of king is necessary and sacred.

This is one of Gluckman's many cases of rebellion, not revolution. There are other cases where the rules of succession are ambiguous, in that they designate the group from which the successor must come, but not the man. Hence a society may be to some extent submissive under the old king, because of its internal dissensions; but it is involved in battle as soon as the king dies. The brothers and cousins form alliances and fight it out till there is a clear acceptance of victory, and it may be wise for the victor (as in the Ottoman empire) to slay all the claimants in his own generation. But there will be a next generation of competitors; and there will be a new battle when he grows feeble or dies. In fact a deadly war may be part of the rules of succession to high office; and yet the office may remain sacred.

One could read much of this into Shakespeare's *Histories*, which are full of 'sad stories of the deaths of kings', and of the calculated brutality of wars of succession. And yet the doctrine of

23. *The Story of Burnt Njal* (trans. G. W. Dasent, Dent; 1911), p. 123.
24. Gluckman (1955), p. 123.

kingship remains; 'Not all the water in the rude rough sea / Can wash the balm from an anointed king.'[25] The throne is handed on securely, and Elizabeth is a divine successor to a true line of kings – 'the imperial votaress passed on, in maiden meditation, fancy-free'.[26]

The Temper of Our Time

The point to be carried forward from this chapter is that we now live in a world of political killing, ranging from assassination to massive civil war. It is not easy to measure the incidence of killing or to assess the trend. What is to count as a political unit? How is one to distinguish political killing from private violence or the maintenance of public order? How long must a régime survive to live down its violent origins and to rank as peaceable and stable? It is easy to change the aspect of the matter by a change of definition. For instance, how should one now classify the régime in Mao's China, as violent or as peaceable?

It may be better to proceed by example than by enumeration. If one takes the latest available list of members of the UNO and seeks cases in which there has been no political killing in the last thirty years, except in international war, the number is exquisitely small, and they lie off the main track of world politics, for instance Iceland, New Zealand, Fiji. Reversing the analysis, one finds that perhaps half of the existing régimes owe their existence to violence within the last generation; in many of these, power is still in the hands of military men, succession is by *coup d'état*, and there is no other rule. Looking at the world from Westminster, we used to think of 'Freedom slowly broadening down, from precedent to precedent'[27] as being the maxim of twentieth century government, and we thought that we could export our peaceful rules of succession to high office. Clearly this was an illusion; one cannot show that over a century violence has increased, but certainly it has not decreased. The rule is still that of succession by violence, violence which changes nothing.

25. Shakespeare, *Richard II*, III, ii. 59.
26. Shakespeare, *A Midsummer Night's Dream*, II, i. 163.
27. Tennyson, 'You ask me, why', (iii).

The prevailing world pattern, on this showing, is that of rebellion, not revolution.[28]

28. The tables related to violence in the *World Handbook of Political and Social Indicators* (second edn, Yale UP, 1972) can most courteously be described as a massive aberration of the human intellect. I should have liked to make more use of Fred R. von der Mehden, *Comparative Political Violence* (Englewood, Prentice-Hall; 1973) which reached me as this went to the printers.

CHAPTER 8

CONTRADICTION

God then will be the only creature, free to be both motionless and alive, a mirror freed at last from all reflection. And yet he will not be free, God will feel the withdrawal of the creatures, see his own death there, and know that he himself must die before our suffering can end. [Lowell, *Prometheus Bound*, pp. 65–6]

THIS was the trouble about Prometheus: he posed radical alternatives. Aeschylus apparently let Heracles talk him out of it in the third[1] play of the trilogy: Shelley gave him victory by meekness – and they all lived happily ever after.

CHORUS OF HOURS

'When come ye, so wild and so fleet,
For sandals of lightning are on your feet,
And your wings are soft and swift as thought,
And your eyes are as love which is veiled not?

CHORUS OF SPIRITS

We come from the mind
Of human kind
Which was late so dusk, and obscene, and blind,
Now 'tis an ocean
Of clear emotion,
A heaven of serene and mighty motion.'

[*Prometheus Unbound*, Act IV, ll. 89–98]

It may seem disrespectful to allocate here only some twenty pages to Marxism directly. My excuse is that in a sense the whole book is about Marxism, indirectly. There are three issues, one personal and two conceptual.

The Temper of the 1930s

The personal issue is one for the whole generation who became alive politically in the 1930s, and are now passing out of politics. In

1. Or the second play; see p. 31, note 18.

a sense we were all *Marxisants*: Marx seemed a pole of rationality in a period of stress and fear, governed by visions of cruelty and madness.

So in Voznesensky's poem 'Ya Goya';

> I am Goya
> of the bare field, by the enemy's beak gouged
> till the craters of my eyes gape
> I am grief
>
> I am the tongue
> of war, the embers of cities
> on the snows of the year 1941
> I am hunger.[2]

'In the night of reason...'

But it was difficult to make contact with Marx. Partly this was because there was no Marx scholarship to speak of. In the absence of open scholarship Marxism was frozen into a propositional system of inter-locking definitions, what we should now call 'vulgar Marxism',[3] and that system became the pulpit language of a tyranny. The contrast between doctrine and practice was as brutal in Stalin's Russia as it had ever been in any Christian or Islamic state.

In that situation, Trotsky did much to save Marxism from the Marxists. It must never be assumed that Stalin was either stupid or illiterate: in practical issues his judgement was better than Trotsky's, and he had a good deal of analytic power when he chose to apply it. Some day scholars will have to come back to Stalin's work, and to puzzle out the different strands in it. But in those days Trotsky's existence and his sheer debating power kept issues open, kept the steel jaws of definitional Marxism from closing.

Nevertheless, while Stalin was alive, Marxism ceased to be intellectually interesting, or even important. The Cold War assumed the aspect first of an old-fashioned power struggle

2. Trans. S. Kunitz, in *Antiworlds*, Patricia Blake and Alex Hayward, ed., (OUP, 1967).

3. Or perhaps 'mechanical Marxism': S. M. Miller, 'Mirror Error', p. 86 of *New Society*, 13 July 1972. But he goes on to say that 'Left-wing Parsonianism' is mechanical Marxism, and I should not wish to adopt that.

between states, then was gradually transmuted by the implications of nuclear war into a concern for global management in a period of rapid technological change. New technology was creating a new world; the relations of production were changing, so was the balance between old and new states and empires.

Stalin's ghost was laid at last by the Cuban missile crisis of October 1962; and through the 1960s the process of pragmatic change went on, till we now have a precarious global balance, very alarming but not in a revolutionary sense. The world we know was made by massive movements of peoples, 'Folk-Wanderings'. That age is surely over? It is clear enough that the *Gast-arbeiter*, or guest-worker, represents one more stage in the human use of human beings; slavery, serfdom, peonage, contract labour in various forms. But this time the hosts will see to it that the guests go home? That they do not stay on, to change the world, barbarians in the Western Empire? *Les Damnés de la Terre* are physically segregated from the affluent; there is really nothing for them to do now but to stay at home and kill one another, quietly. They are 'functionally superfluous', like most Blacks in the USA.

This situation, that of the so-called 'external proletariat', has been one factor in Marxist revival. The analysis of 'neo-colonialism' is not dependent on Marxist concepts; indeed, Bishop Helder Camara and many others have shown that Christian concepts can do the job equally well. But there has been a mingling of Marxist and other languages, rhetorically effective but not scientific in any sense, Marxist or positivist. Hence a challenge to more rigorous analysis of the world system of politics, as it now is: at the same time has come the publication of works by Marx hitherto little known, and the emergence in Europe of serious scholarship concerned to understand Marx's thought in its changing contexts, from his earliest youth. This scholarship is by no means detached from practice, as it is concerned with the intellectual biography of a man who thought he had found the key to method in the sustained unity of theory and practice.

I do not think it is necessary here to call the roll of Marxist concepts, as they appear (above all) in the *Communist Manifesto*. They contain plenty of puzzles, in particular dialectic, alienation, ideology, class; and the world changes; but no one can doubt their systematic power in their original context. And in that context they were concerned above all with revolutionary practice and the emergence of what is radically new in human social organization. Four practical and ethical points, quite briefly:

(1) Revolution is a matter of power to act.

(2) It acts to shatter old frameworks and release new energies; to end alienation.

(3) Force is necessary, but instrumental; in Lenin's words in 1917, 'In Russia, we must at once occupy ourselves with the building of the proletarian Socialist state.'[4] Victory is only a beginning: a revolution is not a popular carnival, nor yet a Freudian catharsis of individual aggression.

(4) Finally, not all is justified: 'an end which requires unjust means is not a just end' – a phrase quoted by Camus in *L'Homme Revolté*, in a passage which emphasizes 'the ethical demands which form the basis of the Marxist dream . . . in them lie the real greatness of Marx'.[5]

These are the points needed for transition to the next section of the book, that on violence. The two conceptual difficulties referred to on p. 102 have a wider range.

The first is that of method, the second is that of will, choice or decision.

The Metaphor of the Dialectic

The metaphor of Hegel's dialectic is quite plain, though it is hard to state. It is not precisely that of Socrates, the midwife eliciting from each man his 'true' view by question and answer. But the starting point is that of dialogue; for instance, Plato's *Symposium*, in which the concept Love emerges from discussion as something wider and deeper than each speaker thinks, yet not independent

4. This is E. H. Carr's translation: *The Bolshevik Revolution, 1917–23, Vol. 1* (Penguin Books; 1966) p. 116.

5. 1951: English translation by Anthony Bower, Penguin Books; 1971, pp. 176–7. Note (1) Camus gives no reference for the Marx quotation, (2) The English title, *The Rebel*, may be misleading. Camus's use of 'revolt' lies somewhere between the English usages of 'rebellion' and of 'revolution'.

of any of them. And the next stage is to a dialogue of the great, pair by pair: Plato to Aristotle, Aristotle to Aquinas, Aquinas to Descartes, Descartes to Hume, Hume to Kant – or as you please. Part of the game of dialectic at that level is to vary the seeded players and the pairings; the essence is that men can advance by argument, that conflict in argument makes change, makes what is radically new. The paradox of radical novelty is resolved (or re-stated) by building novelty into man's life. Human society is conflict; conflict is the re-building of society. The phrase 'conflict is necessary to society' may be so used as to seem functional; but a theory of radical conflict can be construed as functional only in a nonsensical sense: no conflict, no society – the relation of conflict to society is not one of part to whole but of identity or inter-penetration.

Hegel's dialectic was one between concepts or conceptual systems, each in turn offering a rational answer to successive 'problematics' about the nature of reality. 'Marx stood it on its head.' Did he ? Certainly he substituted a dialectic of technologies for a dialectic of philosophical concepts. But a great deal is left standing, in particular, the concepts of rationality and contradiction; so that much serious work is needed, and has been begun, on the implied logic and epistemology. Clearly Hegel and Marx both belong to the vast European tradition of 'systematic', in which an attempt is made to build an edifice of understanding which stands by the coherence of its arched and buttressed structure. But Hegel and Marx were both very learned men; and Marx at least (though he was sometimes hasty and bad-tempered) respected facts as his masters. Mao certainly represents him correctly in these two passages (the first of them quoted earlier):

> If you want knowledge, you must take part in the practice of changing reality. If you want to know the taste of a pear, you must change the pear by eating it yourself.[6]

> To be superficial ... means to deny the necessity for probing deeply into a thing and minutely studying the characteristics of its contradiction, but instead merely to look from afar and, after glimpsing the rough outline, immediately to try to resolve the contradiction

6. Mao Tse-Tung: *Selected Works* (1967), Vol. I: 'On Practice', p. 300.

(to answer a question, settle a dispute, handle work, or direct a military operation). This way of doing things is bound to lead to trouble.[7]

But can a systematic intellectual structure be refuted by facts? Are we liable to be involved in a 'dialogue of the deaf' between the European tradition of grand system, and the English (and Viennese!) tradition of piecemeal empiricism.[8] Sir Karl Popper has had his say about *The Poverty of Historicism*;[9]

It really looks as if historicists were trying to compensate themselves for the loss of an unchanging world by clinging to the belief that change can be foreseen because it is ruled by an unchanging law. [p. 161]

European scholars, even non-Marxists, are likely to retort that, in Oakeshott's sense,[10] English empiricism is 'merely impossible; the product of a misunderstanding.'

Nothing whatever can be constructed out of disintegrated refutable propositions. Such propositions do not make sense without a context; you are committed even by your 'problematic', even by the questions you ask, and the honest inquirer will seek to set down as lucidly as possible the context of his questions.

The exchange of gibes has become pointless, yet it is not easy to find common ground. Mao, so far as I can judge from the texts readily available, has been inclined to treat Marxism as a tool for inquiry about the real world rather than as a description of it, whether literal or metaphysical. And probably both Marx and Mao would use the concept of *praxis* to explain that the structured system, the philosophy, is part of the real world and is in continuous interaction with it, that the system is a tradition, not a dogma.

7. 'On Contradiction', p. 324.
8. 'Testing individual propositions separately' is seen by Boulding (1970), p. 24, as *the* method of science. But this is only part of it? (See also Boulding, p. 96.)
9. Routledge & Kegan Paul; 1957.
10. 'Political Education' in Oakeshott (1962), p. 115.

The Paradoxes of Choice

But the concept of Praxis introduces the second main problem. There was a time at the end of the nineteenth century, when the German Social Democratic Party,[11] the greatest of Marxist parties, was prepared to sit back and let history do its work. And certainly the faith of Marxists has had an eschatological colour, like that of the early Christians: 'the future is on our side'. But for Marx and the greater Marxists the doctrine has been one not of destiny but of human action and choice; the future does not yet exist,[12] it has to be made by the will and intelligence of men. But can men choose between these futures, which do not exist? And choose collectively? These are the subjects of the last part of the book: I pause here only to indicate the double paradox: choice? collective choice?

Conflict is built into the dialectical understanding of society. Conflicts will be confused and overlapping;

> Therefore, in studying any complex process in which there are two or more contradictions, we must devote every effort to finding its principal contradiction. Once this principal contradiction is grasped, all problems can be readily solved.[13]

This will then indicate which is 'the right side' in the conflict, the side of the future: and then success in the conflict, earned by resolution and skill, will enable the victors to make the revolution. But what then? The whole theory is one of how things are made radically new; and looking at history, and above all at 'the bourgeois revolution' in Europe from the fifteenth century, this is indeed what happened. But no-one 'chose' that outcome; indeed

11. Two classic texts: Edward Bernstein: *Evolutionary Socialism: a criticism and affirmation* (1899; trans. E. C. Harvey, New York, Schocken Books; 1961); Karl Kautsky: *Ethics and the materialist conception of history* (1906; trans. J. B. Askew, third rev. edn Chicago, Kerr; 1909).

12. Contrast SciFi speculations about the actual existence of an infinite number of branching futures (John Wyndham), or an infinite variety of pasts (Brian W. Aldiss: 'Danger: Religion!' in *The Inner Landscape*, Corgi Books; 1970), or a logically unbreakable cycle (Robert Heinlein, 'His Bootstraps' in Kingsley Amis and R. Conquest (ed.)., *Spectrum I* (Gollancz; 1961).

13. 'On Contradiction', p. 332.

the German feudal lords, the Germans of the mercantile cities, would have been horrified alike if they had seen that the wave of the future would sweep them all into the Prussian bureaucratic state.

Indeed, how are you to know that there has been a revolution, except in retrospect? A nasty idea, for all of us; perhaps the techniques of production have already switched, now, the relations of production, so that this thing we live, called 'the corporate society' 'the post-industrial state', 'state capitalism', East and West, is already the post-revolutionary society, the choice of history?[14] Perhaps these arrangements (pragmatically modified) are the best we are going to get for the next troubled phase of global history, the period we can see ahead in the relatively short run. To put the same thing in a different way, has anyone a better plan than this for getting through fifty to a hundred years, a period of an increasing gap between rich and poor, a world population stabilizing slowly, a realization that resources are finite and must be rationed? Even if we could find a world Napoleon, a world Stalin, would we like it better?

But suppose that in a historical sense the past sixty years of killing and invention have been *the revolution*? The Marxist answer is clearly that still conflict is built into the technological basis of society; still it will give rise to contradictions, subsidiary and principal; the revolutionary must pick himself off the floor, choose his side, and get to work again, rationally and instrumentally, to make the next revolution.

But the myth will still be that of Prometheus, not that of Dionysus; that of reason, not that of the God of ecstasy, who swept his worshippers, the suffering women, away to the high mountains – in Gilbert Murray's too Swinburnean verse:

A MAIDEN

O glad, glad on the mountains
To swoon in the race outworn,
When the holy fawn-skin clings,

14. C. B. Macpherson argues well *against* this; 'Politics: Post-Liberal-Democracy' (1964) in *Ideology in Social Science*, Robin Blackburn, ed., Fontana Books; 1972). But I am not sure what in this part of his paper he is arguing *for*.

And all else sweeps away,
To the joy of the red quick fountains,
The blood of the hill-goat torn,
The glory of wild-beast ravenings,
Where the hill-tops catch the day;
To the Phrygian, Lydian, mountains!
'Tis Bromios leads the way.

ANOTHER MAIDEN

Then streams the earth with milk, yea, streams
With wine and nectar of the bee,
And through the air dim perfume steams
Of Syrian frankincense; and He,
Our leader, from his thyrsus spray
A torchlight tosses high and higher,
A torchlight like a beacon-fire,
To waken all that faint and stray;
And sets them leaping as he sings,
His tresses rippling to the sky,
And deep beneath the Maenad cry
His proud voice rings:
'Come, O ye Bacchae, come!' . . .

O, then, like a colt as he runs by a river,
A colt by his dam, when the heart of him sings,
With the keen limbs drawn and the fleet foot a-quiver,
Away the Bacchanal springs![15]

And men similarly were swept away by the woman goddess of possession, as was Attis in Catullus's poem written in the most hysterical of Latin metres –

15. Euripides, *Bacchae*, 11.135–53, 165–9. Gilbert Murray, *Euripides* (fourth edn, Allen & Unwin; 1908), pp. 85–6. I believe there is now a version by Wole Soyinka, but I have not been able to find a copy. He may get the colour of the passage better: but readers should perhaps be warned that there are real difficulties in the Greek, involving the identities of God, priest and Bacchae. My guess is that Euripides built in the ambiguities, and Murray's version gets this. But see E. R. Dodds's commentary on *The Bacchae* (second edn, Oxford, Clarendon, 1960), and the translation by W. Arrowsmith in D. Grene and R. Lattimore, ed., *Euripides V* (Chicago UP; 1959). See also Appendix I on 'Maenadism' in E. R. Dodds: *The Greeks and the Irrational* (California UP; 1951).

Attis even while the blood was falling, freshly falling upon the grass,
Attis, now a man no longer, seized with delicate hands the light
Tambourine, the mighty mother's instrument ceremonial,
Then to shake the hollow oxhide with the tender hands began,
And to chant in tremulous accents thus, amid his company.
'Seek the forest depths together, all the Mother's priestesses,
All together, roving herds of her the queen of Dindymus,
You that, into trackless exile hurrying very far from home,
Following my rule, the comrades who have chosen me to lead . . .'[16]

Nor will a new Marxism be akin in spirit to the ecstatic fire and brimstone of the Book of Revelation –

And after these things I saw another angel come down from heaven, having great power; and the earth was lightened with his glory.

And he cried mightily with a strong voice, saying, Babylon the great is fallen, is fallen, and is become the habitation of devils, and the hold of every foul spirit, and a cage of every unclean and hateful bird.

For all nations have drunk of the wine of the wrath of her fornication, and the kings of the earth have committed fornication with her, and the merchants of the earth are waxed rich through the abundance of her delicacies.

How much she hath glorified herself, and lived deliciously, so much torment and sorrow give her: for she saith in her heart, I sit a queen, and am no widow, and shall see no sorrow.

Therefore shall her plagues come in one day, death, and mourning, and famine; and she shall be utterly burned with fire: for strong is the Lord God who judgeth her.

And the kings of the earth, who have committed fornication and lived deliciously with her, shall bewail her, and lament for her, when they shall see the smoke of her burning.

Standing afar off for the fear of her torment, saying, Alas, alas! that great city Babylon, that mighty city! for in one hour is thy judgement come.[17]

Postscript 1

Readers of Camus will see what this formulation owes to him.

16. Hugh Macnaghten, trans. (Cambridge UP; 1925).
17. Ch. XVIII, verses 1–3, 7–10.

He does not write about 'rebellions' in the usage of English social anthropologists, armed fights for office within an ongoing system: but draws a contrast between two traditions of revolution, Marxist and nihilist. The former he respects; he would however maintain that victory is logically impossible, but that honourable men will nevertheless join battle – revolt, not revolution.

Postscript 2

This Part of the book was written before I had seen Kenneth Boulding's *Primer of Social Dynamics*, and I find that our arguments are parallel though distinct. It is not possible here to set out his argument in detail: to put it very briefly he distinguishes three processes, threat, exchange, integration, and argues that the first of these has a fairly limited range of application. There are things in his argument I should wish to debate; for instance, about the 'fairness' of markets and of integration. But he does not directly oppose the line of my own argument; that if one is to grasp the concept of power it must be through the acceptance that conflict is real. It is one step further to say that conflict may be creative; yet another step, to say that conflict alone is creative. I doubt if the last step is taken except by 'vulgar Marxism' (out of sheer stupidity) and by various forms of violence-creeds (Boulding, p. 97). The second last is taken by Boulding himself, rather hesitantly: I should accept it more firmly. Power is real and may *decide* to change things in the real world.

Boulding (p. 108) recognizes 'market power' and 'integrative power'; yet he writes also (p. 89) 'Only the alienated can change society'.[18]

18. *A Primer of Social Dynamics: History as Dialectics and Development* (New York, Free Press: 1970).

Part Three

VIOLENCE

You will see that the River of violence now runs across this land like a scar. [Lowell, *Prometheus Bound*, p. 41.]

CHAPTER 9

SEMANTIC

... you taught me a secret you did not perhaps mean to impart,
That one must speak lightly, and use fair names like the ladies,
They used to call
The Eumenides.
[Stevie Smith: 'A Soldier Dear to Us', in *Scorpion and Other Poems*.]

ONE would not be listened to if one said there was no problem about violence. Wherever one turns, whatever one reads, one meets cases of violence and of the word 'violence'.[1]

Usages and Theme

Some simple classification of usage is possible:

'Violent crime'; meaning cases of physical assault or the threat of it, as between individuals.

'Violence in the streets'; meaning provocation, demonstration, and its escalation by 'police violence' or partisan 'counter-violence' to a state of 'internal war'.

'External war', or at least those aspects of it which involve destruction beyond what is clearly instrumental in conflict between armed forces.

Perhaps 'violence to oneself'; the incidence of suicide and (probably a more frequent usage now) the incidence of compulsive self-destruction by the use of alcohol and other drugs of addiction.

Perhaps – though it may be felt that this stretches usage, in a journalistic way – 'violence at the wheel'; the increase in killing by accident, which turns out on inspection to be more closely related to personality traits and to self-intoxication than to technical factors and risks.

Certainly, 'violence in the media'; a supposed syndrome, in which news of violence (or fiction about violence) meets a craving

1. 'Ce n'est point, aujourd'hui, le temps de la violence, mais celui de la conscience de la violence.' Ellul (1972), p. 7.

for the stimulus of watching violence, so that reporting of violence is further stimulated – and so in a spiral. The notion is popular, the evidence rather weak; and there is even less evidence that the supposed syndrome of the *voyeur*, of violence-watching, builds up to an explosion of external violence.[2]

And then a final twist, 'non-violent violence', the paradox or metaphor that a personality may be destroyed as effectively by indirect methods as by physical brutality.[3] In one sense we owe the concept to the more sophisticated practitioners of police interrogation; in another to theorists (I am thinking of Herbert Marcuse and R. D. Laing in particular) who find social violence in 'repressive toleration' and other compulsions to conformity, family violence in patterns of inter-personal relation which leave no escape open except into madness.

Even laughter may be violence.

This is not easy to clarify, because there are many variations and probably no single theme. If there is one theme, it is that of the dark side of human nature, a man's hatred of himself and others. The associations culled from the NED and quoted in Chapter 2 point that way, to darkness and to death;[4] a theme better handled by myth than by analysis, the Eumenides in Aeschylus's play, the Furies in Shelley's *Prometheus Unbound* –

> *First Fury.* We are the ministers of pain, and fear,
> And disappointment, and mistrust, and hate,
> And clinging crime; and as lean dogs pursue
> Through wood and lake some struck and sobbing fawn,
> We track all things that weep, and bleed, and live,
> When the great King betrays them to our will.
>
> [Act I, p. 214, ll. 452–7.]

2. Among much other inconclusive documentation, BBC Audience Research Department: *Violence on Television: Programme Content and Viewer Perception* (BBC; 1972). Note also the Open University Mass Communications Study Centre, in the USA the Surgeon-General's Commission on Violence on Television, and an article by Alasdair Clayre in *The Listener*, 28 December 1972, p. 885.

3. Cf. Etzioni, p. 8, fn. 7.

4. An unlucky phrase used of Jomo Kenyatta in Kenya, by a governor who meant well: 'the leader to darkness and to death', to Mau Mau, secret oathing, murder and self-destruction. See Jeremy Murray-Brown, *Kenyatta* (London, Allen & Unwin, 1972), p. 301.

Or this by Robert Lowell, translating the poet Mandelstam, a Russian Jew arrested by Stalin's police in 1934:

> We live. We are not sure our land is under us.
> Ten feet away, no one hears us.
>
> But wherever there's even a half-conversation,
> We remember the Kremlin's mountaineer.
>
> His thick fingers are fat as worms,
> His words reliable as ten-pound weights.
>
> His boot tops shine,
> His cockroach mustache is laughing.
>
> About him, the great, his thin-necked, drained advisors,
> He plays with them. He is happy with half-men around him.
>
> They make touching and funny animal sounds.
> He alone talks Russian.
>
> One after another, his sentences hit like horseshoes; he
> Pounds them out. He always hits the nail, the balls.
>
> After each death, he is like a Georgian tribesman,
> Putting a raspberry in his mouth.[5]

Force and Violence

Rather more will be said below (Chapter 10) of violence as being itself symbol and metaphor. But the problem here is to relate the problem of violence to that of political power, treating political power as a necessary basis for collective decision-making. There is here a network of semantic questions, which can perhaps be brought to an issue by discussing the relationship between 'force' and 'violence', as words in English usage.

Is there in fact a workable distinction at all? I should like to be able to say that 'force' is neutral, 'violence' is loaded; that 'force' is instrumental, violence may be desired for its own sake. But (firstly) the distinction may not work in the same way in all languages. For instance, the French word *force* sometimes has to be translated as 'strength', not as 'force', as in the proverb

5. Quoted by George Steiner (1972), p. 151.

l'union fait la force. In the *Prometheus* the two 'hard men'[6] who see to the binding of the Titan are called Kratos and Bia; it would be legitimate to translate this as Power and Violence, but Lowell makes it Power and Force and can scarcely be faulted. But in Latin there is a workable distinction between *vis* and *violentia*, the latter meaning in effect the improper use of force.

That raises (secondly) the endlessly discussed theoretical question: is force the basis of the state? Or, reversing the question, there is the tag from T. H. Green, that 'will, not force is the basis of the state'.[7] We should be saying something different, and slightly paradoxical, if we made it 'will not violence is the basis of the state'?

Thirdly, we cannot get out of difficulties, as we sometimes try to do, by talking of 'legitimate force' as the basis of the state, because by definition it is the state, or an equivalent authority, which constitutes the legitimation of force. But one might say that the two words represent sub-classes of a larger class, for which there is no handy single word, but which could be described perhaps as 'physical intervention'. And perhaps there is a third sub-class; a mother (we should say) uses 'strength' to lift her two-year old child, not 'force', nor 'violence'.

In fact, then, force (except in the fixed terminology of physics) also carries an implication of conflict and compulsion, and it shares that affective tone with the word 'violence'.

It is not therefore quite safe to say that in its use the word 'force' is neutral. It is distasteful, though not perhaps as distasteful as violence; when it comes to the use of force, we salve our consciences by adjectives, its 'proper' or 'legitimate' use.

Nor is it quite safe to say that force is instrumental, violence is always chosen for its own sake. After all, it may be tactically best to open an assault with a 'violent' blow; though we may in addition feel pleasure in its violence, even if it is unsuccessful.

6. So far as I know, only A. J. Podlecki (*The Political Background of Aeschylean Tragedy* (Michigan UP; 1966), p. 107, has noted that Bia, Violence, is feminine. This adds a *frisson* – but I doubt if Aeschylus felt it in that way.

7. T. H. Green: *Lectures on the Principles of Political Obligation* (1941 reprint), p. 121.

At most, perhaps, one can say that violence is more subjective in use than force; it is an emotion, as well as an action, an emotion evaluated morally according to rather puzzling criteria.

There are less important problems about the boundary between force and non-force, violence and non-violence. Can one 'use force' by talking, or by sitting down, by fasting? Certainly, if the effect (intended or not) is compulsory in character. And what is 'compulsory'? Such that it seeks to influence choice by creating an unpleasant option for the chooser, and throwing that option into the scales, as the Gaulish king Brennus threw his sword into the scales when assessing the ransom for captured Rome. There seems to be no difference between force and violence in these respects; the basic metaphor is one of physical action, and in some sense the ultimate recourse is to conflict and trial of strength in battle. Marcuse and Laing are entitled to bring out this point: but in fact no-one knows where the line comes between threats which refer directly to physical action, and those which are as far removed from it as are our bank accounts from the gold reserves. It makes good sense also to take the opposite point of view, that threats like money rest on credit, and that the essence of the compulsion is a matter of social confidence, not of force or violence. Kenneth Boulding[8] stresses that 'threat power' will work better if supported (in his terminology) by exchange value and social integration, which correspond to transactional systems and functional systems in the first part of this book. Similarly, this is the point of T. H. Green's catch-phrase, already quoted, that 'will, not force is the basis of the state'.

But in practice force must generally be *organized* force, *a* force consisting of specialized people, with their own training, equipment and social norms. Even 'a United Nations Force' has the characteristics of an organization, many of which are not attractive; for instance, hierarchical order, a code of mutual support in face of outside criticism or attack, a natural history of exponential growth halted only by counter-vailing power. Brian Chapman in his book on *The Police State*[9] is right in emphasizing both the rational, indeed benevolent origins of organized police, and the

8. (1970): for instance at p. 70.
9. Pall Mall; 1970.

successive distortions through which police organization becomes parasitical and in the end dominant in régimes which depend on it. The individual faced by an organization often has good reason to use the language of violence. There is extreme stress if an individual confronts an organization, especially a well-equipped one, a human being faced by a non-human force.

Word-play

Beyond this lies word-play, deliberate or unconscious.

Force-violence seem to be used as a 'we-they' pair, like 'we are patriotic they are jingo', 'we are resolute they are fanatics', 'we are careful they are mean', and so on. 'We' use force, 'they' use violence. A Rugby correspondent paying tribute to a pack of forwards might call them 'rugged' or 'vigorous' or even 'forceful'. But to say 'violent' would be to say that they go beyond the limit of the rules as 'we' understand them. Violence is dangerous play. A government will find it to its advantage if 'the other side' (pickets in an industrial dispute, for instance) can plausibly be accused of violence, as in the 'battle of Grosvenor Square', a demonstration on 17 March 1968 which was destroyed politically by a photograph[10] of one demonstrator holding a policeman while another kicked him in the face.

Conversely, wise leaders will plan a non-violent demonstration: and will look for a chance to criticize the violence of the police. And wise police leadership will turn that threat aside; foolish leadership will be trapped into escalation.[11] Our images of political violence are those of armed against unarmed, organized against disorderly; photographs of the French riot police at work in May 1968,[12] of Mayor Daley's Chicago police at work in

10. Reproduced in *The Listener*, 17 February 1972, with an article by Richard Wollheim on 'Democracy and Violence'.

11. 'Policemen are a critical variable in the generation of violence. They are at once the symbolic cause of violent unrest and the agency charged with restoring order.' D. H. Bayley and Harold Mendelsohn: *Minorities and the Police: confrontation in America* (New York, Free Press; 1968).

12. For instance in Patrick Seale and Maureen McConville: *French Revolution, 1968* (Penguin Books; 1968).

August 1968;[13] the story of the Protestant attack on civil rights marchers in January, 1969, which began the period of violence in Northern Ireland.[14]

It is prudent to entrap the other side into violence if there is in fact a watching public which is capable of reacting against those who break the rules. But that is not a usual situation anywhere in the world.

It is harder to cool violence than to escalate it; one of the graffiti of May, 1968 was (inevitably) '*Contre la violence policière la violence dans la rue.*'[15]

As early as 1912 Georges Sorel had tried to twist usage one turn further to the advantage of revolution. 'We use the terms *force* and *violence* in relation to acts of authority and to acts of revolt. But clearly the two cases work in quite different ways. I think it would be helpful to adopt a terminology free from this ambiguity and to keep the word *violence*, for the latter case, that of revolt. We should then say that to use *force* is to impose a social order ruled by a minority, to use *violence* is to destroy that order'.[16]

This word-play is part of his exercise in building myth, and his myth is that of the Revolution as destructive violence. Sorel sets himself up in antithesis to the Marxist tradition and to some anarchist traditions, in that for him the Revolution is in itself a definitive act. It is not an act for the sake of building a new society, it is not instrumental for anything but itself and those identified with it as participants. There is an inter-play of revolution-destruction-violence. Its myth is that of the General Strike, escalating into violence; the myth strengthens the workers' solidarity, nerves their resolution, makes them men among men, free men not wage slaves. And this inward change is itself the Revolution; and it exists for a moment, or for all time; once found, it can never be lost.

13. For instance, in the Walker Report, *Rights in Conflict* (New York, Bantam; 1968).

14. C. R. Rose (1971), p. 104.

15. Photograph in Walter Lewino: *L'Imagination au Pouvoir* (Paris, Losfeld; 1968).

16. Georges Sorel: *Réflexions sur le Violence* (Paris, Rivière, eighth edn, 1936), pp. 256–7: my translation.

It is, in a phrase of Nietzsche's, the *Umwertung aller Werte*, the transvaluation of all values. The mood is that of the fallen Archangel –

> What though the field be lost?
> All is not lost; the unconquerable Will,
> And study of revenge, immortal hate,
> And courage never to submit or yield.
> And what is else not to be overcome
>
> The mind is its own place, and in itself
> Can make a Heav'n of Hell, a Hell of Heav'n.
>
> Better to reign in Hell, than serve in Heav'n.
>
> So farewell Hope, and with Hope farewell Fear,
> Farewell Remorse: all Good to me is lost;
> Evil be thou my Good.[17]

By a strange twist, Satan becomes the emblem of heroic violence, the bad Prometheus.

17. Milton: *Paradise Lost*, Book I, 105, 254, 263; Book IV, 108.

CHAPTER 10

IMAGES OF VIOLENCE

> Truly poetry is international, just like music,
> And falling bombs and death and destruction
> And misery and pain and wastage,
>
> Truly we only need one poet in the world
> Since local references can be inserted by editors,
> Theatre managers or clerks in the Culture Ministries.
>
> [D. J. Enright, 'Streets', in *Daughters of Earth*]

Stasis at Corcyra

I HAVE already mentioned (p. 50) the mythological and dramatic element in Thucydides's history of the war between Athens and Sparta, a war in which he took part and which he observed as a spectator of tragic drama. There are various set pieces within his narrative each of which is used to indicate a theme, and these episodes together constitute one of the masterpieces of political reflection; theory set out in images and debates, not by continuous exposition.

One of his themes is that destruction feeds on itself, violence escalates, and that fully escalated violence is the negation of society. The set-piece regarding this negation must in one sense be read with the speech of Pericles on the perfection of man in society; the account of the plague at Athens, that is to say, the physical degradation of man's image; the Athenian arguments for empire as power freed from morality, as in the dialogue with the Melians.[1] I quote a good deal of his account of social degradation, as a lead to what follows in this Chapter.

... the Corcyraeans continued to massacre those of their own citizens whom they considered to be their enemies. Their victims were accused of conspiring to overthrow the democracy, but in fact men were often killed on grounds of personal hatred or else by their debtors because of the money that they owed. There was death in every shape and form. And, as usually happens in such situations, people went to

1. Thucydides: *The Peloponnesian War* (trans. Rex Warner, Penguin Books; 1954), pp. 115, 123, 359.

every extreme and beyond it. There were fathers who killed their sons; men were dragged from the temples or butchered on the very altars; some were actually walled up in the temple of Dionysus and died there.

So savage was the progress of this revolution, and it seemed all the more so because it was one of the first which had broken out. Later, of course, practically the whole of the Hellenic world was convulsed, with rival parties in every state – democratic leaders trying to bring in the Athenians, and oligarchs trying to bring in the Spartans. In peace-time there would have been no excuse and no desire for calling them in, but in time of war, when each party could always count upon an alliance which would do harm to its opponents and at the same time strengthen its own position, it became a natural thing for anyone who wanted a change of government to call in help from outside . . .

So revolutions broke out in city after city, and in places where the revolutions occurred late the knowledge of what had happened previously in other places caused still new extravagances of revolutionary zeal, expressed by an elaboration in the methods of seizing power and by unheard-of atrocities in revenge. To fit in with the change of events, words, too, had to change their usual meanings. What used to be described as a thoughtless act of aggression was now regarded as the courage one would expect to find in a party member; to think of the future and wait was merely another way of saying one was a coward; any idea of moderation was just an attempt to disguise one's unmanly character; ability to understand a question from all sides meant that one was totally unfitted for action. Fanatical enthusiasm was the mark of a real man, and to plot against an enemy behind his back was perfectly legitimate self-defence. Anyone who held violent opinions could always be trusted, and anyone who objected to them became a suspect . . .

Revenge was more important than self-preservation . . .

Love of power, operating through greed and through personal ambition, was the cause of all these evils. To this must be added the violent fanaticism which came into play once the struggle had broken out. Leaders of parties in the cities had programmes which appeared admirable – on one side political equality for the masses, on the other the safe and sound government of the aristocracy – but in professing to serve the public interest they were seeking to win the prizes for themselves . . .

. . . their one standard was the pleasure of their own party at that particular moment, and so, either by means of condemning their enemies on an illegal vote or by violently usurping power over them, they were always ready to satisfy the hatreds of the hour . . .

. . . everyone had come to the conclusion that it was hopeless to expect a permanent settlement and so, instead of being able to feel confident in others, they devoted their energies to providing against being injured themselves. As a rule those who were least remarkable for intelligence showed the greater powers of survival . . .

. . . human nature, always ready to offend even where laws exist, showed itself proudly in its true colours, as something incapable of controlling passion, insubordinate to the idea of justice, the enemy to anything superior to itself; for, if it had not been for the pernicious power of envy, men would not so have exalted vengeance above innocence and profit above justice.[2]

Corcyra, thus wrecked, played no further part in the politics of Greece: but the infection ran through the Greek cities, fermented to some extent by external enemies, the Persians, and it was one factor among others in limiting the further advance of Greek freedom. The images of darkness and blood overcame those of brightness and clear sky.

The Romantic Agony

These dark images have at various times possessed European art. On the whole, political theories of violence follow a step behind aesthetic theories, at least in the nineteenth century.

It is true that Elizabethan and Jacobean tragedy 'supp'd full with horrors'.[3] It is true also that Milton's Satan was perceived later as the essential hero of *Paradise Lost*, the eternal enemy of an evil god. Both these episodes had their social and political roots, no doubt. But from the late eighteenth century the imagery of artists outran political imagination, and the political philosophers did not seize the point promptly.

There was also a gentler, Wordsworthian, theme in the roman-

2. Warner, pp. 208–11. The word 'revolution' is used to translate the Greek word στάσις which has nothing to do with 'revolution' in the sense that word acquired in 1789. It is a question of social death, not of social promise.

3. Shakespeare, *Macbeth*, V, v. 9.

tic age; and John Stuart Mill acknowledged that debt. But for the adoration of violence one looks first to Mario Praz's remarkable book on *The Romantic Agony*, first published in 1930: Frank Kermode 'places it among such books as have, in the depth of their insights, power to alter a reader's understanding of the history of his society, and perhaps of his own history'.[4] and he does not seem to me to exaggerate.

Here there is a different Prometheus.[5]

> The tragedy interprets with unusual boldness the myth of Prometheus – the necessity of crime which weighs upon the man who is intent on raising himself to the condition of a Titan; it confers a kind of savage and pathetic ardour both upon the reiterated efforts of each single will to reach the universal, and upon the mad desire to break the shell of the individual and to feel oneself as the unique essence of the Universe.

This is Prometheus as Satan, crime as necessary to creativity, violence as bad and *therefore* good.[6]

> For the Romantics beauty was enhanced by exactly those qualities which seem to deny it, by those objects which produce horror; the sadder, the more painful it was, the more intensely they relished it.

Mario Praz and others find the first cravings for 'the Horrid and the Terrible' not long after the middle of the eighteenth century, and trace the sequence as far as 'that extraordinary conflagration of cerebral lechery which occupied the end of the (nineteenth) 'century'.[7] Intelligent best-sellers such as Ian Fleming have been aware of this literature, and have used it with a touch of parody. Frankenstein ('the modern Prometheus') and his monster[8] have had a most extraordinary career in Modern Pop Art. But probably in the twentieth century so much vulgar art, so much actuality have explored the delights of torture that serious artists have become less naïve.

4. At p.v of Foreword to the 1970 Edition (OUP).

5. Quoted by Praz (p. 276) from D'Annunzio's preface to his own play, *Più che l'amore*.

6. Praz, p. 27.

7. Praz, p. 395.

8. p. 32 above; Christopher Small (1972); and Brian Aldiss, *Frankenstein Unbound* (Cape, 1973).

Certainly, I feel that 'naïve' is the word, from Sade through Swinburne to Genet: the *frisson* often fails to generate literature, and remains funny, dirty, or pathetic. But there is also greatness, perhaps above all in the great French and Russian novelists, Stendhal, Flaubert, Dostoyevsky, and in Baudelaire. The American Poe was one of the founding fathers. Here is a passage from 'The Black Cat', which was translated into Freud by Baudelaire himself.[9]

And then came, as if to my final and irrevocable overthrow, the spirit of PERVERSENESS. Of this spirit philosophy takes no account. Yet I am not more sure that my soul lives than I am that perverseness is one of the primitive impulses of the human heart – one of the indivisible primary faculties or sentiments which gave direction to the character of Man. Who has not, a hundred times, found himself committing a vile or a silly action for no other reason than because he knows he should *not*? Have we not a perpetual inclination, in the teeth of our best judgment, to violate that which is *Law*, merely because we understand it to be such? This spirit of perverseness, I say, came to my final overthrow. It was this unfathomable longing of the soul *to vex itself* – to offer violence to its own nature – to do wrong for the wrong's sake only – that urged me to continue, and finally to consummate the injury I had inflicted upon the unoffending brute. One morning, in cold blood, I slipped a noose about its neck, and hung it to the limb of a tree; – hung it with the tears streaming from my eyes, and with the bitterest remorse at my heart; hung it *because* I knew that it had loved me, and *because* I felt it had given me no reason of offence; hung it *because* I knew that in so doing I was committing a sin – a deadly sin that would so jeopardise my immortal soul as to place it, if such a thing were possible, even beyond the reach of the infinite mercy of the Most Merciful and Most Terrible God.

Certainly *les poètes maudits* had as hard a life of it as any hippies, yippies or zippies, and worked miserably through the curriculum of drug addiction and debased magic. But it is hard to show that they did much harm to anyone except themselves, physically or spiritually, and very few indeed were concerned with revolutionary *praxis* after 1848.

9. Quoted by Praz at p. 146, in French. It appears in Edgar Allen Poe, *Works* (Philadelphia, Lippincott; 1905), at p. 233.

But there may be a concealed point here, in that existentialism as 'hidden opposite' to Marxism began to take shape in the hands of Kirkegaard at about that time. His work had no immediate impact: but by hindsight one can talk of the existential element in Baudelaire and in Dostoyevsky, the language of loneliness and inward responsibility. Since then, the doctrine has passed through many hands, and we have Christian, humanist, Marxist existentialisms. On the one hand, the existential point of view is imaginatively richer than the cult of evil for its own negative sake. Existentialism arises out of a man's crises of personal identity – 'who am I?' – and can sharpen the imagination, whereas violence blunts it. On the other hand, it is very hard to make a fighting creed out of it. 'One is one and all alone and ever more shall be so'.[10] *L'enfer c'est autrui*: with whom can an existential being find solidarity? The act must be judged for its authenticity alone: how can it be criticized instrumentally? Sartre as dramatist is a gifted maker and user of myths, Sartre as philosopher is hard for us to take, because he is committed deeply to the European tradition of reverence for great systems, referred to on p. 106 above.

But in him and others one can trace a series of links of an intellectual kind through the history of art and literature to a serious contemporary search for a doctrine which might enable you to have your revolution and also to eat it, emotionally, to the last crumb.

Here are some of the *graffiti* of May, 1968; it scarcely needs a literary historian to place them in context:

Créativité, spontanéité, vie
Éjacule tes désirs
Ça saigne
L'ennui pleure
Soyons cruels
Défense d'interdire
A bas le crapaud de Nazareth
A travail aliéné, loisir aliéné
L'imagination prend le pouvoir[11]

10. 'The Lily-white Boys': *Sing Together* (OUP; no date).
11. All from Walter Lewino (1968).

Politics Imitating Art?

It is easy for artists to make play with the doctrine that absolute evil, absolute violence, are the sole and absolute measure of politics: to put the Stasis at Corcyra in place of Pericles' Funeral Speech. But a political theorist needs plausibility, a certain persuasiveness; and there are very few who would be persuaded to accept absolute destruction as a collective enterprise. This seems to be so even now, in a period when it is relatively easy to contrive a universal holocaust. Yet Hitler in his last weeks deliberately sought a *Götterdämmerung* for Germany, and one can at least make science fiction out of Dr Strangelove, the lover of death.

This might be shaped into a sadistically coherent doctrine; but only for the mad and isolated? Brady and Hindley? Charles Manson of California and his harem? It is not in fact easy, skipping through theoretical works of the left since the Great Revolution, to find a clear case of the political philosophy of destruction. The books always refer to Nechayev, and the *Revolutionary Catechism*:

> The revolutionary is a man under vow [says the *Catechism*]. He ought to occupy himself entirely with one exclusive interest, with one thought and one passion: the Revolution . . . He has only one aim, one science: destruction . . . Between him and society there is war to the death, incessant, irreconcilable . . . He must make a list of those who are condemned to death, and expedite their sentence according to the order of their relative iniquities.[12]

It is not easy to pin down what Nechayev wrote, or what he did, though it is convenient to take this as the limiting case to which others converge. But none reach it; others regarded as prophets of violence do preach its divinity, but generally with an escape clause – violence is to be in the end instrumental.

It would be difficult to prove that negative proposition, especially as the published work on anarchic theories is itself anarchic. But perhaps one can distinguish two lines of thought, one collective, the other more individual. For the former, one can cite

12. George Woodcock: *Anarchism* (Penguin Books; 1963), p. 160. The last sentence might serve as epigraph for John Farris's novel of such a group in the USA: *The Captors* (New York, Trident; 1969).

Bakunin, Sorel, even Frantz Fanon;[13] the experience of violence warms the heart, leads a man to recognize himself as man, is in itself a liberation. To be set free without violent revolution is to remain in bondage: nevertheless freedom is an end more absolute than revolution. Even Trotsky's *permanent* revolution would end at the end of a period of history.

This doctrine is not the same as the doctrine of planned terror. The latter had the same point of departure, in that it denied totally the legitimacy of existing public authority, so that murder and robbery were in a sense a continuous series of acts of revolution. But it added tactical considerations, above all that of terror as propaganda. In situations of oppression, speech and publication are both suicidal and ineffective; terror is suicidal too, but cannot be concealed; the régime itself must publish the death of a Tsar or President, a Chief of Police, a colonial governor, a Stolypin. In doing so, it must add explanations: isolated enemies will construe these explanations in reverse, and will know that secretly they have allies. More than this; the murder of the Empress Elizabeth of Austria in 1898 was no more than the killing of an innocent and unhappy woman, 'news' and no more. But the shots that killed the Archduke Franz Ferdinand in Sarajevo in June 1914 'rang round the world', and provoked war (though they did not cause it) as specifically as did the execution of Louis XVI and his queen in January, 1793. 'The propaganda of the deed' is not to be laughed off. Nevertheless, this pair of doctrines, revolutionism and terror, constitute together the Marxist-Leninist category of 'adventurism'; they are naïve in their analysis of cause and effect.

And that sceptical orthodoxy may tell against official Communist parties in situations like that of Paris in May, 1968, and in many post-colonial countries.

A second main line includes doctrines of the great man, the unlimited individual. This might perhaps include Max Stirner, isolated in an extreme position: but the interesting cases are those of Carlyle and Nietzsche, particularly the latter.

13. See the article by Paul Nursey-Bray, 'Marxism and Existentialism in the thought of Frantz Fanon', in *Political Studies* 20 (1972), p. 152.

Carlyle is perhaps under-rated, and due for revaluation.[14] Nietzsche is now in the full tide of fashion, with a learned year-book, *Nietzsche Studien*, and a vast edition of published works and letters is in progress. Yet the views of Nietzsche 'professionals' are not yet very clear, and a general reader is not adequately guided.

For my generation the starting point is that the Nazis picked up and used so much of Nietzsche's language. So perhaps did the Italian Fascists, but domesticated (as it were) through Sorel, Pareto, D'Annunzio, Gentile. Nietzsche had quarrelled with Wagner, yet the two were mixed together in the Nordic brew concocted by Rosenberg and others,[15] from whom Hitler in turn drew his rhetoric, reacting instinctively to his audience. Even now, political scientists merely hold their noses and turn aside; yet the Hitler case offers a manageable area within which to test the interactions of ideas and rhetoric at four levels – creative imagination as in Nietzsche and Wagner; a mixture of learning and obsession, as in Spengler and Rosenberg: a group of gangsters using the techniques of mindbending, as well as those of gun and rubber truncheon; the diverse audiences with whom these 'orators' interacted.

Each of the higher echelons will blame the audiences, hungering for words of violence. The audiences, if indicted, could make a defence based on the conditions of society, education, war, unemployment. And this in turn demands analysis at a deeper level.

In spite of that unlucky reference to the 'blond beast' (and probably he meant no more than the 'fair-headed Achaeans' of Homer),[16] Nietzsche had no concern at all with pseudo-scientific

14. Alan Shelston, ed, *Thomas Carlyle: Selected Writings* (1971).

15. Nietzsche's sister Elisabeth Förster-Nietzsche survived till Hitler's day, and shared responsibility for this. See Walter Kaufmann's article on Nietzsche in *Encyclopaedia Britannica*, 1961 edn.

16. 'Blond Beast' is in *The Genealogy of Morals*, translated by Francis Golffing (New York, Doubleday Anchor Books; 1956), at p. 175. See also Robert Cecil, *The Myth of the Master Race: Alfred Rosenberg and Nazi Ideology* (Batsford; 1972), and an article by H. R. Trevor-Roper in *The Listener* in January 1973, p. 101.

racialism. And his system of thought, exclamatory and fragmentary as it is, is nevertheless a serious analysis of 'the death of God', into which fit the twin pair of sayings 'if nothing is true, all is permitted', 'if nothing is true, nothing is permitted'; Dostoyevsky against Nietzsche, the nihilism of rule destruction, against the asceticism of self-discipline. 'Superman' and 'the will to power' may seem to be lurid catch-phrases for the vulgar; but in Nietzsche their meaning is that a man can rise only by 'a sojourn in the desert', by sacrifice and loneliness, and that in this individual drive lies the only real power, the only escape from the wheel, the endless cycle of human events. He too was to himself Prometheus.[17]

It is perhaps strange that Nietzsche was read at all. But one has to remember that he was an exact and brilliant classical scholar, in a great period of German scholarship: his reflections on Greek art and thought are to this day a powerful stimulus to serious work; he was a professor at twenty-six, not in one of the greatest chairs, but nevertheless in a strong Swiss university, that of Basel. From the base he widened his scope across the European art and literature (not science, apparently) of his time; he was a gifted musician; and the German he wrote (though a foreigner is no judge) shines through the murk of German academic prose.

Perhaps this caught his audience; and a *fin-de-siècle* public was ready for a man who attacked all established institutions alike; God and the State; administrators and scholars; Jews and anti-Semites equally; all philosophers (save Schopenhauer), all historians (save Plutarch); democracy, socialism, nationalism; war and revolution; above all, the ordinary plodding man. He abandoned his chair through ill-health; lived on a meagre pension, wandering about Europe, in a sort of bed-sitting-room life, keeping away from the academic circles in which he had grown up. And yet he was fashionable, at many different levels; has

17. *The Birth of Tragedy* (Golffing's translation, as above) is full of references to Prometheus: pp. 17, 30, 34, 48, 62–5.

contributed much to the style (if not the content) of European thought; and has even survived the degradation of the Nazi period.[18]

What has this to do with violence? In the end, very little; the Nietzschean superman works on men not through violence but by the character of his existence. He possesses a power which should transcend violence; he is too great to fight; once tempered, he has a power above conflict.

And so on. Nietzsche did not formally construct a system of nihilism, was indeed conscious of the 'absurdity' of such an attempt. But isolated phrases and apothegms, perilously near to nonsense if taken alone, do in fact work powerfully in context, and go at least some way to flesh out the ideal of greatness as tragedy,[19] a Stoic, not hedonistic nihilism of the individual; quite distinct (I should claim) both from the hedonistic individual nihilism of Nechayev, and from the political ecstasies of Bakunin and Sorel. Perhaps not truly a political doctrine; yet adopted now as a constituent part of the tradition of political thought in the west – a line that did not end with Herbert Read,[20] nor with the Stoke Newington Eight, whose hagiography will certainly begin before this book is in print.

18. I have used mainly Walter Kaufman, with Lou Andréas-Salomé, *Frédéric Nietzsche* (French translation by J. Benoit-Méchin; 1932, reprint, Gordon & Breach; 1970), and R. J. Dupuy, ed., *Politique de Nietzsche* (Paris, Colin; 1969). But I have not caught up with the recent work referred to in Kaufman's third edition, 1968.

19. I got my education in this from Joseph Conrad; in particular, *Lord Jim*, *Victory*, *Nostromo*; perhaps he had never read a word of Nietzsche.

20. George Woodcock: *Herbert Read: The Stream and the Source* (Faber; 1972).

CHAPTER 11

INDIVIDUAL AGGRESSION

Cruelty is his form of courage. [Lowell, *Prometheus Bound*, p. 4.]

Millamant – O I ask your pardon for that – one's cruelty is one's power, and when one parts with one's cruelty, one parts with one's power; and when one has parted with that, I fancy one's old and ugly. [William Congreve: *The Way of the World* II. iv.]

VIOLENCE has been a challenge to behavioural analysis, and there is a large and difficult social science literature. Perhaps it is useful to distinguish between psychological theories of the individual (in this Chapter) and sociological theories of the mob or mass (in Chapter 12), so long as one recognizes that much of the best work is concerned to bridge the postulated gap between personality and society.

Definition

The first problem for a behavioural approach is to operationalize, and this means that one must begin to work with stipulated definitions of violence.

OBJECTIVE VIOLENCE

A preliminary assumption is that violence has two faces, objective and subjective. What is violent behaviour, what is a violent feeling?

One approach to the former is to work in terms of crimes of violence, as defined by courts of law. This is not illegitimate, in that the problem of controlling violence presents itself through police, judges and prisons: and these institutions face the demands of victims and potential victims that violence be stopped.

But a researcher (or, indeed, an experienced policeman) is bound to say that the criterion of conviction in court is in some respects formal and arbitrary. Those who graduate by conviction n court as violent criminals may be freakish and isolated individuals; or they may be selected almost by accident from social groups within which violence is a normal pattern of behaviour. In either case, if one abandons the legalistic definition one will have to define 'acts of violence' in a way independent of trial and conviction by law. This is not easy, because a great deal depends on context; scrapping in a school playground or on the football terraces is not the same as scrapping in the House of Commons, or indeed on the floor of a factory engaged on production. Some acts – the use of a gun or knife – we should label as violent in any context, even that of self-defence: but the classification of physical contact short of attempted murder or rape depends very much on *milieu* and *mores*. And so of course does the use of 'violent' language; indeed, violence generally contains a message of some sort, and has a place in the spectrum of human communication. 'Couple it with something: make it a word and a blow'.[1]

SUBJECTIVE VIOLENCE

But to write of 'communication' carries the problem one stage further: what is communicated? a state of mind? In particular, how are we to relate 'violence' in behaviour to the subjective sensation of 'anger'? I think we should wish to say that when we lose our tempers we have a subjective experience of violence; and that to hold our tempers is to control that violence ('that deep deep bloody deep well of violence', as the scriptwriters once made *Callan* say).

This raises two issues. One of them is normative: it is not self-evident that anger ('rage', 'fury', 'indignation' and so on) should in all circumstances be controlled. The expression of righteous anger, not only in words but in violent acts, may help to improve society more effectively than pretended acceptance; and it is arguable that rage bottled up may distort and damage a personality.

The other issue is that of measurement. Violent acts and words transmit a message about a subjective state. Is it possible for the observer to obtain independent inter-personal evidence about a

1. Mercutio, in *Romeo and Juliet*, III. i, 43.

state of mind? A plain answer (which may prove difficult if fully analysed) is that mental states are accompanied by physiological signs not directly under conscious control, such as flushing, sweating and moving restlessly, and that the onset and intensity of these signs is measurable. It is difficult but not impossible to build an 'anger detector' on the lines of a 'lie detector'; the real difficulty is to use such techniques on human beings without interfering with spontaneous reactions and without transgressing moral norms. There is, as it were, a scale in our attempts to measure human violence, with juridical criteria at one end, physiological criteria at the other. At the latter end of the scale we reach criteria which men in some degree share with other animals; but we can use such measures far more easily with animals than with men.

Animal Aggression

The result has been a mix-up of terminology in the discussion of animal and of human violence. Perhaps it would be better if we did not use the word 'violence' about animal behaviour at all, because the word derives much of its force from what we know of our own subjective states, and can guess about those of others. Lions are stronger than pygmy shrews, the smallest of mammals, which may weigh only a fraction of an ounce; but lions fight among themselves less than do shrews.[2] We should not wish to say that shrews are more 'violent' than lions; and in fact a separate terminology has been evolved for the study of animal 'aggression', terminology which has fed back into talk about human 'aggro'.

The former can now be regarded as 'normal science' in the sense suggested by T. S. Kuhn; an enormous amount remains to be done, but there is a convincing general model, as a basis for further analysis, observation and experiment. On the one hand, observed encounters between animals of the same species have been placed effectively in context. There is a theory which links the 'fight-flight' reactions of individuals to social concepts of territory, dominance and food resources; and these in turn are

2. 'The nightlong frenzy of shrews' (Ted Hughes, 'Mayday on Holderness', at p. 32 of *Selected Poems, 1957–1967* (London, Faber, 1972).

linked to the physiology of breeding and to the dispersal and maintenance of populations in conditions of competition for resources. On the other hand, the behaviour of individual members of the species in particular social contexts can be linked to physical conditions in the central nervous system and other systems of the body, and scientists can experiment with these systems under strict laboratory conditions. Holding the social situation constant, the experimenter can manipulate the behaviour of the individual within it.

Human Aggression

It is not in doubt that man is mammal and primate and shares much of his physiological inheritance with other members of that class and order. Nor is it in doubt that some of the primates (particularly chimpanzees and baboons) are relatively flexible and adaptive in social structure, relatively open to learned patterns of behaviour. It is possible to make guesses, to tell SciFi stories about how these gaps were bridged; but explanation of the great leaps forward made during the last three million years still lies outside the range of normal science.

Certainly one dimension of human violence is physiological, and tests of drugs and surgical procedures applied to other animals are not irrelevant to the control of human moods. But this is an area touching human personality, an area in which experiments seem particularly abhorrent, with or without consent. But in extreme cases the conscience of physician and friends may prefer some action to no action, may hope that a personality apparently destroyed can be inexplicably restored. In consequence, much knowledge has accumulated, in an unmethodical and sporadic way which frankly alarms laymen on the basis of what little they know[3] – it so much resembles the attempt to re-start an ailing watch by tapping it with a hammer.

3. A situation 'claimed by the Medical Committee on Human Rights to be a threat to political militants and dissenters of all sorts'. *Radio Times* note on 'Horizon' programme, 'The Surgery of Violence', 31 July 1972. See also P. A. Freund, ed.: *Experimentation with Human Subjects* (Allen & Unwin; 1972). Along with examples of work by Skinner and by Laing and his

Yet there is ample evidence that in some cases surgery, shock treatment, drug treatment are followed by a diminution of aggressive behaviour.[4] From which it follows, in reverse, that abnormal aggression may in some cases be due to functional disorders of brain and nervous system, or to excess or deficiency of certain substances. But not much seems to be known directly of aggression as a disease physically based on abnormalities in the individual. Views differ radically about the propriety of interfering, not quite blindly but in the half-dark, in matters affecting the physical basis of human personality; this has become a proper subject for controversy on the stage as well as in the professional press.[5]

The problem is made more difficult in that human cultures differ very greatly both in general tone and in their capacity to tolerate and manage deviants who are in some way abnormal. This richness of variation in personality and culture is one of the most valuable of human resources, and it makes it very difficult to define what is 'normal' except by using social standards appropriate to the context: what does society regard as crime, what as disease, what as irritating (or even useful) eccentricity. Dr Thomas Szasz may or may not be helpful to his patients, but he renders a logical service in noting that it is very difficult to make 'mental illness' match the text-book characteristics which define a 'disease'.

---

associates, I include in the book list some examples of 'middle of the road' work in 'psycho-physiology'. The current 'state of the art' is summarized in D. M. Vowles: *The Psychobiology of Aggression* (Edinburgh UP; 1970), pp. 19–29, and in the OECD Science Policy Study, *Brain and Behaviour* (Paris, OECD 1972).

4. For paranoia see D. W. Swanson, P. J. Bohnert, J. A. Smith: *The Paranoid* (Boston, Little Brown; 1970): for the definition of psychopathic cases see Ch. 15 of D. Graham: *Moral Learning and Development: Theory and Research* (Batsford; 1972) and sources cited there.

5. See Pinter's *The Caretaker*; David Mercer's 'A suitable case for treatment' in *Three TV Comedies* (Calder & Boyars; 1966); *A Clockwork Orange*, for which Kubrick now shares credit with Burgess (see Chapter 15, p. 185 below). For another twist to the debate between orthodox and unorthodox psychiatry see Henry Miller's fierce review of Thomas Szasz's book, *The Manufacture of Madness* (Routledge & Kegan Paul; 1972) in *The Listener*, 23 May 1972.

An extreme view would be that it is misleading to write of individual aggression at all, that aggression is a social condition, the performance of a role in socio-drama, and that the actor plays the part attributed to him, even if it is a part of extreme violence. Lear is unintelligible, has no part to play, except in the context of his daughters. 'Pity the poor paranoid, for he really is persecuted.'[6] It is perhaps socially impossible to hold this view consistently, because the psychologist or psychiatrist is himself within society, and subject to pressure from its language and its necessities. He also has his role set down, and it requires him to do *something* (no matter what) in cases held to be socially intolerable.

Behavioural therapy spans almost as wide a range of theories and dodges as physiological therapy, and these are relevant in the present context because they play upon the theme of individual and society, using social conflict as metaphor for conflict in the individual, and also in reverse. The two symbolic figures are B. F. Skinner and R. D. Laing, in that each strikes public attitudes and is conspicuous in the confused debate. So they merit at least some mention here.

Nietzsche wrote of the death of God; Skinner takes from the late C. S. Lewis the abolition of man. 'What is being abolished is autonomous man – the inner man, the homunculus, the possessing demon, the man defended by the literatures of freedom and dignity'[7] In other words, the soul of man, the little man inside us, the will, all these and other variants are abstract entities like those already swept out of the natural sciences. As some nineteenth century scientist said of God, 'je n'ai pas besoin de cette hypothèse', similarly the explanation and manipulation of human behaviour do not require us to postulate anything but behaviour. In this vein, Skinner extrapolates from the model built in his fictional utopia, *Walden Two*, to the possibility of designing and building a new culture, of a kind adapted to the next phase of man's life in what is now 'the global village'. And to reduce opposition, he would do this by positive rather than negative

6. Remark attributed to Ernest Hadley: *The Paranoid* (1970), p. 13.

7. B. F. Skinner: *Beyond Freedom and Dignity* (Cape; 1971), p. 200, and his article, 'Freedom and Dignity Revisited' in the *New York Times*, 11 August 1972.

conditioning, rewards not penalties, lollipops not concentration camps – and what moral objection could there be to that? Certainly Skinner (though he is nòt explicit) would include himself in his own scheme, as an entity conditioned to play a role in human social adaptivity. Yet he is not in the old-fashioned sense a determinist; he writes not to decry freedom and dignity, decision and choice, but to show that language of that sort is obsolete, is useless in giving us a grip on reality.

Behavioural therapy, based conceptually on Skinner language, has had success with individuals and groups which cannot be laughed off. It works: but within what limits? It is very difficult to state the problem of building a personality or a culture except in terms of branching paths labelled according to criteria of value, and Skinner is hard put to it (ingenious though he is) to keep the words 'good' and 'bad' out of it when he is writing about the future of man on earth. Nor is he altogether happy with the problem of identity and self-knowledge.[8]

It is puzzling but important that Skinner's psychology can coexist in the scientific world with that of Ronnie Laing (taking each man as representative, not as individual). The former treats behaviour as plastic, the latter treats personality as unique; the former is of the international establishment, the latter of the international Left; the former (though not philistine) is prosaic, the latter poetical. Yet both have done painstaking and well planned research, which is clearly within its limits (still to be explored) convincing. This seems to be a case of ambiguity built into the world, not of personal or social divergence. Each school makes blunders in statement; neither can be dismissed as empty. Both ask the question 'What is Man?', both are committed to the improvement of man, as individual and as social species.

The importance of Laing in the specific context here is that on one side he draws through Sartre[9] on the philosophical and political tradition of existentialism (or existentialisms) already referred

8. ibid. p. 193.

9. 'Je tiens – comme vous, je crois – la maladie mentale comme l'issue que la *libre organisme*, dans son *unité* totale, invente pour pouvoir vivre une *situation* invivable'. Sartre's Foreword to *Reason and Violence*, p. 7, my emphases.

to in Chapter 10 (p. 128), on the other side he bases his work on clinical observation of schizoid patients, serious scientific work, though no-one can say how valid his sample is, nor is it easy to define a 'cure'.

The word 'schizophrenia' perhaps by accident emphasizes division; and in Laing's scheme conflict and violence are traced back to conflict within the personality and to failure to establish a secure identity. This approach is held in common by psycho-analytic schools: it has been extended, largely by Laing and his colleagues, to include interaction with the most immediate group, that of the family. Lack of love, conflicting imperatives, constitute violence, and violence of this kind can be escaped only by with-drawal – escape to a different social world or escape inward (the methodological difficulty is that the latter are available for study as 'cases', the former are not). The nuclear family, of whatever class, is encapsulated in the social system of its country, and that in turn is encapsulated in the world system of late capitalism, or state capitalism, or whatever it is to be called; 'the context of all social contexts, the *Total World System* (TWS)'. Laing does not go beyond *The Politics of the Family*; not all families go queer, not all the children of queer families go schizoid, and the methodo-logical puzzle remains.[10] Cooper pushes it to *The Death of the Family*,[11] a phrase which makes a link with Nietzsche's death of God, Skinner's death of man.

This exposition may be enough to show connections linking the pathology of individual violence to political doctrines of individu-ality and violence, and to the problems of collective decision dealt with in Part IV. The immediate link is to violence in groups, mobs and societies.

10. *The Politics of the Family and Other Essays* (Tavistock; 1971), pp. 81, 48.
11. (Penguin Books; 1971).

CHAPTER 12

COLLECTIVE VIOLENCE

AGAVE: He wakened his Mad Ones
A Chase-God, a Wise God!
He sprang them to seize this!
He preys where his band preys.

CHORUS-LEADER: In the trail of thy Mad Ones
Thou tearest thy prize, God!

[Euripides, *Bacchae* (trans. Murray, 1908), p. 142. 'This' in 1.3 is the head of her son, who had been torn to pieces by his mother and the other Bacchae.]

VIOLENCE in groups, violence in mobs, violence in sub-cultures, violence in society. This catalogue may perhaps serve for analysis, with the usual proviso, that categories interlock. In each case one looks uncertainly for an operational definition, facing the same difficulties as in the previous section.

Violence in Groups

In protecting public figures, police and secret service have to worry as much about 'loners' as about groups, because they are more difficult to find. It is scarcely conceivable that a group of killers could put into action an assassin as effectively cut off as was Lee Harvey Oswald[1] who shot President Kennedy in Dallas on 22 November 1963. Clearly Oswald was in some sense 'mad': but in what sense? and how can such 'madmen' be identified in advance? They are dangerous but anonymous: such a man may shoot a President, or slaughter his own wife and family, or lie hid at a window and shoot passers-by. Retrospectively, warning symptoms can be recalled: but nothing has happened to force

1. H. D. Lasswell: *Psychopathology and Politics* (Glencoe Free Press; 1930) refers to Booth and Guiteau, assassins of President Lincoln and President Garfield. Contrast the organized assassinations of Alexander II and of the Archduke Franz Ferdinand; David Footman: *Red Prelude: A Life of A. I. Zhelyabov* (Cresset; 1944), and V. Dedijer, *The Road to Sarajevo* (MacGibbon & Kee; 1967).

these indications on the attention of a skilled observer. And even alerted professionals can make mistakes, as is shown by the rare but alarming relapse of killers released from mental hospitals.

It is, I suppose, a principle of investigation[2] that even these isolates are in some sense products of society: but it is very difficult to find a basis for valid generalization in that. Police action means primarily vigilance and control of weapons.

It is much easier to generalize about the violence of men in groups; to predict and within limits to control. As Professor Tiger says, 'there is a predictable pendulum effect in the earnestness and success of attempts to relate biology and social science',[3] and the pendulum is now swinging away from the all-embracing claims of Lorenz, Ardrey and Desmond Morris about the animal heritage of man, *The Naked Ape*.[4] But Tiger makes a persuasive case for seeing 'the male bond' as one resource for human social invention which has genetic roots.

There are some animals (the roe deer or the raven, for instance) for which the basic social unit is the breeding pair, continuing from season to season; and this is not incompatible with participation in larger social units, such as Lorenz's flocks of geese or jackdaws. Other animals have a sort of 'extended family', generally dominated by an adult male, but including females, younger males, infants of various ages. George Schaller's account of gorilla society[5] reminds one of Laurens van der Post's accounts of the family groups of Bushmen in the Kalahari,[6] and also of the difference between animals and men. Jane Goodall's chimpanzees[7] have another social pattern; a weaker form of the closely struc-

2. 'Violent acts, and violent interactions, do not make sense when viewed in isolation.' Hans Toch: *Violent Men: An Enquiry into the Psychology of Violence* (Penguin Books; 1972), p. 39.

3. *Men in Groups* (Nelson; 1969), p. 195. But participants in the small 'biology and politics' section of the IPSA Munich conference in 1971 were surprised at the wide range of topics which emerged. There is more in it than the biologists have yet realized. See also L. Tiger and R. Fox, *The Imperial Animal* (London, Secker & Warburg; 1972).

4. D. Morris (Cape; 1967).

5. *The Mountain Gorilla: Ecology and Behavior* (Chicago UP; 1963).

6. *The Lost World of the Kalahari* (Hogarth; 1968) and *The Heart of the Hunter* (Hogarth; 1961).

7. *In the Shadow of Man* (Collins; 1971).

tured organization of baboons, on which Tiger bases his case[8] for the bonding of males, in structured age groups, as an important factor in the solidarity and defence of the society.

First one must again emphasize the gap; and (secondly) that male bonding is only one of several tools at the disposal of human social adaptibility. Perhaps it needs also to be said that homosexuality is a different question; whatever may be latent, male 'hunting-groups' in human society, primitive or modern, are in general aggressively heterosexual, and are quite effectively related to systems of marriage and child-rearing. Subject to these precautions, one can then point to the functional role of male peer groups in many pre-literate societies as hunters, as fighters, as graduating through a sequence of age groups and rituals to the status of collective leaders. And once this is recognized, one can find equivalents in modern social organization, in male gangs, clubs, teams, secret societies, cliques, and indeed professions. Going a little further, and speaking analogically, Dr Tiger writes:

> Male bonding I see as the spinal column of a community, in this sense: from a hierarchical linkage of significant males, communities derive their intra-dependence, their structure, their social coherence, and in good part their continuity through the past to the future.[9]

Apply the analogy, and one has a better feeling of what Women's Lib has been up against, in 'spinal' areas of the great Western communities, such as politics, war, finance, journalism, religion, industry, farming. These structures can be understood in an important way as links between male groups: not that this is the only way, nor that it is unchanging.

Accepting this, tentatively, how is it relevant to violence? In two ways at least, more tenuously in a third.

Firstly, the male bond has played a traditional part in organized force. The images are easy to find: Chaka's Zulu Impis; the 300 Spartans combing their long hair as they made ready for their fight to death at Thermopylae; the building of professional armies, privates on the parade-ground, officer-cadets in the intense and ritualized atmosphere of military academies.[10] The principle is

8. E.g. at pp. 24–8. 9. (p. 60).

10. A rich breeding ground of unpleasant novels: try Robert Musil: *Young Törless* (trans. Eithne Wilkins and E. Kaiser: Panther Books; 1971).

that of mutual support in face of death, based on interaction which has become spontaneous and unthinking, a way of life.

This is controlled violence; built into it, sometimes deliberately, is the possibility of uncontrolled violence as release; the drunken and licentious soldiery, hungry for a town to sack.[11] Or it can happen without foresight. Bayley and Mendelsohn[12] note the case of the police, a group of men shut in on themselves, and placed under great strain on occasions of public violence. It is not contrary to expectation that discipline should break down into a 'police riot' as in Chicago in August 1968. There (and on the Cathedral steps in Cape Town in July 1972) one saw the image of senior officers trying physically to hold and beat back their own men.

Secondly, there is the street gang, essentially the adolescent gang, primarily social rather than criminal, but dangerously explosive in predictable ways. One is tempted to think that Universities have in fact become less violent in the last twenty years, as they have become more heterosexual. Before the war, as Evelyn Waugh put it, an Oxford college dean would have an ear attuned to 'the sound of the English county families baying for broken glass'[13] and would know the appropriate tactics; and the Rectorial battles in Scottish universities were once severe.

This has perhaps been sublimated into pop, pot, demos and the pill; but not so on the street corner. Quite adequate models were built by William F. Whyte in *Street Corner Society*;[14] and by McArthur and Long in *No Mean City*,[15] and nothing has changed fundamentally. The violence is most often between gangs: but this is in itself enough to enlist recruits for the prison system, and in addition violence spills over into attacks on citizens at random and into vandalism analogous to that of the old upper-class gangs of mohocks, mashers and bloods.

11. *Was für Plunder!* – 'what a city to sack!'; the remark attributed to Marshal Blücher when he first visited London after Waterloo.

12. *Minorities and the Police: Confrontation in America* (New York, Free Press; 1968), p. 55.

13. *Decline and Fall* (1928; Penguin Books; 1937), p. 10.

14. *The social structure of an Italian slum* (1943; Chicago UP, second enlarged edn, 1955).

15. (1956; Corgi Books; 1964).

These outbursts have the characteristics of explosion, a metaphor that implies pre-existing stress or strain;[16] and there is indeed stress in the adolescent situation. But the precipitating causes seem to lie in the structure of adolescent groups rather than in poverty alone or in the perception of relative deprivation.[17]

Thirdly, should one link the fighting group, formal or informal, with the secret society? The latter pattern of organization has played an important part in violent politics; it is easy to find models both in the social anthropology of initiation and in the fanciful ceremonies of Freemasons and other 'secret' bodies. These models are not conspiratorial: and indeed (as is stressed in J. M. Roberts's book)[18] the models embody mythology rather than practice. But sometimes a terrorist party is truly an oath-bound fraternity, held together by mutual fear, the natural bond reinforced by lessons from tradition and fantasy.

Sub-cultures of Violence

The phrase is loaded; it implies that a 'great society' may include in it sub-cultures which are both deviant and encapsulated; so that the society as a whole is in equilibrium and untainted, in spite of violence contained within it. It is fair to say that the implications are now perfectly clear to American social science, largely through the learning experience of the 1960s.[19] The two great American compendia of concepts and research are Neil Smelser's *Theory of Collective Behavior*, published in 1962, and Ted Gurr's *Why Men Rebel*, published in 1970. I think it is in general terms fair to say that Smelser adopts the Parsons model, taking structure and function to be in equilibrium, and regarding violent behaviour as a pathological deviation which will bring balancing forces into play: whereas for Gurr political violence (though he doesn't like

16. The latter is Neil Smelser's word: *Theory of Collective Behavior* (Routledge & Kegan Paul; 1962).

17. There are abrasive comments on this in Daniel P. Moynihan; *Maximum Feasible Misunderstanding. Community Action in the War on Poverty* (New York, Free Press; 1970).

18. *The Mythology of Secret Societies* (Secker & Warburg; 1972).

19. D. O. Arnold, ed., *The Sociology of Subcultures* (1970).

it) is normal, equilibrium (or 'self-adjusting conflict') is an ideal not reached in practice. The contrast must not be made too sharp: Smelser's dedication is to one who taught him 'that both conflict and stability are essential for growth', and Gurr's index has eighteen references to Smelser for five to Marx, two to Engels, two to Lenin – but seven to Mao. There is however generous recognition of a changed point of view in the volume on *Violence in America: Historical and Comparative Perspectives*, edited by Ted Gurr and H. D. Graham for the President's Commission on the Causes and Prevention of Violence, June 1969.[20]

The new position is quite succinctly and precisely stated in *Why Men Rebel* (p. 160).

> Some of men's perspectives on violence are psychocultural in origin, the result of socialization patterns that encourage or discourage outward displays of aggression, and of cultural traditions which sanction violent collective responses to various kinds of deprivation. These perspectives are underlying attitudes about, or normative predispositions toward, violence. There is considerable variation in such attitudes within most cultures; evidence also suggests that modal dispositions toward violence vary significantly from one nation to another and from one subculture to another within nations. These underlying attitudes are separable from the doctrines that men accept in the course of their lives which provide them with specific justifications for violence in response to their immediate political circumstances. Such doctrines conventionally are categorized as 'ideologies'...

and so to a closely related but distinct topic. 'Obfuscating jargon',[21] says Lawrence Stone: but he goes on to tip his hat respectfully to his Princeton colleague.

The essence of Gurr's statement lies perhaps in the distinction between structure and culture. 'Environmental imperatives' within certain limits determine structure: on that perhaps Marx

20. They note ironically (p. xv) that 'Violence' does not even rate an entry in the new *International Encyclopedia of the Social Sciences*, published in 1967, after five or six years' gestation. The chairman of the Commission was Dr Milton S. Eisenhower, and a 'confrontation' about its work is effectively presented in H. D. Graham, ed.: *Violence: the Crisis of American Confidence* (Johns Hopkins UP; 1971.)

21. *The causes of the English Revolution, 1529–1642* (Routledge & Kegan Paul; 1972).

and Parsons as structuralists might agree, before parting company. For both, culture appears to be epiphenomenon: it doesn't matter what language the proletariat talk, their dances, their dress, their patterns of friendship, love, enmity and violence are secondary in importance, as are religion and ideology. As will be obvious, this book leans to the opposite, equally necessary view that 'poets are the unacknowledged legislators of the world',[22] and that the rhetoric and style of human action are as much worth attention as its structure. It would be asking for trouble to allege 'causation': can one perhaps say that there are 'repetitive patterns which have some predictive force'?

What Gurr is saying, in his dehydrated way, is that America has always been, by any operational criteria one cares to use, a violent culture, one in which men talked and lived the language of physical conflict: that this general pattern was masked by internal divergence of sub-cultures, between (one might say) the holy and the rough; and that it is not for Americans to say dogmatically whether their culture has been more or less violent than that of the English, the Russians, the Chinese, the Bantu – divergencies will be found, doubtless, but the questions have not even been asked, yet, in a serious and careful way.

Gurr's language dries out the life of culture; but it is easy enough to reconstitute that by injecting images from movies and comic strips. Marketable 'socio-drama' can be generated very easily from the clash between American sub-cultures.

'Socialization patterns' in that language means that children learn a culture pattern as they do a language or (in Basil Bernstein's terminology) a 'speech code', a variant within 'the English language'.

So far, then, I have sketched out a relationship between speech codes and socialization through the organization of roles through which the culture is made psychologically active in persons. I have indicated that access to the roles and thus to the codes is broadly related to social class. However, it is clearly the case that social class groups today are by no means homogeneous groups. Further, the division between elaborated and restricted codes is too simple. Finally,

22. Shelley: 'A Defence of Poetry', at p. 197 of R. A. Duerksen, ed., *Shelley, Political Writings* (New York, Meredith; 1970).

I have not indicated in any detail how these codes are evoked by families, and how the family types may shape their focus.[23]

And he goes on to the vivid and exact example of how lavatories differ in different family houses (or the common lavatory, on the common stair). And from that one can move to Michael Argyle on *Social Interaction*[24] and the growing understanding of how posture and gesture are linked to language in patterns of interaction between people.

Certainly, there are more violent and less violent codes of talk and gesture. Certainly, within each culture coexist the peacemakers and the quarrelsome. But sometimes 'the chips are down' (cut to any old movie of Spencer Tracy – for instance, 'Bad Day at Black Rock'), and in that culture the pacific too must defend his identity by physical violence. Not so at High Table; nor on the Stock Exchange. But these may also be structural components within a violent society.

Such analysis is not very remote from the confrontation between the supporters of Glasgow Rangers and the Spanish police in the Barcelona stadium in 1972 (two violent sub-cultures?), or from the pages of newsprint spent on violence on the terraces, destruction outside the ground. 'Glasgow, he said, is possessed of a football madness. It is, like crime, simply part of the evil of the city ... It would take at least four generations to breed this madness out of the city ... The rest of the supporters ... may not go berserk themselves, but they enjoy having it acted out for them by the hooligan element ... In many respects, then, it is exactly like crime in our city – a trait of society.'[25] Mr Ratcliffe is a wise policeman, and certainly sociological analysis does not go further than he cares to go. 'For all my experience and connection with

23. *Class, Codes and Control, Vol. I, Theoretical Studies towards a Sociology of Language* (Routledge & Kegan Paul; 1971), p. 184.

24. (Methuen; 1970); see also his *Psychology of Interpersonal Behaviour* (Penguin Books, second edn; 1972).

25. Assistant Chief Constable W. T. Ratcliffe of Glasgow City Police, reported in the *Scottish Daily Express*, 4 August 1972, after a bad start to the football season. See also the reports on *Football* (HMSO; 1968), on *Crowd Behaviour at Football Matches* (HMSO; 1969) and on *Crowd Safety at Sportsgrounds* (HMSO; 1972, referred to as 'Chester', 'Lang', and Wheatly', respectively.

this problem, I am only able to say that I haven't thought of a solution. And I don't think there is one.'

One of the paradoxes is that a society may be twisted towards violence in some respects only. There is pretty general agreement that the working-class, Catholic and Protestant, of Belfast and Londonderry, are 'respectable' not 'rough': decent people, with conservative standards in family morality and personal dealings, not generating much of a 'criminal element'.[26] Yet one twist of escalation, and there is a killing war: in England and Wales, say forty-nine million people, deaths by deliberate violence in 1969, perhaps 125; Northern Ireland, say one and a half million, during 1972, about 320 civilians, about 150 soldiers and policemen; attempted murders in 1970, 12 – in 1971, 298 – in 1972, 1210.[27a]

Violent cultures are not all alike. Sociology (and the police) have posed the problem: one then begins to see the difficulties of research and action.[27]

The Riot in History

The riot (as one might say) is the efflorescence of a violent subculture. It is short-lived, visible, makes an impact, can be vividly described. And perhaps it has been exhibited almost too well; on the one hand, riot is mistaken for revolution, on the other hand riot is taken out of its cultural context.

The rules of the riot game were perhaps first elaborated in England, where the urban mob[28] was for about a century and a

26. As in the Republic, the recorded suicide rate is by Western standards very low; but the record itself may be a 'social construct', in that in a socially conservative society suicide is disgraceful to the family, and is not recorded as such (Erwin Stengel: *Suicide and Attempted Suicide* (Penguin Books, Rev. edn; 1970), p. 23). There may be a reciprocal relationship between homicide rates and suicide rates. D. J. West, *Murder Followed by Suicide* (Heinemann; 1965), p. 5.

27. R. W. Conant and Molly A. Leven: *Problems in Research on Community Violence* (New York, Praeger; 1969). This handles conceptual perplexities well, but not those of 'field work'. See also Colin Greenwood, *Firearms Control* (Routledge & Kegan Paul; 1972) and his article 'Controlling violent crime' in *New Society* 24 (31 May 1973), p. 491.

27a. See also R. Cooper and Theresa O'Shea, Northern Ireland: a survey of the social trends: *New Society*, 7 June 1973, p. 552.

28. The word 'mob' came into existence late in the seventeenth century as a piece of politicians' slang for the *mobile vulgus*.

half a weapon of some value in political struggle within a stable system. Montesquieu, Rousseau and de Lolme commented at the time on the curious character of English elections; other contemporary observers (above all Hogarth and Dickens) pictured more vividly the part of the English mob in sustaining English liberty. Indeed, more recent observers[29] have described the great period of Whig ascendancy as one of oligarchy tempered by riot; as in the remark about nineteenth century Russia, 'Every country has its constitution; ours is absolutism moderated by assassination.'

English law, by tradition and by statute, was much preoccupied with popular violence, and had till recently an elaborate repertoire of crimes and penalties, such as rout, affray, unlawful assembly, unlawful drilling, tumultuous petitioning; but undoubtedly the queen of the battlefield was riot, defined as

> a tumultuous disturbance of the peace by three or more persons, who assemble together, without lawful authority, with an intent mutually to assist one another, by force if necessary, against any who shall oppose them in the execution of a common purpose and who actually execute, or begin to execute, that purpose in a violent manner displayed not merely by demolishing property but in such manner as to alarm at least one person of reasonable firmness and courage.[30]

This was a common law misdemeanour; what about 'reading the Riot Act', one of the great rituals of the English political tradition, at home and in the colonies? As early as 1411, the sheriff with the *posse comitatus* was enjoined to suppress riot: in 1714, in a moment of political danger, a Cabinet which depended precariously on a new, foreign and unpopular dynasty (which in fact survived) passed the Riot Act. So far as the United Kingdom is concerned the Act disappeared unnoticed in 1967: but it had been a mainstay of colonial police, and one may guess that it survives intact in the law of many new states.

Its rule has the brutal elegance of a simple age. If there is a riot of twelve or more people the justices must go to it and read the proclamation annexed to the Act. An hour after the reading, the

29. M. Beloff, *Public Order and Popular Disturbances 1660–1714* (1938, Cass; 1963) and F. C. Mather, *Public Order in the Age of the Chartists* (Manchester UP; 1959).

30. *Halsbury's Laws of England* (third edn) Vol. 10, p. 587, 590 (1955).

rioters are in effect outlawed; judicial penalties are enormously increased; and it is the duty (not merely the right) of all officials, soldiers and citizens to attack and destroy the riot. They are liable to penalties if they fail. When the Act was passed there were only 16,000 troops under arms,[31] to oppose invasion and contain rebellion in a country of some nine million people;[32] and there were no organized police. Politically, the mob began to decline with the invention of urban police in the 1820s; but it had been a dangerous beast, easily provoked, easily exploited, but difficult to kennel – 'the beast with many heads', 'the mutable rankscented many'.[33] Yet somehow James Mill and Francis Place[34] had managed by 1830 to find intermediaries, and to create at least a show of revolutionary organization good enough to frighten the establishment into a Whiggish show of revolution.

There followed swiftly in the 1830s the emergence from the mob of a movement; the appearance of an organized and conscious working-class which perhaps deceived Engels (who was on the spot), and thus Marx, into an anticipation of history. Certainly there is in England a clear line of descent from town mob to working-class movement.

Perhaps this was exceptional; European and American sociologists were fascinated first by the irrationality of the mass, not by its solidarity, and there is good analysis (perhaps begun by Carlyle[35]) of the way in which men may be moved like a flock of starlings by some common impulse or infection. The crowd has coherence, it might be said, but not reason. *Ergo*, man in the mass is a sub-human entity, less than the additive sum of its components: a degraded whole, not an organic one.

Collective Behaviour

Discussions (Le Bon, Trotter, Christensen, Martin Conway)[36]

31. Basil Williams, *The Whig Supremacy, 1714–1760* (OUP; 1939), p. 151.
32. André Armengand, *Population in Europe, 1700–1914* (Fontana Books; 1970). p. 12.
33. Shakespeare, *Coriolanus*, IV. 1 and III. 1.
34. Joseph Hamburger, *James Mill and the Art of Revolution* (Yale UP; 1963): Graham Wallas, *Life of Francis Place* (Allen & Unwin, rev. edn; 1918).
35. For instance, *Selected Writings* (1971), p. 125.
36. See Book List.

in the early period of academic sociology were perhaps obliquely anti-Marxist and anti-proletarian: but not in a structural sense, as were Max Weber in one way, Pareto and Mosca in others. These were men of independent imagination, and set going the notion of something called 'collective behaviour'[37] which is neither individual, nor organized, and which is quite distinct from the 'collective' reactions of a small 'face-to-face group', accustomed to interaction. One author[38] refers to its first defining characteristic as 'restlessness which is communicated by a process of circular reaction'. This communicates vividly the image of 'collective behaviour' in birds, beasts or fish: in applying it to men one must add the characteristic of a '*mass* phenomenon',[39] that is to say, that collective behaviour is a phenomenon among strangers, stripped of structural relations except such as are generated by 'the wave' itself.

Smelser's own definition is 'mobilization on the basis of a belief that redefines social action'. Each term in this is chosen with precision, and would need technical explication. Crudely, it means that men in the crowd are primed for action on the basis of common consciousness that there is a new factor: there is a whiff of smoke, a cry of fire; each and all perceive that there are only three exits from the theatre – the audience's situation is abruptly redefined. Basically, however, Smelser's definition is an ostensive one; he points at five kinds of behaviour which seem to have something in common: (1) the panic, as in face of fire, flood or defeat in battle; (2) the craze, which will include rather more stable phenomena such as fashions, 'ad-mass' heroes ('Beatlemania'), financial booms and slumps, revivalist religious meetings; (3) what he calls 'the hostile outburst', in fact the riot as collective violence; (4) finally 'movements' of two different types; (*a*) norm-oriented, which aim to change law and institutions (Women's Lib is a good contemporary case, and the example given in Chapter 2 is relevant here in that it has emotional as well

37. Smelser (p. 2, footnote 1) attributes this to R. E. Park in the 1920s and 1930s. I was startled recently to find that there is a *physics* journal called *Collective Phenomena*, concerned with 'many-body systems' wherever they occur.

38. Blumer, quoted by Smelser (p. 7, footnote 1).

39. R. Brown, quoted by Smelser (p. 2, footnote 3).

as instrumental content), (*b*) value-oriented, which aim to change men, not law, to make a new heaven and a new earth, to enable men to be born anew.

My own view is that it is right to point to these phenomena and to associate them: but that they cannot satisfactorily be brought under a single analytic definition. The gap is too wide between the first three phenomena, which are essentially explosive and short-lived – orgiastic, one might say, remembering Dionysus and the *Bacchae* in ecstasy in the mountains; and the fourth group, which involve perhaps the same explosive forces but only when they have been harnessed and given continuity by specially gifted leaders and (at quite an early stage) bureaucratic organization. The last group is too big and complex to be subsumed under a single explanatory structure. A panic may last ten minutes and sweep a theatre; a movement may last a thousand years and sweep the world.

Canst thou draw out leviathan with an hook? or his tongue with a cord which thou lettest down?

Canst thou put an hook into his nose? or bore his jaw through with a thorn?

Will he make many supplications unto thee? will he speak soft words unto thee?

Will he make a covenant with thee? wilt thou take him for a servant for ever?

Wilt thou play with him as with a bird? or wilt thou bind him for thy maidens?

When he raiseth up himself, the mighty are afraid: by reason of breakings they purify themselves.

The sword of him that layeth at him cannot hold; the spear, the dart, nor the habergeon.

He esteemeth iron as straw, and brass as rotten wood.

He maketh a path to shine after him; one would think the deep to be hoary.

Upon earth there is not his like, who is made without fear.

He beholdeth all high things: he is a king over all the children of pride.[40]

40. *Job* 41, verses 1–5, 25–7, 32–4.

Yet Leviathan, a great movement of men, is made of the same flesh as the rest of us.

Here social science meets history in debate about strategy for the study of great revolutions and great movements. One might perhaps refer to the scientism of the sociologists, the historicism of the Marxists, the particularism of Western academic historians – and to the present serious and anxious search for a synthesis, with which to re-shape our model of mankind in crisis. Smelser's book is massive in structure and learning, but that problem is too big for it.

It will be enough for the present theme to illustrate two of his major arguments, which I should on the whole adopt: 'strain' and 'value-added'.

STRAIN

Would it be agreed that in our usage the panic, the craze and the riot share a sense of pent-up energy discharged not instrumentally (as in the explosive running of a race) but because the dam breaks at its weakest point and there is an 'irrational' discharge, as of lightning from a cloud? This is not Smelser's language, but it seems to be his picture: two things are emphasized, 'explosion' and lack of collective rationality, and together they imply stress, strain or pressure against a barrier.

This is an implication of the image; and does not tell us anything about the character of the strain. The image can be applied psychologically to conflicting drives within the personality, or to 'cognitive dissonance'; for Smelser, as sociologist, it is appropriate to refer to structural strain, related to the components of social action rather than to strains within individuals. 'Strain, then, always expresses a relation between an event or a situation and certain cultural and individual standards' (p. 51). Smelser emphasizes cultural standards: but there is a sense in which in panic or riot (but not in craze or fashion) it is each man for himself.

Ted Gurr's theory of *Why Men Rebel* is built round the concept of relative deprivation, a perception that I am worse off than you and that the gap might be bridged by my action; Smelser alludes to the theory (p. 51, fn. 1) but does not explore it further. On the whole, it seems too rationalistic to explain the basic phenomena of violent outbursts: one has to stretch it rather too far if it is to cover the *kamikaze* pilots, the drunken hunting men of pre-war Oxford, the weekly football orgy, our memories of our own childish tantrums and vandalism. D. H. Lawrence was not much of a psychologist or physiologist, but one would as soon believe his image of the strong-backed obstinate man-child –

> When a child stiffens and draws away, when it screams with pure temper, it takes no note of that from which it recoils. It has no objective consciousness of that from which it reacts, the mother principally. It is like a swimmer endlessly kicking the water away behind him, with strong legs vividly active from the spinal ganglia. Like a man in a boat pushing off from the shore, it merely thrusts away, in order to ride free, ever more free. It is a purely subjective motion, in the negative direction.[41]

Smelser would (I am sure) deplore such language: but he seems closer to this view than to Ted Gurr's.

VALUE-ADDED

As is to be expected, Smelser is very cautious indeed about the concept of causation: but he has a useful device called 'value-added' which enables him to avoid some of the difficulties and which may be useful in later discussion of 'decision' – is a decision a cause?

Probably the phrase 'value-added' was never very happy, even when it was new: and it has now been further addled by the invention of 'value added tax', VAT. The picture is however simple enough in essence, and is similar to that of the 'funnel of causation'.[42]

The funnel is however shaped in stages not in continuous flow, and the stages can occur only in logical order, when the situation has been made ripe for each by what precedes it. 'As the value-added process moves forward, it narrows progressively the range of possibilities of what the final product might become.' 'Iron ore, for instance . . .'[43] and so forth, following the analogy of a production process. Smelser's model has six stages.

41. *Psychoanalysis and the Unconscious* (1923, Penguin Books; 1971), p. 226.

42. Angus Campbell, Philip E. Converse, Warren E. Miller, Donald E. Stokes: *The American Voter* (New York, John Wiley & Sons; 1964).

43. P. 14.

(1) *Structural conduciveness.* A 'physical' panic is literally structured by its setting: a panic at theatre exits, the panic at a Paris *Métro* staircase as an O A S bomb was feared. Analogically, a stock exchange panic is structured by the working pattern of the market; without the market the panic cannot take place in that way at all. But the structure is not shaped *for* the panic: it is shaped for something else, and generally works well – but it can serve also by a sudden transformation as setting for panic.

(2) *Structural strain.* However one construes 'strain', the model is obvious; there is a pile-up somewhere in the flow, normality is distorted, strain can only be relieved if something gives. Notice that up to this point the model is mechanical and objective: on 2 January 1971 sixty people died at a staircase in a Glasgow football ground because their team scored a goal in the last seconds, as they were leaving – there was no panic fear, merely 'ambiguity', as some turned back, some went on. Yet they died just as they would have died if they had believed there was a bomb on the terracing.

(3) *Growth and spread of a generalized belief.* Some may prefer to be more strictly behavioural: but it is simplest to say that 'belief' can kill – they 'believe' there is a fire, they 'believe' all the doors are locked but one. In the classic case of Orson Welles and the Martian invasion of New York, there was a 'generalized' belief in bogey men from Mars, a belief usually quite remote from action. But Orson Welles's radio play, misheard as a news-bulletin, provided the minor premise, and New Yorkers fled the city in thousands.[44]

This sort of latent major premise is implicit in race riots, lynchings and pogroms,

[(4) *Precipitating factors*] but since Smelser wrote, massive evidence has accumulated of the way in which a small incident between a Negro and a policeman, during the 'long hot summer' may act as detonator in an explosive situation. The incident starts in a trivial way; negro or policeman acts so as to provoke escalation; there is a single violent incident; rumours start to fly,

[(5) *Mobilization of participants for action*] a crowd gathers, a

44. H. Cantril (with Helen Gaudet and H. Herzog): *The Invasion from Mars* (Princeton UP; 1947).

single policeman is about to be overwhelmed, shoots or calls for reinforcements, the crowd increases, the rumours get crazier, there is a battle and the crowd breaks into a dispersed riot. 'In this stage of mobilization the behaviour of leaders is extremely important' (p. 17). I would add that the availability and action of leaders may depend on gangs and culture: it may conceivably (though this is rare) be a matter of organized and integrated leadership. But this is so difficult to achieve, given the step-wise process of mobilization, that the conspiracy theory is generally wrong in fact, though it may be important as myth for both sides.

(6) Finally, *the operation of social control.* In other words, mobilization produces counter-mobilization, or fails to do so. Carlyle's account of *non*-mobilization against the Paris mob on 14 July 1789, is a superbly presented example, standing at a key point in his history of the French Revolution:[45] and there are obvious parallels in the Russian Revolution of 1917. But generally (as in the 1905 Revolution) social controls will operate like a military defence in depth, a net which yields but grows stronger as it gives back, and eventually smothers the outburst. But the social cost of the experience may be so heavy that this alone is enough to enforce social change.

I am not altogether happy with the picture of social control as No. 6, 'long stop', lender of last resort. The advantage of the model is its simplicity (contrast Smelser's trouble later in the book with a sevenfold model [p. 92] which has an almost magical quality).[46] But social control is the continuous outcome of a social learning process, and in fact it feeds back from the violent episode (or the episode narrowly escaped) into each of the four preceding stages.

One can in fact use the *schema* to formulate recommendations, working backwards from No. 6.

(5) If shooting starts, shoot accurately to put the leaders out of action: the key rule in the handbook for colonial police.

(4) But recognize explosive situations and teach your policeman tact.

45. *Selected Writings* (1971), p. 118.

46. 'Seven for the seven stars in the sky' and 'Four for the Gospel makers'; *Sing Together* (OUP; no date).

(3) A stage further back, strike as convincingly as you can (and perhaps it is too late now) at the 'generalized belief' that 'police are pigs' (and so is Whitey, and anyone over twenty-five).

(2) and (1) And in the last resort modify 'structural conduciveness', without yielding power; the policy (so the textbooks say) of the English establishment after its experiences in the 1640s and 1650s, the first 'Great Revolution'.[47]

This would serve quite well as an analytic model of what has happened in America since Smelser wrote. It has very little predictive force: but would be a good basis for police strategy and tactics in face of collective violence.

47. Lawrence Stone's category: p. 3.

CHAPTER 13

THE MANIPULATION OF VIOLENCE

Zeus sits in an armory of power, all force at his fingertips, but he himself . . he is not powerful. [Robert Lowell, *Prometheus Bound*, p. 43.]

Force signals weakness in politics, as rape does in sex . . . [Murray Edelman, *The Symbolic Uses of Politics*, p. 114.]

THIS discussion of violence has been built first on language and myth, secondly (and less securely, I feel) on biology and social science.

It is not at all easy to gather from these other disciplines what violence 'is', subjectively and objectively. There is meaningless or non-instrumental violence at the level of individuals, groups and cultures; at the first level there are found physiological correlates, and for the social levels there are analogues to be found in social biology. But there seems to be no agreement whether violence in any or all of these senses is pathological and needs cure; or cathartic in relation to the discharge of stress; or functional as an aspect of aggression, the place of which in social biology is now fairly well understood.

Someone or other wrote that the violence that needs therapy first is the word 'violence'. This is probably a wrong approach, in that the thing 'violence' as it appears in our awareness of ourselves and others is well represented by the confusions of the word. Hence my feeling that the problem is better stated by myth than by definition, until such time as the specialists in each discipline have established more precisely what 'violence' means to them operationally, in terms of prediction and manipulation. Still better if bridges could then be built between them.

The myth makes this appeal directly and universally, because, like the corresponding religious ritual, it symbolizes what does happen, and what ought to happen, and what ought not to happen, in the inner development of any human life.[1]

1. F. M. Cornford: *The Unwritten Philosophy* (1950, Cambridge UP; 1967), p. 8.

One would wish to add, 'in the political development of any society'.

The sense then is one of darkness and blindness; the black rage, the red mist before the eyes. Murder and suicide,[2] assassination and self-destruction.[3] Violence is impotence, not power.

But there is no power without violence? This will follow if the conclusion of Part II is accepted, that the concept of power implies conflict, and also the resources to achieve victory in conflict.

But blind violence wins no battles; the gigantic berserk chewing his shield and screaming is a joke, even in Sagaland;[4] he is not the hero. Power therefore depends on organized violence, the gold which supports credit. 'Violence is necessary and it's as American as cherry pie', says Rap Brown, as quoted by Henry Bienen.[5] 'I suppose I had better begin by stating the obvious: that a degree of controlled violence is essential to government as we understand it'; Sir Robert Mark, now Commissioner of the Metropolitan Police.[6]

One can make a working distinction between violence growing wild (like Lévi-Strauss's *La Pensée Sauvage*)[7] and violence cultivated.

Violence Growing Wild

One of the dirtier (but necessary) arts of politics,[8] and of police in politics, concerns the management of spontaneously generated

2. 'Something like a half of murders in England are followed by the suicide or attempted suicide of the aggressor.' D. J. West, (1965), p. 3.

3. See Ali A. Mazrui, *Violence and Thought* (Longmans; 1969) Ch. 9. 'Thoughts on Assassination in Africa' and Ch. 16 'Sacred Suicide'.

4. For instance, in *Hrolf Gautreksson*, trans., H. Palsson and P. Edwards, (Southside; 1972), Chs. 16 and 20.

5. *Violence and Social Change: a Review of Current Literature* (Chicago UP; 1968), p. 13.

6. In a paper on 'The containment of social violence', given at Bramshill Police College: reported in *The Times*, 20 August 1971.

7. Paris, Plon; 1962.

8. 'Politics, Gorky once said, is similar to the lower physiological functions, with the unpleasant difference that political functions are generally carried out in public'. From a *Listener* review by Stuart Hood of Gorki's *Untimely Thoughts*, trans. H. Ermolaev (Gainstone; 1971).

violence. It concerns equally those who are ready to mobilize violence in a conflict over power.

Clearly there are three fundamental manoeuvres: to escalate, to de-escalate (if there is such a word), to divert.

Escalation is very easy:

> Our province and our native land is poisoned with fear. More and more citizens seek to banish their fear by reaching for their guns . . . First we have fear. Then we have hatred. After that comes violence, followed by open war which is eventually replaced by still deeper hatred. These deep-seated fears are the souvenirs bequeathed to us by our honoured forefathers.[9]

Not much skill is needed to play on these deep-seated fears in Northern Ireland; in other communities it may be harder to create and polarize fear, so that escalation begins. But few communities lack fertile soil.

If the soil is fertile, escalation may be used as a technique of police control. So far as the record shows, British police in Ireland have used agents but not *provocateurs*. But it is easy, as in the days of 'Oliver the spy'[10] and other Home Office agents in the bad days of the Liverpool régime after Waterloo, for the undercover man to establish his *bona fides* by his extremism, and to please his masters with stories of extremist talk – stories which he knows to be true, since it was his own talk. It is an easy step from that to deliberate provocation. The leaders of a peaceful demonstration will know their own violent men, anxious for escalation, but will not find it easy to control them. Add a few skilled *provocateurs*, and a peaceful crowd may be led on till it is discredited and destroyed morally, so that it can be destroyed physically and its leaders made harmless (as euphemism has it).

To de-escalate (to get down the stairs again) is harder; the tactics are known, but difficult. To strike a sharp quick sobering blow, though with inferior forces? To divert violence from a collision course into wider spaces? To await weariness and drunken sleep?

9. 'Souvenirs of Ulster', by the Rt Rev. Robin Williamson: *The Listener*, 25 May 1972.

10. First effectively exposed by J. L. and Barbara Hammond: *The Town Labourer, 1760–1832: The New Civilisation* (Longmans; 1917).

To let the impact fall on the non-violent community, in such a way that it mobilizes itself as moral and physical control?

On the whole, the European Resistance, led by very small groups of violent men, forced the German occupying armies into escalation and so destroyed Hitler's strategy of 'collaboration'; and this was perhaps as important morally as was its military contribution to victory. Violent negro leadership in the USA has largely been contained, but at high social and political cost. In Northern Ireland the process of escalation went on, step by step, from a Protestant attack on Catholics in January 1969 to an armed Protestant response to armed Catholics in the summer of 1972. As this is written, there are a few weak but classical signs of de-escalation; the road is long, slow, and uncertain.

The third option is *to divert*, to twist violence side-ways against groups hostile, or at least indifferent, to those in power. Thus the powers in England in the eighteenth century could turn mobs against Catholics, dissenters, radicals: how pleasant for rioters to be both violent and patriotic. And anti-Semitism in Europe had a similar but longer and more tragic history. And in general a race riot in any setting is a diversion of the collective violence of poverty away from a revolutionary target.

Violence Cultivated

On the other hand, violence cultivated becomes organized force: and one returns to the classic ground of politics as force organized for external war and internal order. Three points only, for the present purpose:

(1) Such organization is to some extent technologically determined. The state and its enemies are potentially engaged in 'a shooting war', external or internal: but weapons are differentiated not only in fire power but also in power of discrimination. In some circumstances a discriminating weapon – a knife – may be superior to an indiscriminate one, such as massed artillery, air bombardment, or a nuclear attack. In Northern Ireland the soldier's best weapon has been individually aimed rifle fire; terrorists have used indiscriminate weapons as well, probably to the disadvantage of their own cause, in the end.

That remains to be seen: the point is that from the level of street fighting to that of thermo-nuclear war the technological potential of each weapon has to be understood in a sophisticated way.[11]

A special case is that of police organization. I quoted earlier from *Minorities and the Police*[12] the saying that the police are also a minority group. Police managers have to be aware that violence grows wild among police under strain, as among soldiers: and that it may destroy their value as a weapon. Once upon a time the Turks ruled in that way: but after the last Macedonian massacres Gladstone turned violence into rhetoric, and drove them out.

> I entreat my countrymen ... to require and insist that our Government ... shall apply all its vigour ... in obtaining the extinction of the Turkish executive power in Bulgaria. Let the Turks now carry away their abuses in the only possible manner, namely by carrying off themselves. Their Zaptiehs and their Mudirs, their Bimbashis and their Yuzbachis, their Kaimakams and their Pashas, one and all, bag and baggage, shall, I hope, clear out from the province they have desolated and profaned.[13]

Similarly Mayor Daley's police provided texts for the rhetoric which expelled him from the Democratic National Convention of 1972.

But how sophisticated can you get?

> The Minister of the Interior also announced that he intended to set up a specialized bureau, which would coordinate operations in the struggle against clandestine extremist groups. Its competence would extend not only to threats to State security, but to the activities of all extremist groups, France's myriad Leftist factions as well as the no less violent far Right. Police officers specially trained in these delicate matters would carry out inquiries under the control of magistrates.
>
> 'We are taking vigorous action against all forms of sedition,' M. Marcellin added. 'I say firmly that nothing like May, 1968 will be repeated, for all the means put at our disposal by the law and the Constitution to prevent it will be used, and, believe me, they will be used energetically to prevent it.'[14]

11. Which would need an extension of Andreski's theme in *Military Organization and Society* (Routledge & Kegan Paul; 1968).

12. See above, Ch. 12, p. 145.

13. Gladstone's pamphlet on the 'Bulgarian Atrocities' of 1876: I quote from R. W. Seton-Watson: *Disraeli, Gladstone and the Eastern Question* (Macmillan; 1935), p. 75.

14. Nesta Roberts's report in *The Guardian*, 14 June 1971.

This would please many faithful Gaullist voters; but it would tend to rally the liberal centre to the more radical left. This shift would be accentuated if the police were caught out in roles of provocation and organized violence. There is an election to be fought in 1973; the Gaullists will lose if there is a rally towards the Republican Left.[15] Extreme police provocation might enable the Government to frighten the centre and move right towards a military régime – then there would be crisis elections, or no elections at all. But then what about France's role in EEC?

That is to say, that the sort of point made about technological weapons can be extended to organizational weapons. It sounds as if M. Marcellin does not know the different uses of an H-bomb and a telescopic sight. Clausewitz again: police work is a continuation of politics by other means. And vice versa.

Secondly, there are organizational questions about the relations between army and police in the control of violence. The relevant points about discrimination in the use of weapons have been made. But this is a long story, perhaps best told in Brian Chapman's *The Police State*[16] which traces specialization of police back to its eighteenth century origins. The Army may grow its own police, as must happen if any military régime is to persist except in very primitive conditions: in Brazil and Peru the régime persists, it fell in Pakistan. Or the police may grow its own army, as did Himmler and Beria: yet neither struck the blow for which he had prepared, though the opportunities were there. In the last resort, they were merely policemen; Fouché, not Stalin. Or (thirdly) there may be extemporization of intermediate forces; in France one has to remember the existence of seven or eight more or less independent entities of which M. Marcellin's Quatrième Bureau of the Paris Prefecture of Police is one only.

This is perhaps the extreme case, and may seem crazy. But it is not, and exemplifies at least two principles. One principle is the political one, divide, balance and control: and there is also a

15. In fact, in the elections of March 1973, the trend to polarization was balanced by the tradition of local particularism and political bargaining: and still the Gaullists have a majority. But the 'scenario' given above can still serve as an example.

16. (Pall Mall; 1970).

technical principle, that of discrimination in the design and use of tools.

(3) The conflict is one of organization against organization. A revolution is not a mob or *Jacquerie*; the outburst may itself be unplanned, but it can make progress politically only if gripped by leaders and given structure. There are as many text-books now about conspiracy as about police, and it seems unnecessary to summarize.[17] But one might perhaps note that they all fight shy of stating what might be called the Dostoyevsky principle, that revolutionaries and police converge. Revolutionaries must learn how policemen are organized and how they think: if they do not learn of their own accord they will be given sharp lessons. And similarly for police. As in any specialized conflict (for instance, that between radar experts and that between spy masters in World War II) the specialists know one another, know their own common idiom, read projects and intentions better than does anyone else in the world.

And so to the Dostoyevsky paradox – who knows which is revolutionary and which is policeman? It is very simple to change sides, even to be on both sides at once.

The Justification of Violence

It will by this time be clear that I am avoiding a frontal attack on the problem 'When if ever is violence justified in politics?'[18]

I hope to blunt its edge *distinguendo*.

METAPHORS

Two things one can put aside not as irrelevant but as requiring no justification. One of them is that of sympathy between human

17. Those who get their images from Sci-Fi might like to 'compare and contrast' the very sophisticated presentations of conspiracy in Kurt Vonnegut: *Player Piano* (1952) and Robert Heinlein: *The Moon is a Harsh Mistress* (NEL; 1969).

18. This relates in particular to Richard Wollheim, 'Ivan Illich' (*The Listener*, 16 December 1971), an article about 'manipulation', and 'Democracy and Violence' (*The Listener*, 17 February 1972): and Eric Hobsbawm, 'Terrorism' (*The Listener*, 22 June 1972).

violence and the violence of nature – Lear in the storm, on the blasted heath:

> Blow, winds, and crack your cheeks! rage! blow!
> You cataracts and hurricanoes, spout
> Till you have drencht our steeples, drown'd the cocks!
> You sulphurous and thought-executing fires,
> Vaunt-couriers to oak-cleaving thunderbolts,
> Singe my white head! And thou, all-shaking thunder,
> Strike flat the thick rotundity o' the world!
> Crack nature's moulds, all germens spill at once,
> That make ingrateful man![19]

The whole romantic period in poetry, prose, pictorial art and music echoes with the crash of thunder, the roar of torrents, the pitiless violence of the glaciers.

> The crawling glaciers pierce me with the spears
> Of their moon-freezing crystals, the bright chains
> Eat with their burning cold into my bones.
> Heaven's winged hound, polluting from thy lips
> His beak in poison not his own, tears up
> My heart; and shapeless sights come wandering by,
> The ghastly people of the realm of dream,
> Mocking me: and the Earthquake-fiends are charged
> To wrench the rivets from my quivering wounds
> When the rocks split and close again behind:
> While from their loud abysses howling throng
> The genii of the storm, urging the rage
> Of whirlwind, and afflict me with keen hail.
> And yet to me welcome is day and night . . . [20]

This is violence in verse; the so-called 'pathetic fallacy' – though I have never been able to see that it is either pathetic or fallacious. One may deplore the metaphors of violence: one might as well deplore obscene words – kill one crop, another will spring up.

IMMATURITY

Nor is it helpful to deplore the violence of the child whom Lawrence describes, stiffening and screaming and beating at the

19. Shakespeare: *King Lear*, III. ii. 1–9.
20. Shelley: *Prometheus Unbound*, Act I, 37–44.

hostile world, including his necessary and repressive mother. To be mature is to learn how to handle this violence in oneself, to harness violence as energy.

SOCIAL DISORGANIZATION

It is very much more difficult to write about the violence of those who were denied the chance of maturity. In Glasgow the myth of violence imposed by society is that of Johnnie Stark – 'they ca' me the Razor King' – in McArthur and Long's novel *No Mean City*: the boy who had no asset, no defence but his own strength, who rose to power, withered in gaol, was felled by thugs of a younger generation. This is in fact the natural history of the slum, a society comparable in its order to the condition of Stasis in Corcyra, described some 2,500 years ago: social disorganization, in which even the most violent are to be ranked as victims.

RESPONSIBILITY

But who then is 'responsible'? Who is to answer the summons 'justify your acts'? Clearly, those who manipulate violence, rather than those who pull the trigger: in terms of the killings at Kent State in May 1970, the State Governor who used the rhetoric of violence in his primary election campaign (the vote was held a few days after the killings – he lost), not the tired and ill-trained Guardsmen who fired the shots, not their officers who mismanaged their tactics, but at least tried to beat down the troopers' guns.[21]

That paragraph is of course rhetoric in its turn. Is it possible to cool the issue? I think not, because we are locked into a circle of violence.

COMMAND

Distinctions flow easily. There is the power to command, and one tends to use American Presidents as paradigms, in that their constitutional power as commanders is clear, they have been to a remarkable extent men who accept publicly the responsibilities of the office – and their acts and thoughts are known in extraordinary

21. I. F. Stone: *The Killings at Kent State: How Murder went Unpunished* (New York, Vintage Books; 1971).

detail. Unfairly, this has put American Presidents in the dock or pillory to a greater extent than Prime Ministers or First Secretaries of the CPSU, adepts in eluding responsibility. Myths of Promethean stature have been, are being, built round the responsibilities of Abraham Lincoln, F. D. Roosevelt, Truman, Kennedy, Lyndon B. Johnson. Their sense, in brief, is that Zeus himself is not free.

MANIPULATION

There are then the manipulators, the *eminences grises*, the boys in the back-room. But who are they? They are by definition those who do not carry the responsibility of issuing commands in public; their political role is very well described in the passage by Stafford Beer quoted on p. 227 below, and that role is played in all big organizations (and small ones too), not merely in the politics of states. It is difficult to imagine politics at all, macro-politics or micro-politics, without the roles of commanders and manipulators. But that is by no means the end of the story.

FACILITATION

Universities like other organizations are structures of decisions, even if decisions merely about the scheme of my/our lectures, the form of my/our examination questions. The politics of American or French universities can in part be stated in terms of commanders or managers: those of British universities in terms only of manipulators, facilitators – and interests. 'The irresponsible interests' appear in this as in other settings: reflecting on my own experience of what Cornford called the Academic Microcosm, I am inclined to think that the ideal is to facilitate, the practice (*mea culpa*) is to manipulate. The norm is that of Mao's 'Hundred Flowers' in 1956:[22] let all flowers bloom. But this is ecologically impracticable, as the Chinese, a nation of gardeners, know very well. Which bloom is to be facilitated? And the minimum political intervention of the University administrator, academic or lay is to choose what and whom to facilitate. But the process of choice is

22. See J. Gray & P. Cavendish: *Chinese Communism in Crisis: Maoism and the Cultural Revolution* (Pall Mall; 1968), and R. MacFarquhar, *The Hundred Flowers* (Stevens; 1960).

easy to disguise, for the sake of harmony and everyone's self-esteem: it is also easy to evade, and British universities are happy homes for non-deciders paid to fill posts of decision.

And how wonderful it is to be a good facilitator, in one's own esteem. Oxford sarcasm between the wars nominated such people of the Crypto-megalomaniacs Cricket Club First Eleven.

WILFUL IGNORANCE

But there are two more stages to come. First, there is wilful ignorance.

> Thou shalt not kill; but need'st not strive
> Officiously to keep alive.[23]

Clough, who wrote these lines, was a mid-Victorian scholar, peerless in his generation, driven by his conscience so that he became one of those whom Florence Nightingale worked to death as seconds in her various enterprises. He knew the many different *milieux* of decision in British society; and pinned down for ever the decision 'not to know'.

This is of course a very difficult and ingenious sort of decision, in that one has to know a bit, in order to decide what it is wisest not to know. Simple ignorance is not a decision, even though one is ignorant of things as dreadful as US killing in Vietnam, IRA/UDA killings in Northern Ireland. The decision is to choose wilful ignorance (or perhaps invincible ignorance, but the latter involves theological questions beyond my grasp): how does one decide what not to know?

We do it all the time, at least those of us who live as 'public persons'. We are not in fact caught doing it – how could we be? We have in fact done 'nothing'. But if we were arraigned (as we should be) we should wish to say (I think) that there are spheres for each man, and priorities within these spheres: and that these mark the limits of each man's personal responsibility and effectiveness. The less I know about the streets of Calcutta the better: perhaps I can 'facilitate' some 'intermediary' there (Oxfam,

23. 'The Latest Decalogue', in *Poems* (Macmillan, eleventh edn; 1885), p. 134.

leach on our consciences, like Shelter, Poverty Action Group and the rest) and give some money – or merely some jumble. But my place is not there.[24]

In which those who read A. C. Bradley will recognize an inferior restatement of his essay on 'My Station and its Duties'.[25] What obligation is there on me to attempt what I cannot achieve? Do I share responsibility for those who die (and this too is political violence) homeless on the pavements of swarming tropical cities?

COMPLICITY

So the circle is then closed against us by the existentialist concept of 'complicity'. I am responsible for what I do not disclaim. Ignorance does not diminish responsibility, not even if it is built into the situation. Society is built step by step from those innocently unaware, through tacit or open intermediaries, to those who command violence. No-one is innocent; we share the sin of violence. There is no salvation, except to deny that this is a sin.

In other words (and I write as a lapsed member of a Calvinist national church), violence in politics is not due to the Fall of man, it is not Original Sin, it does not distinguish the Elect and the Damned to all eternity. It is (to repeat a quotation) 'as American as cherry pie': 'this is the way the world ends' – and to reverse T. S. Eliot ('not with a bang but a whimper'), it ends as it began, violently. We need not worry much about the special sins of each one of us: in Nietzsche's phrase, the problem is *menschlich, all zu menschlich.* In so far as there is responsibility, we share it.

24. Blake had no doubts about the case in England:

> Because of the Opressors of Albion in every city and Village.
> They mock at the Labourers limbs: they mock at his starv'd children
> They buy his Daughters that they may have power to sell his Sons:
> They compell the Poor to live upon a crust of bread by soft mild arts:
> They reduce the Man to want, then give with pomp and ceremony:
> The praise of Jehova is chaunted from the lips of hunger and thirst.

Quoted by J. Bronowski (1972), p. 97. But Blake also wrote:

> 'Sooner murder an infant in its cradle than nurse unacted desires' (Proverbs of Hell).

25. Essay V in *Ethical Studies* (1876: OUP, second edn; 1927).

Part Four

DECISION

When we speak of the science of politics, we mean the science of power. Power is decision-making. A decision is a sanctioned choice, a choice which brings severe deprivations to bear against anyone who flouts it.

[H. D. Lasswell, N. Leites and Associates, *The Language of Politics*, p. 8.]

When I must shipwrack, I would do it in a Sea, where mine impotencie might have some excuse; not in a sullen weedy lake, where I could not have so much as exercise for my swimming. Therefore I would fain do something; but that I cannot tell what, is no wonder. For to chuse, is to do: but to be no part of any body, is to be nothing.
[John Donne, 'Letter to Sir H. Goodere', *Complete poetry and selected Prose*, John Hayward ed., Nonesuch Press, 1929, p. 454 (Quoted by A. Alvarez, 1974).]

CHAPTER 14

CAT'S CRADLE

Oh, a sleeping drunkard
Up in Central Park,
And a lion-hunter
In the jungle dark,
And a Chinese dentist,
And a British queen –
All fit together
In the same machine.
Nice, nice, very nice;
Nice, nice, very nice;
Nice, nice, very nice –
So many different people
In the same device.

[Kurt Vonnegut: *Cat's Cradle*, p. 8.]

Recapitulation

The quotation at the head of Part IV may serve to mark the point reached so far in attempting to relate our experience of power and violence to our experience of decision-making in politics. Part II followed a familiar path of academic analysis, and set out a sequence of models or metaphors related to the place of power in society. Part III was concerned with violence, a word perhaps stronger as image than as concept, in that violence engages the public mind more and more, not perhaps because violence increases but because its salience increases.

This may be due partly to an increased level of expectation about the way we ought to live, partly because news gathering and mass communication makes it easier to show violence publicly and to engage attention by the juxtaposition of images. But the study of violence is still fragmentary: if the image were not so strong one would be tempted to say that violence is a non-subject, a word which should be expelled from our vocabulary of concepts, because it disintegrates in face of attempts at definition.

Yet these ambiguities lend strength to the image, which shifts and changes as the light falls on it.[1] Prometheus Bound has

1. '... both psychoanalytic theory and linguistic theory make much of

served as such an image for perhaps 2,500 years now. Its effective creator, Aeschylus, handled it so as to reflect his own ambiguities about divine and human reason, tyranny and justice. The myth had strange fortunes in the Middle Ages, re-emerged as a central theme of neo-classicism and was enlarged in scope by those who found treasure in it, people as different as Goethe, Shelley and Mary Shelley, Coleridge, Marx, Rimbaud, Nietzsche, Camus, Simone Weil,[2] Lowell.[3] A fuller anthology of Prometheans might have enriched this argument, but perhaps enough has been said to illustrate the relevance of explanation by myth and context in areas hard to unify conceptually.[4]

Choice and Decision

The difficulties of exposition increase when one comes to the concept of decision.

A problem at the outset has been whether to accept the word 'choice' as synonym for 'decision'. Sometimes I have found it natural to do so, without much thought; yet the words do not quite coincide in modern usage. One could perhaps express the

---

man's tendency to employ the same symbol to connote opposites: that is, to name a category of perceptions grouped between two poles which powerfully focuses attention, anxieties, and hopes.' Edelman (op. cit.), p. 160.

2. In particular, *Intimations of Christianity among the Ancient Greeks* (1951, 1952: ed. and trans. Elizabeth C. Geissbuhler (London, Routledge, 1957)). But I think the analogy with crucifixion is a mistake.

3. Shakespeare has one powerful use, at the crisis of *Othello*:

> Put out the light, and then put out the light:
> If I quench thee, thou flaming minister,
> I can again thy former light restore,
> Should I repent me: – but once put out they light,
> Thou cunning'st pattern of excelling nature,
> I know not where is that Promethean heat
> That can thy light relume. When I have pluckt the rose,
> I cannot give it vital growth again,
> It needs must wither . . .' [Act V, Scene II.]

But probably he knew nothing of Aeschylus.

4. See also the somewhat fuller note at the end of Ch. 2.

shade of difference by saying that it is hard to say 'choice' without postulating a chooser, not so hard to say 'decision' without postulating a decider. Certainly there have been two strong examples of the latter in recent academic discourse; the emergence of 'decision theory' as a branch of mathematical logic, yielding algorithms for decision by computer; the reference to politics as a 'decision-making process',[5] a flow of outputs explicable in terms of inputs and system structure.

What is it to 'choose'? The question once put, one realizes that there is a constellation of words in this context, and that they are difficult words: what is it to act, to be a person, to will or wish, to contemplate ends and means? To be Prometheus? It has already been noted that for some time now there has been a convergence towards theories of action, theories which attribute importance and reality to this constellation of images and concepts. Gouldner[6] notes that the whole drift of Parson's thought is to the effect that human will, purpose, choice will have real effects, but not those anticipated by the chooser; whereas Lenin's extension of Marxism insisted that the chooser (or band of choosers) might choose and win, might indeed shape the future.

(One must note a counter-current: *The Times* (23 December 1972) presented a Christmas article by a Benedictine on the contemplative and mystical strain in Christianity and extended an ecumenical hand towards Buddhist and Hindu concepts of meditation and Nirvana, the negation of concepts of 'real choice'.)

The Postulates of Choice

What then are the requirements of 'real choice'? This not in the sense of free will versus determinism, but in terms of consensus about the use of language.

First, there is the problem of polarity between ends and means. If one has indeed chosen, one should be accountable, in the sense

5. The Open University uses this approach (with ingenuity and caution) in the first two 'levels' of its Politics course. See for instance D. J. Murray and others '*Patterns of Decision making*' (Block VIII 'Decision making in Britain) (Open University Press, 1972).

6. Gouldner (1970), p. 190.

of being able to give an account of one's choice. 'Why did you do A?' The 'explanation' is that one did it as a step towards B. 'Why did you do B?' And so on, till regress is stopped: 'X is what I wanted to get'. But other chains of explanation may lead to Y and Z, other ends or purposes which are not means to one another, and are therefore commensurable only by the process of 'knowing one's own mind'.

'To know one's own mind' is not necessarily a fluke, an accident. It may be referred logically to a settled view of the world and man's place in it; non-rationally, to a settled cast of mind, a tradition of behaviour.

But (secondly) there is the problem of passing from individual preference to public choice, which can in principle be solved either by the operation of a free market (see Ch. 5 above) or by a stipulated procedure. The problem is not quite as bad as it seems, in that the distinction of 'I' and 'we' is never absolute; we are all (or almost all) participants in some instances of the first person plural. To repeat what was said about choice of ends, choice of identities is a matter of 'knowing one's own mind'; and that may be based either on a settled view of the world or on a settled cast of mind, or on both.

Nevertheless, the problem of amalgamation of preferences is as difficult as that of assessing ends.

Thirdly, there is choice between different means to an agreed end. This is our common experience and most of the time we do it without thinking. If 'we stop to think', then things become harder: but if the end is settled then it is not hard to agree on a framework of thought for a choice of means.

But (fourthly) the choice of means is in any real situation restricted by lack of information and lack of power. The problem is to do the best we can with what we have; the algebras of maximization and probability exist, and can be used to place us as near to the peak as we can get by rational combination.

And (fifthly) the computation can tell us when it would be rational to spin a coin and take a fifty-fifty chance rather than to expend time and resources in trying to gain better information and better resources. Temperamentally, you may prefer to withdraw rather than to stake all on the spin of a coin. That in turn is an intelligible statement about your choice of ends.

Finally, there are problems of indecision, non-decision and decision by default.[7] We know these as individuals, but it is simpler to build a formal model of them in terms of the control of business in a committee, an assembly or any large-scale use of voting. In the last resort, decision is defined by voting procedure: and that will affect the tactics of the leaders. But there are two other keys to power; the power (whether violent or legalistic) to bring matters to an issue at a chosen moment, or to let them sleep, so that failure to decide becomes by lapse of time decision by default; the power to control the agenda, so that among many courses of action, many candidates, public choice is restricted to a few.

A Crisis of Choice

This discussion is by no means abstract and theoretical. At the individual level it seems as if the attainment of universal education in the West, the approach to affluence, have promised freedom of choice not previously available. When choices are foreclosed against him, the individual today is 'alienated', is no longer carried passively by the movement of society; and perhaps (taking the issue narrowly) the present cult of alienation represents a more vigorous assertion of choice than did the previous cults of integrated personality, integrated society.[8]

At the social level, too, there is a crisis of choice, and in one sense this too arises from a sense of increased resources. Human resources of energy and productive skill have increased to a huge extent in the last century; great engineering jobs such as those involved in the H-bomb and the moon missions can be executed over a long span of time and within available resources, provided that top priority (that is to say, supreme power over the allocation of resources) is conceded and can be sustained and enforced.

7. A debate begun by P. Bachrach and M. S. Baratz, 'Two Faces of Power', (*American Political Science Review*, 56 (1962), p. 947–52) and continued in their book, *Power and Poverty; Theory and Practice* (OUP; 1970).

8. 'Anomic disorder may unbind wasted energies, sever fruitless commitments' (Gouldner; 1970, p. 224). It may – or it may not. Similarly with 'alienation'.

There is no doubt that the same would be true of engineering to improve water resources, to breed new varieties of crops and animals, to harvest the sea. This technological confidence is one aspect of the Delphi technique, used by Olaf Helmer, then of the Rand Corporation,[9] to provide a basis of long-range planning. In each of49 technological areas, experts were asked to guess separately at the time needed to invent, develop and use radical innovations; and the point to make in the present context is that there was a considerable measure of consensus within each field about what could be done, and about the time required for it.

But such a study could not embrace the dimension of power and priorities, which are no easier to foresee than (say) in the fifteenth century, before the technological revolution gathered force. It is not too much to say that man for the first time sees mankind as a whole, and can specify the world and its resources as a whole.[10] It is easy for man to reduce the world surface to a radio-active cinder; rather harder, yet still within the scope of engineering, to make it a Garden bringing forth every living creature in abundance after its kind.

There has emerged a gap between what is technically possible and what is politically possible. There have been real advances towards good sense and adaptivity in world politics: but nevertheless the gap has widened, and its reality has been illustrated by a world-wide rubbish dump of abandoned projects, of failures, of disastrous side-effects. Everyone knows something of this, because it has affected our lives; about aircraft projects that went wrong, about misuse of water resources, about unexpected pollution of air and sea, about rich and poor, health and sickness, birth-rates and death-rates. Chaotic results are associated with the highest

9. Olaf Helmer, ed.: *Social Technology* (New York, Basic Books; 1966), App. 1.

10. Two good popular expositions are the Verney Working Party report, *Sinews for Survival* (HMSO; 1972), prepared as part of a brief for the Minister for the Environment at the UN Conference on the Human Environment, Stockholm, June 1972; and Barbara Ward and René Dubos, *Only One Earth: The care and maintenance of a small planet* (prepared for the same Conference) Penguin Books; 1972. There is a more technical exposition with case studies, in Walter Isard, ed., *Ecological-Economic Analysis for Regional Development* (New York, Free Press; 1972).

echnical competence; we know what men could build by the 'ear 2,000, we have very little confidence about what they will in act decide to build or choose to build. The dimension space vithin which 'we' could choose has been immensely enlarged; ur capacity for collective decision has increased, but at a far lower rate. Olaf Stapledon, writing in the late 1920s,[11] postulated he discovery of nuclear fission about AD 2,200, the final crippling of Western Europe, Germany and Russia by that date, a struggle between the USA and China resolved about AD 2,300. We have already begun to play Stapledon's scenario, and think it reasonable to postulate a 'make or break' situation between the USA and China within a generation, say fifty years: Stapledon allowed nearly 400 years. We have a sense of change accelerating, of a time scale drastically shortened.

Perspectives

Hence catch-phrases about decision-making in 'the global village',[12] such as 'credibility gap', 'future shock', 'goal scepticism'. These are no more than catch-words, conveying no clear image or concept. Nevertheless, there can be built imaginative and symbolic structures which will contain them. There are the philosophies of *Ohne Mich*, 'Count me out', 'Stop the World I want to get off', which can be stated very persuasively and advertised as the creation of a new non-Protestant ethic for a new age. There are philosophies of revolution, the feeblest based on conspiracy theories of the way the world is run, the best seeking earnestly and scrupulously for the Archimedean lever,[13] the fulcrum point at which to move the world. And there are theories of politics as a symbolic activity, not a practical one, a field in which collective decision is an illusion but a necessary one. A paragraph from Edelman may make this clearer.

11. *Last and First Men* (1930, Penguin Books; 1972.)

12. 'Global village' is said to be McLuhan's phrase; *Future Shock* is by Alvin Toffler (Pan Books; 1971); the others I have not traced.

13. By radical student groups, 'dialectical materialism is seen as the only available scientific-redemptive method, an Archimedean point, which allows one to grasp the world in its present structure and contradictions and lift it out of its position.' F. G. Friedmann: *Youth and Society* (Macmillan; 1971), p. 43.

Because it is apparently intolerable for men to admit the key role of accident, of ignorance, and of unplanned processes in their affairs, the leader serves a vital function by personifying and reifying the processes. As an individual, he can be praised and blamed and given 'responsibility' in a way that processes cannot. Incumbents of high public office therefore become objects of acclaim for the satisfied, scapegoats for the unsatisfied, and symbols of aspirations or of whatever is opposed. To them are constantly ascribed careful weighing of alternatives and soul-searching decisions. That the premises for the decisions are largely supplied and screened by others and the decision itself frequently predetermined by a succession of subordinates' decisions is not publicized. Decision-making at the highest levels is not so much literal policy-making as dramaturgy.[14]

I have not chosen, in this last Part of the book, to take up these attractive themes, each of which can be deployed very vividly and with great mythological and symbolic force. Instead, I have tried to follow the clue of rationality in collective decision-making, a drier theme and one beset by ambiguities and pit-falls. It is in fact a less attractive argument than the three others to which I have referred (p. 181), and it is riddled with difficulties. But it seems to me that it must be stated, and must be scrupulously weighed, in that it represents the only viable project for world management by reasoned collective choice.

The scheme of exposition is as follows.

Chapter 15, Individual Choice, follows through the point made in Chapters 11 and 12, Individual Aggression and Collective Violence. The individual, it is true, cannot be understood except in a social setting, and with the aid of social metaphors. But if one accepts 'the Judaeo-Christian ethic' (as Anthony Burgess calls it; see p. 185 below), then there is a stronger current from individual to community than in the reverse direction. Our vision of collective decision is derived from ideal language about individual choice.[15]

14. Edelman, op. cit., p. 78.

15. It can be put more sociologically in Gouldner's language. Gouldner (1970), p. 220. 'Human beings are as much engaged in using social systems as in being used by them. Men are social system-using and social system-building creatures. They are not merely viewed inadequately when seen one-sidedly as "social products" ... but are also seriously misunderstood if

But if collective decision is to come within sight of the standards of good sense we set ourselves as individuals, then there are three additional obstacles which need not be faced in the analysis of individual choice. These are, in sequence, the aggregation of individual preferences, the negotiation of agreement on the choice of means, the struggle to increase social learning and social adaptivity – the problem of learning how to learn how to . . ., at the level of a continuing social entity. These problems are taken in sequence in Chapters 16, 17 and 18; but they must be handled together, as a *troika*.

---

viewed simply as *social* beings, if by that is meant *sociable* beings, friendly little fellows eagerly waiting to cooperate with others'.

CHAPTER 15

INDIVIDUAL CHOICE

Go!
Never again elude the choice of tints!
White shall not neutralize the black,
nor good
Compensate bad in man, absolve him so:
Life's business being just the terrible choice.
[Robert Browning: *The Ring and the Book*
Book X, line 1233.]

Social Identity and Personal Choice

THE disjunction between individual and collective choice has no absolute validity. It is commonplace that the criteria of choice used by an individual are socially derived; and that any specific social choice (as distinct from the abstraction, social choice in general) is to some extent the product of the idiosyncrasies of individuals.

Furthermore, we get the two sorts of choice mixed up in our metaphors. Each of us, asked to describe the process of individual choice, does so in metaphors drawn from various types and levels of debate about action. The dialectic of reason is such a metaphor, and probably Hegel would have wished it to operate not as a metaphor but as an identity, God or the Absolute thinking in and through men's arguments.

Conversely, 'we' (confounded word) have great difficulty about when to use the first person singular, when the first person plural. This book began with a discussion of words in contexts; one of the hardest semantic puzzles in politics is about the 'proper' use of the word 'we'. Undoubtedly, 'I' tends to impose his 'we' on the 'I's of others. Undoubtedly he often fails, and others fail too, so that the word 'we' is used ambiguously in social discourse, at all levels, from that of R. D. Laing's schizophrenic families to that of the politics of all mankind. Who are 'we'? Simply an extension of the personal identity laboriously gained by each child in the process of development?

A happy solution might be the interpenetration of 'I' and 'we', of personal and social identity. We perhaps credit 'primitives' with this, our analogue for the primitive communism of Marx and

Engels. And possibly also we see in these terms ultimate communism, the anarchist utopia expressed by a familiar quotation in Lenin's *State and Revolution*;[1] 'from each according to his ability, to each according to his needs!' The appeal is powerful, but as myth: the real world is one in which 'I' is a member of a range of distinguishable 'we's', and in the management of collective choice 'we' must have regard to that.

Here is a paragraph by Anthony Burgess, commenting on Kubrick's film of his book, *A Clockwork Orange*, and on B. F. Skinner.

> Theologically, evil is not quantifiable. Yet I posit the notion that one act of evil may be greater than another, and that perhaps the ultimate act of evil is dehumanization, the killing of the soul – which is as much as to say the capacity to choose between good and evil acts. Impose on an individual the capacity to be good and only good, and you kill his soul for, presumably, the sake of social stability. What my, and Kubrick's, parable tries to state is that it is preferable to have a world of violence undertaken in full awareness – violence chosen as an act of will – than a world conditioned to be good or harmless. I recognize that the lesson is already becoming an old-fashioned one. B. F. Skinner, with his ability to believe that there is something *beyond* freedom and dignity, wants to see the death of autonomous man. He may or may not be right, but in terms of the Judaeo-Christian ethic that *A Clockwork Orange* tries to express, he is perpetrating a gross heresy. It seems to me in accordance with the tradition that Western man is not yet ready to jettison, that the area in which human choice is a possibility should be extended, even if one comes up against new angels with swords and banners, emblazoned *No*. The wish to diminish free will is, I should think, the sin against the Holy Ghost.[2]

Skinner might reply that this is a misunderstanding of his position. But the sentiment wins an echo?

Given then that Burgess is right, that our Western souls twang in harmony with these sentiments, and that we believe, dogmatically and neo-colonially, that they are right for all men at all times; man *qua* man is a chooser. Yet it is not easy to get agreement beyond that point.

1. Ch. 5.
2. *The Listener*, 17 February 1972.

The Character of Individual Choice

There are at least four points of view about the character of individual choice; and one needs to add three further dimensions, rational/irrational, conscious/unconscious, self/others.

To take the four points of view.

WISDOM AND FREEDOM

First (*honoris causa*) is the arrogant intellectual tradition (arrogant, though presented by Socrates with irony) that wisdom and only wisdom gives free choice. Here is Cornford, stating (not necessarily endorsing) the Socratic view.

> The only thing in the world that is really and intrinsically good for man is the perfection of his own nature . . . Now, no one will believe this truth until he can see it for himself with the inward eye of his own soul; you cannot persuade him to act as if it were true until he knows it, with entire conviction, from his own experience. When he does know it in this complete sense, then he will act upon it unfailingly; his knowledge must determine his will, for no man will sacrifice his true happiness for pleasures he can see to be illusory. This knowledge is wisdom; and the man who gains it becomes thenceforth morally autonomous: everything he does is determined by his own inward light; he will not be guided by any external authority, but will claim the unconditional freedom of self-rule.[3]

And here is the Christian view, or one version of it, as expressed by Dante at the end of the *Purgatorio*, with four lines of comment by Cornford:

> 'When the whole stair was passed and now beneath us, and we were on the topmost step, Virgil fixed his eyes upon me, and said: "My son, thou hast seen the temporal fire and the eternal, and thou art come to a place where, of myself, I see no further. I have led thee hither with intelligence and art; henceforward take thine own pleasure for guide; thou hast come forth of the steep and narrow ways.
>
> See there the Sun, which shines upon thy forehead; see the tender grass, the flowers, the young trees which here the Earth of herself alone brings forth.
>
> While those fair eyes with joy are shining, whose weeping made me come to thee, here mayst thou sit and walk among them.

3. Cornford (1950), p. 59.

Await no more word or sign from me. Free, right and sound is thine own will; and not to act according to its prompting would be a fault. Therefore I give thee, over thyself, the mitre and the crown".'

The mitre and the crown are the signs of sovereignty, spiritual and temporal. Dante, now purified, is subject to no external power; because his own will has become right, sound and free, and cannot lead him astray. Hence he is made priest and king over himself.[4]

Bourgeois ideology? I am not sure that in this respect Marx or Lenin had different ideals. Mao is more enigmatic.

THE CURSE OF FREEDOM

Secondly, there is the converse position. Freedom of choice is not a privilege but a burden; the the curse of freedom is imposed on each man alike. Hence one strand in the existential tradition; each man must pick up the burden of identity, authenticity, commitment – or be convicted of complicity or bad faith.

This too wins echoes? At a simple personal level, the relief of finding that really you have no choice; remarks like 'won't *you* please choose?' or 'I'd rather spin a coin than brood about this.' At a cosmic level, the Agony in the Garden:

> 'O my Father, if it be possible, let this cup pass from me: nevertheless, not as I will, but as thou wilt . . . O my Father, if this cup may not pass away from me, except I drink it, thy will be done.'[5]

An *agon* is a kind of conflict,[6] and the word is used technically by Aristotle for the tragic conflict in Greek drama. *Prometheus Bound* is Agon: later comes Reversal and Explication. On this has been built by Coleridge,[7] Nietzsche and others the image of tragedy and the tragic character of man; an aspiration for a deeper insight than that of the Romantic Agony. Violence is in this too, and pain: but by conflict a transcendence of Sadism and Satanism.

4. Cornford, ibid., p. 80.
5. *Matthew*, Chapter XXVI, 39, 42.
6. And Kotarbinski: *Praxiology: An Introduction to the Science of Efficient Action* (Warsaw, Polish Scientific Publishers; 1965) postulates 'agonology' as a field of general theory (p. 158).
7. 'The Prometheus of Aeschylus . . . of which it may be truly said, that it is more properly tragedy itself in the plenitude of the idea, than a particular tragic poem.' 'On the Prometheus of Aeschylus', at p. 323 of *Literary Remains*, Vol. 2 (H. N. Coleridge, ed., London, Pickering; 1836).

Cornford weaves this also into his discussion, using *The Brothers Karamazov*. The Grand Inquisitor asks Christ why he has returned 'to hinder the work of the Church':

> The Church has relieved mankind of that intolerable burden of freedom, which the stranger [i.e. Christ at his first coming] had promised them. 'We have paid dearly for that promise,' says the Inquisitor. 'For fifteen hundred years we have been wrestling with that freedom, and now it is ended. The people have brought their freedom to us, and laid it humbly at our feet'. The Church has given them, instead of freedom, authority; instead of knowledge, mystery. And men rejoiced that they were again led like sheep.[8]

Nietzsche's first book was on the birth of tragedy. On this view, men hunger after the death of tragedy.

THE ILLUSION OF FREEDOM

Thirdly, there is the perhaps comforting thought that choice is an illusion. The historic argument about freedom and fate seems to have died out.

> Others apart sat on a Hill retir'd,
> In thoughts more elevate, and reason'd high
> Of Providence, Foreknowledge, Will, and Fate,
> Fixt Fate, free will, foreknowledge absolute,
> And found no end, in wandring mazes lost.
> Of good and evil much they argu'd then,
> Of happiness and final misery,
> Passion and Apathie, and glory and shame,
> Vain wisdom all, and false Philosophie . . .[9]

This is seventeenth-century language, surviving now only in academic essays. Now we are reasonably well briefed on contingencies, idiosyncracies, random distributions, indeterminacy. We are free from both masters: God who predestined each to salvation or perdition, and whose saints prevail against even the gates of Hell: nature, an infinite and perpetual clock in which each of us is meshed like a cog.

The figure of the Laplacian Demon was a very striking symbol of

8. Cornford, ibid., p. 66.
9. Milton: *Paradise Lost*, Book II, 1.557.

this: Imagine, says Laplace, a Being who knows the position and momentum of every particle in the universe, together with the laws of motion governing such particles; such a Being would be able to predict all subsequent states of the universe.[10]

Determinism as such is not now a bogey: we are at least confident that the future is uncertain.

But this also is an unhappy state: we are not predestined but we are infinitely small. That we are random is part of nature; I know that I choose, and that my choice is not an illusion. The illusion is that it makes a difference what I choose. What is random in me is swallowed up in probabilities for the whole. I choose but do not 'significantly' (a nice technical word) affect the future for me or for the whole.

To be free is to be powerless.[11]

FREEDOM AS POWER

And therefore, finally, to be free must be to have power. A tragic view is that the hero, damned by his own flaw, seeks escape from personal freedom by claiming power over others: Zeus, Julius Caesar, Macbeth, Napoleon, even Hitler and Mussolini sought to play the part. Perhaps every man and woman has something of this in him or her; to seek to actualize 'my' identity by dominance, and to fail.

And this is a bridge to the question of collective choice. 'The commander' may seek to express his identity through the execution by others of his commands; *pari passu*, the manipulator. But one can reverse the language and regard each as 'functional' in the process of collective choice. The collectivity, 'we', could not 'decide' without manipulator or boss.

And perhaps there is a third dimension of power, that of the 'midwives', those who facilitate the initiatives of others, that sort of don whom pre-war Oxford called 'crypto-megalomaniac'; 'but for me it would never have happened'. Where this is done consciously, as by some civil servants skilled in the English

10. William Barrett: *Irrational Man: A Study in Existential Philosophy* (Heinemann; 1964), p. 33.

11. Cf. Gouldner (1970) (at p. 193) quoting Parsons on alienation as the condition of man's humanity and freedom.

manner, one must surely classify this as a kind of power, even though these are only the serving-men or valets of history. But the facilitation may well be unconscious, a trait of personality and position.

Dimensions of Freedom

Three further dimensions are required.

RATIONALITY

Rationality can be construed in a substantive sense or in a formal one. The substantive sense is that of Dante quoted above, or of the opening words of the Gospel of St John: 'In the beginning was the Word, and the Word was with God, and the Word was God.'

Logos, here translated as Word, is a difficult and confusing concept. C. H. Dodd traces its ancestry in Greek and Hebrew thought, and through the gnostic philosophies of the late Hellenistic period, and offers various paraphrases.

> The Logos of Christ is the Logos of God, and that is Truth, the ultimate reality revealed.

> It is a rational content of thought corresponding to the ultimate reality of the universe.

> It is the rational principle in the universe, its meaning, plan or purpose, conceived as a divine hypostasis in which the eternal God is revealed and active.[12]

This is so difficult to seize that one is tempted to say that Logos, 'substantive reason', is not a concept but a word, intelligible only by observing its use and contexts, and its imperfect identity of meaning as it passes in translation through many languages. But this does not release one from the problem and the challenge, in that Logos and its kindred have been and still are words of power, transmitted through Judaism, Christianity and late Greek philosophy to the Middle Ages, to Dante, to the originators of modern science, to a lineage of saints, poets and philosophers; to Hegel and perhaps even to Marx, who might in some

12. C. H. Dodd: *The Interpretation of the Fourth Gospel* (Cambridge UP, 1953), pp. 267, 280.

moods have accepted the second of Dodd's formulations as applicable to the dialectic; to Wordsworth, Blake and Shelley,[13] among many others. 'And ye shall know the truth, and the truth shall make you free.'[14]

For the formal sense of rationality, I quote from Anthony Downs:

> A rational man is one who behaves as follows: (1) he can always make a decision when confronted with a range of alternatives; (2) he ranks all the alternatives facing him in order of his preference in such a way that each is either preferred to, indifferent to, or inferior to each other; (3) his preference ranking is transitive; (4) he always chooses from among the possible alternatives that which ranks highest in his preference ordering; and (5) he always makes the same decision each time he is confronted with the same alternatives.[15]

Such austerity is not to be condemned as trivial. No-one has climbed the mountain of Purgatory with Virgil and Dante; few even believe that they have. But all (if they can even add and subtract) claim formal rationality; that measure of agreement lies at the heart of the rhetoric of combined action. If we cannot even agree on adding up the bill, how can we cooperate?

This is perhaps more important in the next three chapters than in this, because formal rationality is our sole lifeline in argument about many joint enterprises. In so far as I choose merely for myself, it might seem appropriate to use the Latin tag:

> *Sic volo, sic iubeo, sit pro ratione voluntas.*
> [Thus I wish, thus I command, let my will stand in place of reason.][16]

But Juvenal's line is put into the mouth of a woman who intends to crucify a slave, for no reason: and perhaps this is as close as one gets in ancient literature to an expression of Sadism, and an attack on it.

13. J. Bronowski (1944), Carl Grabo: *Prometheus Unbound: An Interpretation* (N. Carolina UP; 1935).

14. *John*, VIII. 32.

15. A. Downs: *An Economic Theory of Democracy* (New York, Harper & Row; 1957), p. 6. (I have already used the quotation at p. 121 of *Politics and Social Science*).

16. Juvenal, *Satires*, VI, p. 223.

IRRATIONALITY

Why then has the other pole, that of irrationality, had any attraction? In its formal sense, it has perhaps had no attraction: given the definition of 2, no one much wants to say that $2+2=5$. But there can be a slide from formal to transcendental, *via* the distinction between contrary and contradictory. 'X is A, X is not A' leads nowhere: but 'X is A, X is not A but B' gets going a discussion or dialectic. And the outcome of the dialectic is a radically new proposition. Formal rationality is barren, the dialectic is fruitful: irrationality is fruitful if it is not mere negation of formal rationality. But what else could it be but negation?

This is another semantic jungle growing wild; it could be reduced to cultivation only by drastic clearance which would destroy what we are trying to explore. Is it possible to tread down a few narrow paths, for the purpose only of the present argument?

First, one must discard the idea that formal rationality is something solitary or anti-social. On the contrary, it is the extreme case of the public character of established science: it is not possible to cooperate in any technical enterprise, or even to buy and sell in a market, except on the basis of a common understanding of arithmetic and geometry. On that simple base is erected the structure of mathematics and a universal and unchallenged language of cooperation. Perhaps the activity of logic or mathematics would be pointless, even inconceivable, as solitary; part at least of their essence is to establish a public world of discourse.

Later, I will refer to the formalities of procedure as necessary to collective decision on any substantial scale.[17] What is formal is not therefore trivial.

Secondly, there runs through the argument the problem of contraries and contradictories. Here is (for instance) Blake's version: 'Negations are not Contraries: Contraries mutually Exist; but Negations Exist Not.'[18] It is possible to label this sort of logic irrational or non-rational; in which case it could be argued that radical innovation or creativity is non-rational.

17. Chapter 16, p. 206.

18. *The Marriage of Heaven and Hell*, p. 639, quoted in Bronowski, op. cit., at p. 130. For Blake's 'dialectical' thinking (by no means Hegelian) see Kettle (1972), p. 11.

Thirdly, it is possible to equate irrationality with the presence of any affect or emotional tone at all; any coloured perspective which might blinker 'the cold light of reason'. To be emotionally involved is to be enslaved. Simone de Beauvoir writes:

> With a severity similar to Kant's, and which has its source in the same puritan tradition, Sade conceives the free act only as an act free of all feeling. If it were to obey emotional motives, it would make us Nature's slaves again and not autonomous subjects.[19]

I am not sure that she is quite right, either about Kant or about Sade; but the point is made. If affect is irrationality, let us be irrational in our choice.

This is perhaps wide enough to sweep in as elements inseparable from choice all the symbolic affects of art, myth and ritual,[20] as well as inter-personal emotions: to 'sweep them in', both descriptively as present everywhere, and normatively as compatible with (perhaps essential to) 'good' decisions.

Fourthly, there is the semantic problem posed by Oakeshott's essay on 'Rational Conduct'[21] and by Gluckman's chapter on 'The Reasonable Man' in Barotse jurisprudence.[22] Oakeshott stigmatizes here and elsewhere the notion that there can exist such a thing as 'rational conduct' if by that we mean that there is an independent entity called 'the mind' which can be trained logically so that it premeditates ends, devises logical means, and puts them into effect.

In Oakeshott's hands this was the basis of an attack on attempts to build a 'rational society' from first principles, and it was in that sense pretty successful. But probably the attack swept in too much. His type case is that of Mrs Bloomer and the invention of 'bloomers' (a sort of divided skirt, pretty long) as 'rational dress' for lady cyclists at the height of the cycling craze: and he points out that 'bloomers' were justified by the rhetoric of rationality, but were in fact a compromise with social norms about

19. (1962), p. 53.

20. The sociological symposium on *Rationality* (Blackwell; 1970), edited by B. R. Wilson, is largely concerned with this sort of irrationality.

21. In *Rationalism in Politics and Other Essays* (1962).

22. In *The Judicial Process among the Barotse of Northern Rhodesia* (Manchester UP; 1955). See also his book *The Ideas in Barotse Jurisprudence* (1965; extended reprint, Manchester UP; 1972).

the exposure of female leg tolerable at that time. Pure rationality (he says) would have led to shorts; rather to tights, I think, in the English climate, but these would also have been socially intolerable – the full outline of the leg would have been deemed as bad as the naked leg. But did Mrs Bloomer know that she was compromising with a social 'idiom' or 'tradition'? Or did she try for a purely rational solution and retire defeated? In the former case she behaved in the sense that Oakeshott wants to give to the word 'rational' (which has, as he says, 'bequeathed a legacy of ambiguity and confusion'; p. 80): late in the essay, he brings in also the word 'reasonable'.

Gluckman's analysis is kindred but distinct, in that he takes the concept of 'the reasonable man' as being a tool of analysis and 'a central figure in all developed systems of law' (p. 83), and also in that of a large, stable and intelligent tribe, the Barotse in what is now Zambia.

'The *kuta*'s main technique in cross-examination is to state the norms of behaviour of a specific position, as the reasonable man would act in a perhaps unique situation' (p. 93). 'The judges operate with a whole set of pre-suppositions about how people of different social position act in Lozi life' (p. 153). 'The reasonable man', he writes, – 'or rather the reasonable incumbent of a particular social position' (p. 94): and in his later book (1965), 'as a reasonable man or woman – or rather as a reasonable brother, sister, uncle, nephew, or general dependent of the new headman' (p. 16).

The two points of view seem to converge towards the idea that to act reasonably is a matter of social context: this does not imply that pre-suppositions about what is 'reasonable' are fixed forever and exempt from growth. But change is a process of growth rather than of engineering.

It is possible to accept all this, and yet to feel that these perceptions under-rate the power of 'human engineering' in big organizations, of *The Sciences of the Artificial*[23] applied to men as well as to other materials. But organization theory as it now stands has made full amends for the abstract rationality of its early days and insists that the manager like the judge must be sensitively

23. H. A. Simon (1969).

aware of social context and of the unforeseen side-effects of 'rational' acts. He will not survive unless he is a 'reasonable man'.

The reasonable man then is a social creature, indeed a creation of society. To be totally unreasonable is to be mad? In that sense one can certainly accept the Laing doctrine of madness as a stigma imposed by society on those whom it cannot manage to contain. We are again in trouble with definitions: does one or does one not set up an equivalence 'irrational' = 'unreasonable' = 'socially outlawed' = 'mad'? This is quite without prejudice to the debate with Skinner about 'behaviour', with establishment psychiatry about 'mental disease'. What one has to do here is to rescue as true participants in choice some of those whom the world calls 'mad': and it is indeed part of the myth of art that artists share in divine madness, that art may be Dionysiac, that perhaps all radically new choice contains an element of isolation, of loneliness, which entail social stigma if the 'maker' fails. The Great McGonagle was mad, and pathetic; not so Blake, Clare, Smart, or for that matter Ezra Pound, Virginia Woolf,[24] Sylvia Plath[25] – and other 'unacknowledged legislators of the world'.

CONSCIOUS AND UNCONSCIOUS

The distinction between 'conscious' and 'unconscious', whatever exactly it means, belongs to a different dimension of analysis. It is now a commonplace that 'mathematics gets done', 'decisions get taken' not in the conscious mind alone. But when one comes to write it down, this unconscious work may have at one extreme the character of formal rationality, as when one wakes up with the proof clear in one's head; at the other extreme, the character of divine madness, as when Coleridge awoke from stupor and wrote down all he could remember of Kubla Khan.[26]

Perhaps this is no more than a statement of the usages I choose for this argument out of the manifold of language. At any rate, I

24. Quentin Bell, *Virginia Woolf: A Biography* (Hogarth Press; 1972).

25. A. Alvarez, *The Savage God: A Study of Suicide* (Penguin Books; 1974).

26. J. L. Lowes, *The Road toXanadu* (1927). I know that Coleridge is now suspected of faking.

should in these senses defend as real and good 'irrational' or 'non-rational' or even 'unreasonable' decisions.[27] This would not entail defending decisions which are 'silly' or 'silly-clever' or just plain 'stupid', though these are very common. It would not entail any distinction in this context between conscious and unconscious decisions. But it would be left with a difficult residuary category of 'mindlessness': a cabbage does not decide. It is in a common-sense way clear what one is saying if one refers to a living being in human form as 'mindless'. Unfortunately, it is by no means so clear what one is saying if one attributes mindlessness, incapacity for decision, to a social entity.

SELF AND OTHERS

Finally, the dimension of self-regarding and other-regarding (p. 191 above).

(1) Formal rationality as defined by Arrow (ch. 15; p. 8). is in an empty sense self-regarding; the preferences fed into the optimizing machine are *my* preferences, and the object of the exercise is to climb as high as possible on *my* preference schedules. These are not 'goods', but revealed preferences; nothing is known or need be known except my observed behaviour.

(2) There can, quite separately, be empirical questions about my expression of these preferences. Partly these are questions about social environment. What information did I have about the choices open? How far can generalizations be made about what I choose? Do these generalizations correspond to social rules learnt in a particular society? Indeed, how far is the language and style of choice explicable in social terms? Partly they will be questions (and I find these more difficult) about my self-image, my personality structure, my emotions of love, hatred, solidarity, and so on, my capacity for rule-governed activity. Together, these are questions of social identity, and they seem to be at least conceptually answerable, given the assumption, methodological and poetic, that 'no man is an island', that self-sufficiency is not even conceivable.

(3) Then, thirdly, there are the metaphysical questions,

27. And in a special sense 'anti-rational' decisions.

unanswerable except in terms of *consensus*. There are doctrines of personal salvation by faith and good works; there is also the contrary doctrine that 'he that findeth his life shall lose it; and he that loseth his life for my sake shall find it';[28] that to act according to the rules of virtue is damnable if done in a self-regarding way, merely as instrumental to one's own good, here or hereafter. And doctrines of wisdom, as in Socrates and Dante, seek to find a higher level, at which personal choice is made at a universal level of identification and understanding which excludes selfishness. Has this any meaning except a mystical one? One can at least say that the aspiration for such wisdom is not Western only but universal.

Summary

All this is difficult – so difficult that a more diffuse statement would not help. With apologies, therefore, I offer only a brief and formal summary.

(1) There is an inter-penetration of individual and society, of 'I' and 'we'. The exposition here is set out within a tradition and a set of ideas which give priority to the individual, in the last resort. To put it in terms of language, there is a two-way traffic in metaphors, but the predominant flow is from individual to collective experience.

This is 'our' way of talking: other ways are conceivable.

(2) Within that tradition, there are at least four points of view about the character of individual choice:

(*a*) To be wise, to attain pure reason, is to be free to choose.

(*b*) Choice is an agony and a burden; men seek to lay it down.

(*c*) I am free to choose, but my choices have no power over events.

(*d*) There is no choice unless I have power to see that my choice is executed. In so far as I choose to make choice an end, I must seek power as means. But power, though ultimately dependent on violence, is social in its character and has many guises; to command, to manipulate, to facilitate. No individual has power except

28. *Matthew*, X. 39.

through society; but the proposition is reciprocal – society can have no power except through individuals.

(3) Substantive rationality or Reason, the Logos, has been set aside in section 2(*a*). There remains formal rationality, which has been attacked many times as sterile. Those who do so perceive choice as irrational or non-rational.

This area is known to be a rank semantic jungle, and I make only four limited points:

(*a*) Formal rationality is by no means empty; on the contrary, it is necessary for cooperation in any technical enterprise.

(*b*) There is the dialectical debate about contraries and contradictories, and about radical innovation. It does not perhaps matter much whether one calls this 'non-rational' or 'super-rational' thinking?

(*c*) Formal rationality may be despised on the ground that it seeks choice free from affect or emotion. But formalism and affect dwell apart; neither can be taken to exclude the other.

(*d*) Oakeshott goes looking for a rationality which is neither formal nor transcendent, and come back with the word 'reasonable', which serves very well in English talk and English law as a semantic bridge between individual and social 'reason'.

(4) There remain two other issues which must be mentioned because they are used in both contexts, individual and social; yet they cannot be explored fully here.

(*a*) Do we exclude unconscious choice from consideration, as not being truly choice? Surely not, in an age which gives full credit to unconscious reason.

(*b*) Need we explore the issue of self-regarding and other-regarding choice? I think not, given what has been said about the inter-penetration of individual and social spheres, subject to the restricted priority conceded to the individual.

CHAPTER 16

THE AGGREGATION OF ENDS

He sat up hear all night in his long coat, makin' speeches to himsilf; but tord mornin' he come over to my place where O'Brien sat with his la-ads. 'Well,' says O'Brien, 'how did it suit ye?', he says. 'It's sthrange,' says Dorgan. 'Not sthrange at all,' says Willum J. O'Brien. 'Whin ye've been in politics as long as I have, ye'll know,' he says, 'that th' roly-boly is th' gr-reatest or-rator on earth,' he says. 'Th' American nation in th' Sixth Ward is a fine people,' he says. 'They love th' eagle,' he says, 'on th' back iv a dollar,' he says. 'Well,' says Dorgan, 'I can't undherstand it,' he says. 'I med as manny as three thousan' speeches,' he says. 'Well,' says Willum J. O'Brien, 'that was my majority,' he says. 'Have a dhrink,' he says. [Finlay Peter Dunne, *Mr Dooley in Peace and in War*.]

Public Choice, Collective Decision

IN the light of recent theoretical and practical work, the problem of public choice has resolved itself into three related problems.

The first is that of the amalgamation of individual preferences so as to constitute a collective decision. In Rousseau's words:

Trouver une forme d'association qui défende et protège de toute la force commune la personne et les biens de chaque associé, et par laquelle chacun, s'unissant à tous, n'obéisse pourtant qu'à lui-même, et reste aussi libre qu'au-paravant. Tel est le problème fondamental dont le contrat social donne la solution.[1]

As will be seen later in this Chapter, professional economists by no means reject the use of the social contract model as analytic tool, but they make it a premise that to will or choose is the prerogative of the individual, and that a general will does not exist except as an aggregation of individual wills. They also make it a premise that where formal criteria of rationality are available they should be applied, and this is possible in two cases:

(*a*) that of tailoring means to resources, so as to maximize the utility of means in pursuit of a given end:

1. J.-J. Rousseau: *Du Contrat Social* (Paris, Flammarion; no date), Chapter VI, p. 17.

(*b*) that of assuring that different ends, each with its means thus formally deployed, are com-possible, that is to say that there is no conflict over the use of resources such as can be resolved only through a choice of ends.

These two are jobs for professional analysts, and inter-personal summation of preferences is needed only for the choice of ends, or for the allocation of an agreed weight to each of a number of ends or purposes, which amounts to the same thing. The ends are now by definition incommensurable, since all the formal measurement and comparison that can be done have already been done by the professionals. The problem is therefore difficult, perhaps formally insoluble.

Add to this, that the whole system of choice is moving through real time, in a real and changing environment. In Heraclitus' phrase, one can never step twice in the same river; the situation at the end of the decision process is not the same as when it began. What is more, there is not only a flow of water (to pursue that metaphor), there are also short-term seasonal fluctuations in flow, and a long-term trend of changes in the landscape, say from river to desert or from river to glacier.

For the sake of argument, I take first the routines for collective choice of ends, reserving choice of means for Chapter 17, adaptivity for Chapter 18. But the distinctions are analytical; in real life 'the public' may be confused as between ends and means, the professional analysts may be biassed or may make mistakes, the process of adaptation to environmental change may not be gradual nor automatic, but may come in waves or bursts such as to enforce very quick reaction, on penalty of destruction. That is to say, for the purpose of found analysis one has assumed away the results of study of politics as a process of power and violence.

In the quotation which heads Part IV Lasswell defined power as power to make decisions, and to enforce them by severe deprivation. Parts II and III have followed the logic of this definition, and have perhaps made good the point that power and violence are necessary conditions of political choice. But do these conditions exclude rationality in the choice of ends and means and in adaptation to change? This has not been shown by the argument hitherto, and I guess that it would be difficult to show except at the cost of abandoning altogether the concept of choice. But, conversely, it is difficult to state the theme of rationality in a way consistent with our experience of political life. As Cicero put it, we have to make speeches not in Plato's Republic but *in Romuli faece*,[2] 'in the sludge of Roman politics'.

Welfare Function and Impossibility Theorem[3]

Political economy created the market model, and yet has from its earliest period felt bound to examine cases in which demands are made 'in the public interest' to mitigate the severities of the market. One set of demands tends towards sustaining the collective power and wealth of 'our' state as against other states; these are claims for restraint of trade by various forms of protection, which tend ultimately towards the participation of governments in international trade. Another set of demands relate to the claims for internal distribution made in the names of political stability, national efficiency, and human decency, as against distribution of resources to individuals by the free play of the market.

The latter have been subsumed under the heading of 'welfare'; in a sense, welfare economics over the last century or so has in various forms explored the possible meaning of Article One, section 8. 1. of the American Constitution which empowers the Federal Legislature to 'provide for the common defense and general welfare of the United States'. How can one state rationally the criterion of general welfare as distinct from the criterion of market outcome?

This was the quest for the 'general welfare function', the formula which would enable one (in a mathematical sense) to 'transform' the utilities or preferences or welfare of individuals into the general welfare of the whole.

Two points have generally been conceded at the outset. The

2. *Ad Atticum*, II, i. 8.

3. I have reviewed much of this material more thoroughly in Ch. 9 of *Politics and Social Science* (Penguin Books; 1967), and in 'Models of collective decision-making' included in the UNESCO collection *The Social Sciences: problems and orientations* (The Hague, Mouton; 1968). I have tried not to repeat myself nor to compete with professionals on their own ground, but to shift the angle of approach somewhat.

first is known as 'Pareto optimality': the collectivity is better off as a result of a course of action if none of its members is worse off and at least one is better off. The second is the assumption of what Mishan[4] calls 'methodological individualism'; that is to say, that the task is to elicit a measure of social welfare (or social preference, or social choice) from the choices of individuals, because it is assumed that only individual persons can have welfare, preferences, choice. So long as these concessions were made, the discussion turned on difficulties of making inter-personal comparisons of utility without denying the premise that each man is the best, or indeed the only, judge of his own welfare. But more recently doubt has been cast on both these concessions. Pareto optimality is not so easy to work in practice as it is in theory, at least in dynamic situations where base-lines are hard to establish and forecasts are precarious.[5] But the main battle has been over the compatibility of the assumption of 'methodological individualism' – one made in the present book – with any aggregation of preferences which one could properly call 'democratic'.

This is the Arrow theorem; the General Impossibility Theorem, proving that a General Welfare Function not possible except on conditions unacceptable for us politically. One succinct expression of this is as follows:

> If we exclude the possibility of interpersonal comparisons of utility, then the only methods of passing from individual tastes to social preferences which will be satisfactory and which will be defined for a wide range of sets of individual orderings are either imposed or dictatorial.[6]

One could put the proposition less rigorously. If we begin by postulating that to decide or choose or prefer (I make no verbal distinction here) is the prerogative of the individual person, then

4. *Welfare Economics: an assessment* (Amsterdam, North Holland Publishing Co.; 1969), p. 26.

5. On the weaknesses of Pareto optimality see in particular M. Peston: *Public Goods and the Public Sector* (Macmillan; 1972), p. 34, footnote 1, p. 35, footnote 2.

6. K. J. Arrow: *Social Choice and Individual Values* (second edn, New York, Wiley; 1963), p. 59.

one cannot get decision in the plural ('we decide') out of decision in the singular ('I decide') unless,

either (1) one attributes personality to the collective 'we'

or (2) one postulates that 'we' is an entity politically structured by relations of power/influence/authority.

Then one rejects the former alternative for various reasons; it seems an improper use of language; it conflicts with the conventional postulates of individual choice; it has been the ideology of bad régimes, and the pretext for crimes against humanity. Are these self-indulgent arguments, less than logical? If one accepts them, one must then move, in Max Weber's phrase, into 'the house of power'[7], the life of politics.

Arrow's statement of this position in logical form has withstood frontal attack for twenty years now. Indeed, the only valid criticism I know is that of Gordon Tullock in an important article[8] in which he seeks to outflank the General Impossibility Theorem by postulating a very large number of choosers whose preferences are independent. This may not be quite the condition we meet with in 'the real world of democracy',[9] in which voting patterns are structured fairly rigidly by the patterns of parties and of social groupings, so that the preferences of our thirty million or so voters are by no means independent, and can be reduced by empirical analysis and observation to a much smaller number of categories, still complex, but offering possibilities of prediction and manipulation. Nevertheless, one must have great sympathy with Tullock's further remark, that 'One of the real problems roused by Arrow's book was why the world democracies seemed to function fairly well in spite of the logical impossibility of rationally aggregating preferences' (p. 49).

7. H. H. Gerth and C. Wright Mills: *From Max Weber: Essays in Sociology* (Routledge & Kegan Paul; 1943), p. 194. (I owe the reference of Dr Ovadia Shapiro of the Department of Sociology, University of Haifa). Weber contrasts the House of Power with the House of Obedience, '"the iron cage" of the specialized division of labour upon which the administration of the modern social and economic order depends.' (Anthony Giddens: *Politics and Sociology in the Thought of Max Weber*, Macmillan; 1972), p. 48.

8. 'The General Irrelevance of the General Impossibility Theorem': in *Towards a Mathematics of Politics* (1967), Chapter III, p. 37.

9. A phrase borrowed from C. B. Macpherson's book, *The Real World of Democracy* (OUP; 1966).

Paradoxes of Voting

But this reference carries forward to another section of the argument. Arrow's presentation relates to any method of aggregating preferences. But it is not in dispute that the argument arose in part from the tradition handed down from the French mathematician, Condorcet (who died in prison in 1794), through the Oxford mathematician Lewis Carroll Dodgson, that there are cases in which the usual procedures for voting in a committee will produce a nonsensical result. Each voter knows his own mind, yet the effect of their votes is that the committee prefers A to B, B to C, and C to A. The paradox actually occurs only in a tiny proportion of decisions by vote: but it is quite formidable because (on the one hand) it can be taken as a case of Arrow's more general proposition about the General Impossibility of aggregating preferences 'democratically'; on the other hand, it is a fact of life in committees. A blundering chairman can get his committee entangled in contradictory motions and reach non-decision. An astute chairman can let the committee entangle itself and then quietly 'impose' (Arrow's word) his solution. Indeed, those who know Cornford's little book on University politics may find pleasure in watching competing masters of tactics, round the table, each waiting (as in a Western movie) for another to 'make his move', which will be at the mercy of later movers, unless the first move is at some distance from the first mover's real intention.

Such games can in fact be very serious, if played in the context of international or industrial negotiation, and this is that rare case in political study, one in which it can be shown that there is an unbroken chain between analytic propositions and the patterns of behaviour which have become second nature for subtle and experienced negotiators.

The chain of argument, if unbroken, would show that voting (whatever the procedure chosen) cannot in all cases produce results of a logically consistent kind. A. Voting is the only quantifiable procedure known to us for aggregating preferences fairly and consistently (note the words 'procedure' and 'fairly' which refer forward to the next section). B. In some cases voting produces nonsensical results, and these cases cannot be foreseen and mitigated by tinkering with procedure. C. *Therefore* we cannot always proceed from methodological individualism to an aggregation of preferences which is not *either* nonsense *or* 'un-democratic'.

The argument turns on these three points, A, B, and C.

A is virtually definitional; the word 'voting' is used here to include all methods known to us for the individual to express preferences in a quantifiable way. But it raises a wider question about procedures and fairness in decision-making.

B has been pushed very hard by Lewis Carroll, his chronicler Duncan Black,[10] and others; the cases in which paradox may arise have been more precisely identified and procedural improvements have been suggested. But there is no claim that a perfectly rational voting procedure can be achieved.

Point C is best met by the brief reply 'so what', in the sense of Tullock's words quoted on p. 203. This amounts to saying that decisions lie in 'the house of power', and cannot be shifted to 'the house of obedience', that of bureaucratic rationality, without losing their essential character as decisions. We get along somehow, and we could not get along at all in any other way. The situation requires that there be rulers, those whose voices count for more; that rationality cannot consistently be attained (not even if there were only one voter); but that reasonable people can use reasonable procedures to reach reasonable decisions. Is that enough?

Procedures and Fairness

This argument has drawn attention to the importance of 'decision procedures'. The phrase has various senses.

The first, in principle the simplest, is that rationality in decision can be maximized by following tested algorithms in calculating the best means to a predetermined end, or to more than one end, if the ends are given weights. But this is concerned with means, not ends, and in logic (not always in practice) belongs to the next chapter.

The second is that the binding force of a decision, general recognition that this is 'our' decision, and also that it is a decision

10. *The Theory of Committees and Elections* (Cambridge UP; 1958).

'for us', depends on the proper performance of a series of ritual acts.

The third is that the formal establishment of such a sequence is a source of power to those holding formal positions, supposing always that the related procedures do in practice retain some binding force and that position-holders cannot be by-passed. Such a formal position is by no means the only source of power; nevertheless, 'it dwells in the house of power' and arguments about procedure are (in general) arguments about power and fairness.

PROCEDURE AS FORMALITY

It is difficult to persuade beginners in politics to take procedure seriously, yet it lies close to the heart of collective decision-making, and Lasswell (in the quotation at the head of Part IV) perhaps under-rates it, though one could doubtless find that he strikes a better balance elsewhere in his work.

First, a quotation from Sir Henry Maine, a lawyer who based his generalizations on the comparative study of Roman, English and Indian law, in a way which has had a continuing influence on studies in the history and sociology of law:

> Not only are formalities of equal importance with the promise itself, but they are, if anything, of greater importance; for that delicate analysis which mature jurisprudence applies to the conditions of mind under which a particular verbal assent is given appears, in ancient law, to be transferred to the words and gestures of the accompanying performance. No pledge is enforced if a single form be omitted or misplaced, but, on the other hand, if the forms can be shown to have been accurately proceeded with, it is of no avail to plead that the promise was made under duress or deception.[11]

His examples lie in that field of private law, but might equally well have been chosen from public. 'There's such divinity doth hedge a king'[12] ... and that follows formally from the correct observance of procedures about succession, coronation and coronation oath. If one attacks a king's power with arms, it is wise also to attack his title with all available resources of legal and

11. Sir Henry Maine: *Ancient Law* (1861; OUP, 1939).
12. Shakespeare, *Hamlet*, IV, v, 123.

ecclesiastical scepticism and scandal. Thus one can attack the man, but not the kingship; for one hopes to attain his title, and must submit to the same formalities.

Here are two quotations from Murray Edelman, in a more modern vein.

> ... So what people get does not depend mainly on their votes.
>
> It does not follow that election campaigns are unimportant or serve no purpose. It is rather that the functions they serve are different and more varied than the ones we conventionally assume and teach. They give people a chance to express discontents and enthusiasms, to enjoy a sense of involvement. This is participation in a ritual act, however; only in a minor degree is it participation in policy formation. Like all ritual, whether in primitive or modern societies, elections draw attention to common social ties and to the importance and apparent reasonableness of accepting the public policies that are adopted. Without some such device no polity can survive and retain the support or acquiescence of its members:
>
> Two symbolic forms that permeate our political institutions are rite and myth. Both of these are commonly associated with studies of primitive tribes, and anthropologists have taught us a good deal about their dynamics, as has psychoanalytic theory. Much that anthropologists and psychologists say about them has its application in political analysis, not simply as interesting analogy, but as a necessary tool for explanation and prediction.
>
> To study the working of ritual and myth in this area is to examine persisting political institutions, in contrast to the passing parade of news. For rite and myth are persistent, in precisely the same sense and for the same reasons that elections, discussions of politics, patriotic holiday ceremonies, legislative postures, judicial dramas of combat, and administrative busyness are persistent.[13]

Procedure, rite, ritual, correctly performed are binding. They *bind* as a spell *binds*, provided that the spell has been performed exactly. If the spell fails to bind, there are various explanations to hand, the simplest being that the spell-binder was ritually impure, or that he got the words wrong, or that he was overborne by a greater magician. Such arguments can sometimes be detected in modern politics, and in most countries there are traditional

13. Murray Edelman (op. cit.), p. 3, p. 16.

formalities (royalty in England, for instance) which could not be abandoned without some loss of binding force within the polity.

But if it is argued (as for instance about the Rent (Scotland) Act, 1971 and Industrial Relations Act, 1971[14]) that what appears procedurally to be a public decision is not binding, the cry now is not generally that the procedure was not observed, but that it was used unfairly or for unfair purposes.

FORMALITY AS FAIRNESS

I am not familiar enough with the work of John Rawls to assess it adequately. But the philosopher's return to social contract theory, 'justice as fairness' chimes in with similar revivals in sociology and in economics.[15]

Rawls's proposition is that a collective decision is binding if reached by a procedure which you would accept as fair even if it were applied to your own disadvantage. In other words, the test of fairness is the application of the social contract model. Supposing I had been a man in a state of nature (a difficult supposition to handle), would I have accepted as fair to me a constitution so drafted?

Approaching the same problem as a sociologist,[16] J. S. Coleman (Johns Hopkins) directs attention to the deviant cases; not to the successes of constitutional procedure but to its failures; disobedience to law, sporadic violence, secession, revolution, phenomena which attract more attention (not always reasonably) than concerted collective choice. 'The construction of a constitution that will allow collective action to proceed without splitting the society apart is nearly equivalent to devising a complete theory of collective action' (p. 30). For this, it is necessary, to 'replace the single action back in its context of a whole set of collective actions' (p. 35). Coleman starts therefore from the concept of power: an actor's 'power, or ability to get what he wants in the system, depends both upon his formal control of various collective actions and on the interest of others in those actions' (p. 36). This approach

14. Rent (Scotland) Act, 1971, (19 and 20 Elizabeth 2 c.28) Industrial Relations Act, 1971, (19 and 20 Elizabeth 2 c.72).

15. *A Theory of Justice* (OUP; 1972).

16. 'Foundations for a theory of collective decisions', in B. Liebermann, ed., *Social Choice* (New York, Gordon and Breach; 1971), Ch. 5.

emphasizes that to occupy a position in a chain of procedure creates bargaining power: whence two points –

(*a*) Substantive power may be required to gain a position in the chain of procedure: but that position (once gained) is itself a source of power, provided that the system holds.

(*b*) Bargaining power can be tested only through time. Give a little here, take a little there: on balance, how am I doing? Once inside the system it is hard to break with it. But perhaps this must be done if I feel that I am losing in a series of deals and can do better outside the system. And this reasoning can be applied to the politics of groups within a constitutional system as well as to individuals in some form of partnership.

The economic model is proposed by Buchanan and Tullock, using the hypothetical case[17] of farmers each having equal plots in a block of land, each equally dependent on public maintenance of roads for their individual economic survival. The case is presented as a formal model, but is related to experience in rural local government wherever there are communities of substantial farmers. One example of their analysis will be enough to indicate the pattern –

> In this model the simple referendum system would result in no local road being repaired because an overwhelming majority of the farmers would vote against the repairing of any given road, considered separately. A logrolling system, however, permits the local roads to be kept in repair through the emergence of bargains among voters.

From that point clearly there will follow the discussion of coalitions,[18] the discussion of interest groups and their weakness under pressure,[19] the theory of political intermediaries and entrepreneurs and their role in manipulating disposable votes (Ch. 5).

Above all, there is Coleman's point,[20] that within the procedural system 'actors are powerful when the [procedural] actions they control have high value'. Conversely, actors bringing power from

17. *The Calculus of Consent: Logical Foundations of Constitutional Democracy* (Michigan UP; 1962), p. 135.
18. W. H. Riker; *The Theory of Political Coalitions* (Yale UP; 1962).
19. Mancur Olson: *The Logic of Collective Action* (Harvard UP; 1965).
20. Coleman (1971) p. 37.

outside the procedural system will require from it controlling positions of 'high value'. A constitution is needed to settle procedure for making constitutions, and so in regress till a point is reached at which power prevails, or there is deadlock: 'talks about talks about talks about . . .', a normal routine in the extra-constitutional situation of international politics, which sounds ridiculous and yet has a logical ground in the paradoxical situation of constitution-making. Procedure is necessary for collective decision; procedure is to some extent the product of tradition, habit, obsessive concern with repetition in detail; but procedure if challenged in a rationalistic society must also have a plausible claim to fairness. Fairness can be debated in the languages of natural rights or of utility as well as in that of social contract. But the social contract model helps one to see that the constitution is in one sense fundamental, in another sense is mere regress towards an underlying situation of power. Hence Coleman's remark, already quoted on p. 208, that 'the construction of a constitution . . . is nearly equivalent to devising a complete theory of collective action'.

One could follow this argument further, in particular into theoretical work on voting procedure which is concerned with fairness as well as with consistency, so that voting is studied as a model for the analysis of links between ethics and logic, a model very remote from the political analysis of real elections.[21]

But the work has become progressively more rigorous in symbolic statement, and perhaps only four points need be made in relation to the present argument.

(1) No way has been found to sum preferences rationally and completely which is consistent with the premise of methodological individualism;

(2) Voting may in some settings present virtually no element of choice; but where it has some role to play (and this is not in many human societies – perhaps one-third of mankind, if one is bold enough to include India) men get on 'reasonably' well. In spite of

21. I am thinking in particular of the elegant work of P. K. Pattanaik, *Voting and Collective Choice* (Cambridge UP; 1971) in relation to the work of A. K. Sen and R. M. Hare. Robin Farquharson and David Chapman are equally rigorous but less remote from the empirical study of politics.

its latent irrationality a procedure for voting may settle down pretty well as part of an on-going political system.

(3) Voting is itself a complex procedure, and even more complex procedures are required to determine the agenda for voting and the options presented. The criterion of procedure which can be respected is perhaps fairness rather than rationality (if these can be distinguished).

(4) But fairness has to be judged in terms of a constitutional bargain, and in the last resort, the bargain concerns power and is settled by power.

Ends are aggregated by power; it can be done in ways that are more or less reasonable, more or less fair.

CHAPTER 17

THE ASSESSMENT OF MEANS

> There is no reason why good cannot triumph as often as evil. The triumph of anything is a matter of organization. If there are such things as angels, I hope that they are organized along the lines of the Mafia – *Winston Niles Rumfoord.* [Kurt Vonnegut Jr., *The Sirens of Titan.*]

Introductory

WELFARE economics has by no means abandoned its concern with the aggregation of ends. But perhaps, in its most modern forms, its main trend is to leave ends to the politicians and to assert its professional concern with means, and only with means.

Hence, in more or less direct line of descent, a new crop of administrative initials, of which perhaps the best known are CBA (Cost Benefit Analysis), PPB (Planning, Programming, Budgeting),[1] PAR (Programme Analysis and Review),[2] CPA (Critical Path Analysis).

These techniques offer to provide advice about the execution of policies. Parallel to them, but distinct, are the various forms of organization theory, which advise about administrative structures apt for various purposes. There was perhaps a common origin in the age of machine-building: indeed, Bentham's *Constitutional Code*,[3] written between 1810 and 1830, anticipates most of the mechanisms and devices proposed and used up to the end of the 1920s. But the position was thereafter complicated by new social sciences using different metaphors; perhaps there has now been convergence towards the use of systems models in the study of

1. C. L. Schultze: *The Politics and Economics of Public Spending* (Washington, Brookings; 1968); and articles by B. M. Gross and A. Schick, referred to on p. 207 of C. D. Foster, *Politics, Finance and the Role of Economics* (Allen & Unwin; 1971).

2. See in particular Treasury evidence to the Steering Sub-Committee of the Expenditure Committee (H.C. 147 of 1971–2), 27 January 1972, p. 14.

3. Vol. 9 of J. Bowring, ed., *The Works of Jeremy Bentham* (Edinburgh, Tait; 1843).

administration, but such models can be built and interpreted in many different ways.

The demand for advice, from public and private sources, has been so overwhelming that each of these two main branches, project evaluation and organization theory, now constitutes an industry or discipline in itself, so much more remunerative than other branches of social science that there may be serious distortion of concepts and objectives.[4] For the purpose of this argument I take two examples only, based on recent British work about Cost Benefit Analysis and about Operational Research; even these examples are treated superficially, and with emphasis on what is relevant to the present essay.

CBA

THE SENSIBLE MAN

It may be best to concentrate on CBA, rather than to attempt a survey of the whole cousinhood of techniques for project appreciation, since CBA seems to be so clear in principle. How else could a sane man proceed in decisions about his own affairs? – perhaps not even excluding matrimony.

First, state the end or ends to be achieved. If there are several ends or purposes try to rank them in order of importance and to allocate a weight to each end in accordance with that ranking. If this cannot be done at the outset see if conflicts are resolved or eased by information that comes to hand during the inquiry. If you still don't 'know what you want', then (says Pattanaik, in a rather different context) 'If the trouble of weighing different alternatives is considered too much, the individual will be perfectly rational to choose at random.'[5]

4. About 1930 – says Coser (1967) – American sociology became an 'applied' discipline, concerned with 'the utilization of the research findings and research personnel of sociology by various public and private bureaucracies' (p. 27). 'Two consequences follow from this: (1) the sociologist who affiliates himself with public or private bureaucracies will be expected to deal with problems that the decision-makers pose for him; and (2) those problems are likely to concern primarily, as Merton and Lerner have argued, "the preservation of existing institutional arrangements".' Daniel Moynihan (1970) confirms this observation for the 1960s.

5. Pattanaik (1971), p. 139.

Towards each end there will be a choice of means. Map these as carefully, explore each as thoroughly, as your time budget and your cash budget allow. For each end there will be a preferred path: or if paths are equivalent, so far as one's investigation budget allows one to explore them, then (once again) it is rational to spin a coin (working a little magic in the side, just as a precaution – it can do no harm).[6]

But some of the means will involve 'externalities': that is to say, they will have side-effects, in physical or social terms. And these may be probable, not certain. If you choose the shortest path, there is a chance of one in a hundred you may bring down an avalanche on you. The shortest path leads through the orchard of a rich and suspicious neighbour, there is a one in ten chance that he will see you, and there will be considerable embarrassment if he does. In fact, any path has aspects of 'snakes and ladders', about it: play the game out in advance, timelessly, so far as your investigation budget allows, and feed the risks into your mental computer.

Taking into account what has been said in Chapter 15, it will be clear that this model of individual choice is not a simple one; especially if one adds that an individual's purpose, though it is formally directed to maximize his own welfare, may be 'to do the best he can' for his dear wife or his dear son or his nuclear family – or even for the church or creed to which he gives his faith. But CBA is committed (as is this essay) to the basic methodological assumption 'that all members of society agree that an individual is the best judge of his own welfare'.[7]

PUBLIC GOOD SENSE

One is bound in this context to indicate the further difficulties that arise if one projects this individual model to the level of collective decision. It is therefore proper to say at the outset, with all possible emphasis, that these are incidental difficulties. It may not work out but it would be crazy not to try. The case is made convincingly

6. Rub your rabbit's foot. There is sound anthropological theory about how sensible people can be both instrumental in their thinking, and also magical.

7. E. J. Mishan: *Cost-Benefit Analysis* (Allen & Unwin; 1971), p. 12.

by the examples of cost-benefit studies which constitute Part I of Mishan's book:[8] for instance, how else is one to conduct an argument, as among engineers and accountants, about the best locations within a river system for dams to control floods and provide irrigation? There will in the end be 'politics': to the pioneer cost/benefit studies of water control in America[9] one must add the political situation of the US Army Corps of Engineers,[10] a historic source of patronage and log-rolling. But good CBA narrows the political options, in so far as its results are made known and earn respect; and this respect is ensured, so far as it is deserved, by the proper canons of science, that all assumptions, data and deductions are set down conscientiously and are laid open for debate by peers in the discipline. PPB in the USA was damaged by L.B.J.'s intemperate enthusiasm, and too many 'bad scientists' were recruited too quickly and were paid too well. But this is only one aspect of the underlying problem of politics and CBA. It should be emphasized that what follows is based entirely on questions raised within the discipline. These are not the sour comments of a political scientist about the political innocence of economists.

PRIVATE AND PUBLIC

Economists, as Mishan rightly says,[11] are brought up to 'regard the allocation of private goods resulting from a price system as more efficient than any directed by a political system', and they can produce good 'systemic' arguments for this. But the arguments may be circular in character, as he goes on to say:

> ... the supposed greater efficiency of the price mechanism for a wide range of day-to-day decisions can hardly be argued ... without reference to some acceptable system of welfare economics.

8. Mishan, (1971)., pp. 9–30.

9. A. Maass and others: *Design of Water-Resource Systems* (Macmillan; 1962). B. H. Davies, 'Waterpower and Wilderness', *Public Administration Australia*, 31 (1972), p. 21.

10. See Chapter 7, Pork in S. K. Bailey and H. D. Samuel, *Congress at Work* (Douglas Saunders in association with MacGibbon and Kee, 1953).

11. E. J. Mishan, *Welfare Economics: An Assessment* (1969), p. 18: see also Mishan, (1971), p. 309.

What then if there is no 'acceptable system of welfare economics'? Or none which is not based on a simulation of the market?

Nevertheless, economists are impelled by the logic of their discipline to enlarge and modify to suit the public sector criteria developed in the first instance for the private sector. In the public sector, says Mishan,

> Instead of asking whether the owners of the enterprise will be made better off by the firm's engaging in one activity rather than another, the economist asks whether society as a whole will be made better off by undertaking this project rather than not undertaking it, or by undertaking, instead, any of a number of other projects.[12]

But the distinction fades away, the crutch of profit-maximization ceases to give support, in a period of long perspectives, of consolidation of business units, of government policies which use subsidies and taxation relief to bias the profit motive. All decisions are thrown into one crucible by the incidence of 'externalities' and 'lumpiness'.

North Sea Oil can serve as an example of the former. Governments (of both political colours) have tried to transfer decisions to huge companies actuated by the profit motive, or at least by the motive of self-preservation. But the externalities accumulate:[13] the short and long term effects on the British economy; the risks of radical changes on the environment of the North Sea and its coasts; the employment pattern within Scotland; its implications for public provision of roads, housing, schools and the rest of the infrastructure. The ultimate extent of oil resources is (it seems) still a geological gamble, and private industry is supposed to earn profit by taking risks. But the risks they bear are a small part of the whole risk: government have not in fact contrived to minimize their risks, in that externalities come home to the public, very quickly and on an enormous scale.

Rolls-Royce or Concorde can stand for 'lumpiness'. Things are too big and too slow for the cash flows available to private industry, even at its biggest. There are risks that even great international

12. Mishan (1971), p. 8.

13. Here Mishan, *The Costs of Economic Growth* (Penguin Books; 1969) is also relevant.

corporations cannot take – or could not take but that governments, advisedly or not, hold a safety net under them. You can't win; Rolls-Royce was treated as private, Concorde as public, and no one has liked the result in either case.

At this point the economist begins to ask difficult questions about his brief.

The first is paradoxical but perhaps has not much cutting edge, except in so far as it reduces to the second question – where does power reside? 'The economist asks whether society as a whole will be made better off' (above, p. 216). How is he to define 'society as a whole' (apart from the basic commitment to individualism)? Economists are well equipped to see what is involved because they are already sophisticated about the problems of what is 'the economy' and what are its 'boundaries'. *Prima facie*, the economist takes his brief about this from 'government': but (says the political scientist) how far does the responsibility of government extend? To those presently within the boundaries of the United Kingdom? To those who own UK land, currency and securities? To citizens of the UK wherever they may be? To partners in the Commonwealth, white, brown, yellow or black? To our partners in the EEC?

Questions are endless: here is one which may at first seem to be a trivial perplexity. 'First, what set of individuals constitutes society? Most cost-benefit analyses restrict the set to the individuals of one nation' (whatever a 'nation' may be ...) 'More important, only the individuals comprising *present* society are counted. One obvious reason for this is that the preferences of future generations cannot be known.'[14] This is by no means trivial, because CBA is in the last resort asked to make recommendations about who shall live and who shall be let die. If decisions are not to be left random, then criteria are needed for the elimination of accident black spots (there is a tariff per death, as in the courts of law); for priorities in the development of medical

14. D. W. Pearce: *Cost-Benefit Analysis* (Macmillan; 1971), p. 9. But the Verney Working Party (1972) 'are quite clear ... that we have a profound duty to posterity. We are trustees and have a duty not to misuse the earth' (p. 4). This is like Burke's vision of society as a partnership 'between those who are living, those who are dead, and those who are to be born' (*Reflections on the Revolution in France*, OUP World's Classics edn, Vol. IV, p. 106).

facilities, as between very old and very young; in general, for public expenditure coming to fruition ten years hence, when more than 10 per cent of us will be dead, and more than 10 per cent with be 'new entrants' in the race.

Our first reaction probably is to say 'these are political questions and require political decisions'. But by this we may mean two quite different things; either 'nobody knows the answer, let's forget it'; or 'these are questions of power and can be, will be, answered only by those who hold power in the community'.

Serious economists choose the second meaning, and thereby converge to the problems posed in this essay. The economist may wish to see himself simply as consultant to the democratically elected representatives of the voters (or equally, one supposes, to an enlightened oligarchy or despot, old or new style). Thus Mishan, for instance, stating not his own view but that of others to whom he refers:

> His is the task of disclosing the implications of the policies being mooted and, perhaps, that also of suggesting alternative policies. By discharging these tasks, the economist enables the elected representatives to select policies having consequences that are consistent with one another, and that accord with the wishes of the majority of the electorate.[15]

One of the difficulties seen by Mishan is that the job cannot in practice be done like that: the politician wants it on one sheet of notepaper, or not at all. If the economist will not draft that (biased and venomous ?) little sheet, others will, in the style of Lindemann, Lord Cherwell, when he was a key man in the court politics of Winston Churchill.[16] The other is that economists are not obliged (any more than are obstetricians or agronomists) to tender professional advice against their own ethical and political beliefs. They remain men and citizens: and (says Mishan – and he notes that his views are in some respects 'very particular'[17]).

> Economists are not alone in being unimpressed by the workaday wisdom of majority rule in modern societies. Notwithstanding con-

15. Mishan (1971), p. 307.
16. C. P. Snow: *Science and Government* (Harvard UP, 1960), p. 63.
17. Mishan (1971), p. 3.

ventional safeguards, a majority in power is capable of irresponsible and, even, tyrannical behaviour towards individuals and minorities. There can be no reasonable expectation, in particular where legislation is influenced by party doctrine, that majority decisions will always respect minority interests, or even views that are widely held in society.[18]

Hence his two reservations, which are in the classical tradition of liberal politics.

The first is expressed as follows:

If we ... regard democratic rule as no more than a majority-rule decision-mechanism then, indeed, the welfare economist has no role to play. But if, instead, we regard democracy as a method of reaching agreement through informed debate, then the principles by which decisions are reached become relevant.[19]

His other reservation is also classical in style:

The consequences of these deficiencies in the working of democracy can be limited by decentralized institutions, and by constitutional restrictions that rest upon a broad consensus. The existence of either, that is, depends on near-unanimous acceptance of a number of ethical premises.[20]

As he says,[21] his view of 'constitution' is related to but distinct from that of Buchanan and Tullock,[22] which was referred to in Ch. 16. Their notion is that of a bargained constitution; his must be that of an entrenched natural law constitution? But this underlying concept is mediated by that of the 'virtual constitution of the community':[23] 'what men of good will regard as reasonable'.[24] The ethic, which is the constitution, links the content of Mill[25] to the constitutional style of Burke.

To sum up, briefly. The CBA economist, like other specialists,

18. Mishan (ibid.), p. 309.
19. Mishan (1969), p. 19.
20. Mishan (1971), p, 310.
21. Mishan (1969), p. 19, fn. 1.
22. J. M. Buchanan and Gordon Tullock: *The Calculus of Consent* (1962).
23. Mishan (1969), p. 21.
24. Mishan (1971), p. 313.
25. Mishan (ibid.), p. 357. I think P. K. Pattanaik: *Voting and Collective Choice* (1971), Ch. 2 would in principle concur: note also Pattanaik's references to Little (at pp. 29–31) and to Harsanyi, p. 159.

dwells in the House of Subservience.[26] But, like the civil servant in Charles Sisson's book,[27] he 'might in the last desperation, exhibit a scruple'. He must not submit to complicity; an arrangement under which he is used as a political expedient, and serves his own career by serving the expediency of politicians.

Is this to ask too much of one, who (though against his will) has been invited to be a guest in the House of Power?

Instrumental Organizations

To some extent, I cheat (it must be confessed) by choosing Mishan primarily to represent Cost-Benefit Analysis, Stafford Beer[28] to represent Organization Theory and Operational Research, in that both are exceptionally perceptive about the political implications of rigorous work in specific technical disciplines. I hope however that this will clarify the main trend of argument without distorting it.

What I have called 'project appreciation' involves now, as I said earlier, a cousinhood of techniques and sub-disciplines. The theory of instrumental organization (one of the 'sciences of the artificial' as H. A. Simon puts it[29]) has an even more complex history, an even more complex relationship to various on-going disciplines, each with its own concerns.

OR; GROWTH AND CHARACTER

Perhaps it is safe to say that Operational Research developed in two dimensions, one conceptual, one situational. The latter is now part of the history of World War II, and can be studied in various war histories and individual memoirs. The memoirs are greatly preferable, as they capture a little of the social and personal flavour of the situation, in which I played a tiny non-speaking part.[30]

26. Or House of Obedience, p. 203 above fn. f.

27. *The Spirit of British Administration* (1959; Faber, 2nd. ed. 1966),

28. *Decision and Control* (John Wiley; 1966); *Brain of the Firm: The Managerial Cybernetics of Organization* (Penguin Books; 1972).

29. *The Sciences of the Artificial* (1969).

30. During World War II, classic, lawyer, half-trained social scientist, I found myself acting as secretary to RAF committees on RDF and OR, both then in their brawling infancy.

This flavour was best exemplified in the very quick and adaptive response of British institutions to the technological breakthrough in RDF or (in the American language) Radar. The first sets were very big and very clumsy: and were virtually hand-made by young scientists of professorial calibre. They worked with their hands as well as with algebra and slide-rules (no working computers, at that date, except desk calculators); and they worked alongside first-rate manual craftsmen, some of them RAF 'other ranks', though not in uniform. This clumsy gear and extemporized organization could 'see' aircraft approaching at least fifty miles off (except at low altitudes): fifty miles meant at least fifteen minutes, enough for Hurricanes and Spitfires to get off the ground and reach operational altitude for interception. This in its turn was partly the result of the technological breakthroughs in engine and air frame design made in the early 1930s: but partly it depended on drills closely coordinated between aircrew, ground staff and communications people. Up to that point, organization could follow technology quite swiftly but at a rather low level. The glory of higher command in the RAF (which might well have been upset by what was in various senses going on above its head) was that it saw quickly what only battle commanders could see, that the crux would come once the fighters were in the air; how to bring together RDF data, make sense of them, pose decisions for the commanders, get these decisions to fighter squadrons in the air, and sustain a flow of decisions without confusion.

This remains the classical example of technological innovation demanding radical change in organization up to the highest level of decision. As the Frenchman said of the original gear-box, *c'est brutale mais ca marche*; and in this case the boffin was the lubricant, in that for men of open mind, high intellect and personal courage it was socially possible to pass freely between university common-room and laboratory, to work with mechanics on the bench, to work with pilots in the air, to work with Group Captains and Air Vice Marshals in operations rooms.

Operational research as I saw it began with the hard grind of making clumsy stations operational, and thence followed the argument where it lead, regardless of rank and education except as relevant to a job which had been given over-riding priority.

The scientific component in the first instance was electronic; but this led with no gap to the work done by Blackett's people in the air/sea war[31a], by Dr Gordan and others on the equally vital problem of RAF maintenance. In both these cases the tempo was slower (minutes and hours, not seconds), the technical developments were less dramatic, the most important innovations were the result of systematic paper work; as for instance in the problem of the most effective search patterns for Coastal Command aircraft in different situations. It is not irrelevant to say that Bomber Command learned late, but to perfection: hence the Dresden raid of 13 February 1945 which must now stand with the Charge of the Light Brigade as the greatest military muddle of all time. Let guilt lie where it falls: at least Hiroshima was 'decided', Dresden was not.

The main stream of this argument is that to a component of social adaptivity there was added a component of mathematical technique, drawing on various branches of mathematics to optimize outputs in relation to quantifiable choice in given technical situations (RAF experience was that the next step might be to pin-point bottlenecks in technology and production, and to give priority to breaking them).[31] Hence, from my limited perspective, the rise of the branch of applied mathematics known as Decision Theory, the biggest technical component of Operational Research. Here I rely primarily on Douglas White's textbook on *Decision Theory*,[32] much of it too mathematical for me; and on Parts II and III of Stafford Beer's *Decision and Control*, which explain these techniques at a high intellectual level but virtually without the use of mathematical symbols.

There has of course been a third component; if it had not been for my own experience of the early days of OR, I should be bound to call this a separate branch of study. That is the development of the study of big organizations, foreseen by Bentham but gathering pace only in the period shortly before 1914, when the impact of big organizations was first widely felt, and indeed resented, from

31. For 'planning on the bottlenecks' I have no better source than Ely Devons, *Planning in Practice* (Cambridge UP; 1950), particularly Chs. 2 & 5.

31a. C. H. Waddington: *O.R. in World War 2; Operational Research against the U-boat* (1973).

32. Allen & Unwin; 1969.

the level of Max Weber's perception that society was becoming through and through 'bureaucratic' to that of assembly line production on the factory floor. After much divergence in lines of investigation there has of late been convergence, first towards formal techniques of project evaluation and secondly to theories of systems organization, in particular theories of self-organizing systems.

Much could be drawn from Beer's book and from his experience, which began with operational research for the British Command in India at the end of World War II and was developed by a very successful period with United Steel. Since then Beer has been President of the Operational Research Society of Great Britain and has taught in universities and business schools. But I limit discussion to three topics which interlock with issues discussed elsewhere in this book. These are, in brief, the adaptive role of OR; the organization as self-maintaining system; the peculiar relationship of top leadership to the organization.

THE ROLE OF OR

The Operational Research Society's definition of its members' role reads as follows:

> Operational research is the attack of modern science on complex problems arising in the direction and management of large systems of men, machines, materials and money in industry, business, government and defence. Its distinctive approach is to develop a scientific model of the system, incorporating measurements of factors such as chance and risk, with which to predict and compare the outcomes of alternative decisions, strategies or controls. The purpose is to help management determine its policy and actions scientifically.[33]

Beer doubtless had a hand in drafting this, but it leaves great scope for variety in interpreting the role. He would himself contrast the true doctrine with recent 'routinization' of the 'charisma' of the original boffins. On the one hand, there is the routine professional, looking about inside the organization for specific jobs or problems, known in advance, to which his tools can be applied: a particularistic and technological approach. On the other hand, there are those who understand science and its method, who are seeking a sense of the whole, who are not happy with any particular

33. Beer (1966), p. 92.

question posed, because it may well be the wrong question, or a non-question. The essential work of the OR man is to find the right questions, in terms of the complex general character of the organization.

TELEOLOGY

Beer is wholly committed to the study of organizations in terms of systems models, and has done much to develop the use of the cybernetic analogy, sketched in Chapter 6 above. His definition of the proper use of a model is rigorous and narrow ('A scientific model is a homomorphism on to which two different situations are mapped, and which actually defines the extent to which they are structurally identical.')[34]; and there are few with a sufficient range of experience to know whether he continues to apply that definition strictly and consistently; that is to say, to sustain the distinction between model and metaphor. But he certainly succeeds in expelling 'function' totally from his analysis, by reinstating 'purpose' in a sense partly old and partly new. He reaches this point by following vigorously the clues given by the late Ross Ashby and others about ultra-stability and requisite variety in electronic and neuro-physiological systems.

His conclusion is that purpose is present in any self-organizing system which does better than chance in the process of surviving in a continually changing environment, 'preserving its identity across the generations, accompanied by a long-term increase in organization'.[35] Key passages in the statement of the argument are as follows:[36]

A system is not something given in nature but something defined.

The philosopher Hegel enunciated a proposition called the Axiom of Internal Relations. This states that the relations by which terms are related are an integral part of the terms they relate. So the notion we have of any thing is enriched by the general connotation of the term which names it; and this connotation describes the relationship of the thing to other things. In fact, Hegel's Axiom entails that things would not be the things that they are if they were not related to everything else in the way that they are.

34. Beer (1966), p. 113.
35. Beer (1966), p. 362ff.
36. Beer (1966), p. 242.

In practice, however, we acknowledge relatedness only when we are ready to declare its relevance . . . When a general pattern of relatedness is detected, we call the set of relationships systematic. Even then, the collection is not dignified by the unitary notion of a system until some unifying purpose is devised for it. Thus there seem to be three stages in recognizing a system as such. We acknowledge particular relationships which are obtrusive: this turns a mere collection into something that may be called an assemblage. Secondly, we detect a pattern in the set of relationships concerned: this turns an assemblage into a systematically arranged assemblage. Thirdly, we perceive a purpose served by this arrangement: and there is a system.

It may be retorted that this is no more than a stipulative definition of the word 'purpose'. But it is a definition within a complex and flexible context, and it serves in that context to make it possible to ask intelligibly whether mankind or any other supposed social entity is or is not a self-organizing system.[37]

TOP MANAGEMENT

The application of this to the real world of management consultancy is to postulate that an organization should be a hierarchy of self-organizing systems, governed by its own purpose and talking the 'language' appropriate to that level and to that purpose. The operational managers[38] run the system and talk the system language. 'The "owners" of the system seek to discuss its future in a metalanguage.' 'At a higher echelon there are the policy-makers . . . those who would re-direct the *motives* of the enterprise as distinct from its *aims*.'

In business, the policy-makers (if they are not – as often – just a lot of silly old sheep) will form a circle of people who interact closely because they must, and who have power to decide – though he prefers the word 'command' to the word 'power'.

37. I suspect that this is analogous to Vonnegut's (or 'Bohonon's') distinction in *Cat's Cradle* between a *karass* and a *granfalloon*. 'Granfalloons' claim to be self-organizing systems but fail the test, such as '. . . the Communist party, the Daughters of the American Revolution, the General Electric Company, the International Order of Odd Fellows – and any nation, anytime, anywhere. As Bokonon invites us to sing along with him: "If you wish to study a *granfalloon*, Just remove the skin of a toy balloon"' (p. 61).

38. Beer (1966), p. 372.

Decision, command (p. 457), and information go together. 'Decisions are always taken by the node, or the plexus of nodes, in a network which has the most information' (p. 435).[39] From information will flow the logic of decision, in White's sense of 'decision theory': but at that node there will also be the process of choice. And the debate over choice will be made in the meta-language of the informal group which shares information and interaction. Choice will not be made without 'vehemence' (p. 435), or 'a tussle between the top men' (p. 513). But (in this gifted group of leaders) vehemence and tussle proceed from information and knowledge.

But managerial systems are enclosed in a political system: what of political leadership? Here the trumpet gives rather an uncertain sound: there seem to be three valid points of view in Beer's book, not unified.

First, he is as respectful to the constitution as are the cost-benefit men. 'These are the gods of the system. To the operational managers they are the directors who represent the shareholders; to the civil service they are (or ought to be) the political masters who represent the electorate'. The gods, talking their metalanguage among themselves, can take the big decisions about motivation 'overnight'. But

> Their problem of control is to know what to do to the ultrastable self-organizing enterprise which will give effect to the new policies which reflect a change of motivation. This need is nowhere more apparent than in the government sphere, since a change of party in power presupposes a change of fundamental political motivation [p. 372].

That is to say, there is a single legitimate authority, but it can work only within the limits of its situation.

But (secondly) there is the politics of manipulation. 'The

39. It is interesting to note the coincidences with Kotarbinski (1965). 'The combination of information with leadership' (p. 66): 'leading a team is a special case of handling a complex object with a highly intricate structure and considerable dynamics . . . That is how a physician handles the organism of his patient' (p. 155). It is not clear to me what has happened to cybernetics in Eastern Europe. Technologically, they are the basis of the Russian space programme as of the American; but their administrative applications have been suspect.

cleverest kind of tyranny is one in which the populace is hoodwinked into believing that it operates as a free society' (p. 462). Equally Machiavellian (Beer quotes Machiavelli with great respect – p. 3) but less brutal is this passage, which deserves to be known to students of politics as a vivid statement, almost in Oakeshottian terms, of one way of understanding politics –

> The job is to modify the structure, without destroying the self-organizing properties of the system, so that the goals it 'just happens' to achieve (the ones recognizable only after the event) turn out to be the goals which the human managers wished to attain all the time. In the arena of policy-making, the brilliant manager (be he government minister or company director) knows intuitively that this is what he has to do. And because the whole of the mechanism by which he operates is verbal, inter-personal and political, he is able to achieve his ends. Politics is the art of building organic structure into a universe of discourse, of debate, of climate of opinion. An analysis of any major policy-making manoeuvre reveals this elaborate structuring of ideas: how certain opinions are used to neutralize each other so that a third opinion (apparently less cogent than the other two) becomes acceptable by default; how individual personalities behave homeostatically and produce the kind of expectant deadlock in which some one personality becomes uniquely acceptable as being the only common member of the sub-sets of preferred states. Then the way in which hierarchical structure in argument and the command of opinion is floated within this self-organizing [system] is also clear: we talk about it in terms of loyalties, of personal ascendancies and of character. But when the same task is faced in the control of the enterprise (which included the political level of control), there arises a much wider realm of things, relationships, and even people which are quite outside the policy-making group.[40]

This is perhaps to facilitate consciously rather than to manipulate?

And yet (thirdly) Beer appeals to the government to be *explicit* in its dealings with the citizens, and that on good conventional grounds –

> What is the law and what counts as the good citizen's reaction to the law are both major determinants of what people and institutions will actually do [p. 463].

The government must talk its own metalanguage and choose; it

40. Beer (1966), p. 380.

must manipulate or facilitate politically a self-organizing society; it must also talk plainly in the language of citizens, in order to identify citizens with the policies decided in the metalanguage of leaders.

This is very like what Mishan says in the passages quoted on p. 219 above, and I find the coincidence impressive. But it is as difficult to express the thought satisfactorily in general systems language as in current English, and it certainly does not promise a 'no-conflict system'. 'In politics we are always living on volcanic soil.'[41]

Summary

I hope that a brief summary will be adequate, as I have simplified the argument about CBA and OR very drastically in order to bring out what I think relevant to the present essay.

Chapter 16 was primarily about rationality in aggregating divergent individual wishes as regards the ends to be pursued in collective action. This chapter was concerned with rationality in choice of means towards agreed ends; CBA works primarily to construct a logical criterion of action, OR to construct a scientific criterion of organization.

Both techniques or disciplines find difficulty in dealing adequately with the point of junction between ends and means. Rational analysis carries them a long way (each in its own style), and must not be rejected as futile or unconvincing. But rational analysis cannot in the end banish decision by politics, by conflict and power.

Both Mishan and Beer, writing as individuals, recommend that politics be (so far as possible) both de-centralized and well-informed, in the interests of reason and adaptibility: Beer goes further to explain adaptibility in terms of information flows, language, and levels of decision.

41. Ernst Cassirer, *The Myth of the State* (Yale UP; 1946), p. 280.

CHAPTER 18

ADAPTIVITY

All men believed or hoped, is torn aside;
The loathsome mask has fallen, the man remains
Sceptreless, free, uncircumscribed, but man
Equal, unclassed, tribeless. and nationless,
Exempt from awe, worship, degree, the king
Over himself; just, gentle, wise: but man
Passionless? O no, yet free from guilt or pain,
Which were, for his will made or suffered them,
Nor yet exempt, though ruling them like slaves,
From chance, and death, and mutability,
The clogs of that which else might oversoar
The loftiest star of unascended heaven,
Pinnacled dim in the intense inane.

[Shelley, *Prometheus Unbound*, III, iv, 1.192.]

It's laughable, that you are called Prometheus, the Foresee-er. As long as the rule and order of the world remain, you will foresee only what you now see: Force. [Lowell, *Prometheus Bound*, p. 4.]

This non-system holds together by having no togetherness, no uniformity, never seeking perfection, no utopias – just answers good enough to get by, with lots of looseness and room for many ways and attitudes. [Robert Heinlein: *Glory Road*, p. 192.]

Utopias

LATE in the nineteenth century they built nice utopias; William Morris's *News from Nowhere* (1890), Robert Blatchford's *Merrie England* (1894), Edward Bellamy's *Looking Backward* (1887),[1] W. H. Hudson's *Crystal Age* (1887). In the first years of the twentieth century they began to build nasty ones; the Ancients in Shaw's *Back to Methuselah*, the Morlocks in Wells's *The Time Machine*, the animals that were almost men in *The Island of Dr Moreau*. The nasty future was sustained by Aldous Huxley (1932) and George Orwell (1949): and then a new phase began.

1. John S. Thomas, ed., (Cambridge, Mass., Belknap Press; 1967).

Futures[2]

The future began to seem very unpleasant and very close; no longer utopias, but scenarios. The tone was hortatory, not speculative; 'act now, or something very nasty will hit you personally quite soon'. This was perhaps not the tone of Bertrand de Jouvenel's *Futuribles*, begun with some Foundation assistance in 1961; nor of his book summing up that phase, *L'Art de la Conjecture* (1964). Their concern was closer to my concern in this chapter; foresight not as prediction, but as a means of social control.

Into the main stream there fed, first, work on the possible consequences of nuclear testing and nuclear war. This ranged from sophisticated scenarios indicating a differentiated spectrum of possible outcomes (the Rand School: Herman Kahn, *On Thermonuclear War*, was published in 1960), to the little gory posters produced for CND (how right we were; and perhaps we *did* move the argument forward). This was generalized into theories of conflict[3] and escalation in games between human opponents; and then passed over into the concept of games between man and nature, non-zero sum games in which the outcomes were more likely to read *minus* than *plus*. In Britain this was slipped into the public consciousness by the TV series, *Doomwatch*, which began in 1970. There had been a UNO Environmental Year announced for 1972; no one noticed at the time, but perhaps some manipulators somewhere had made a plan – and bits of it came off.

Meantime, the big organizations became sensitive about the importance and difficulty of technological forecasting. The failures of brilliant British technology in the production of aircraft, computers and nuclear power stations are now familiar; during 1971 and 1972 there emerged piece-meal in the City pages the story of miscalculation and over-provision in chemical investment. We had in fact, taking the first three fields together,

2. There is now a serious journal of this name, launched in 1969 with the sub-title 'the journal of forecasting and planning': it had a special issue in February 1973 on the limits of growth controversy.

3. T. C. Schelling: *The Strategy of Conflict* (Harvard UP; 1960).

4. Herman Kahn: *On Escalation* (Pall Mall; 1965).

and all nations together, expended marvellous efforts in research and manufacture which added up in the end to nothing; unemployment relief, digging holes and filling them up again, the Reeks and Wrecks of Vonnegut's *Player Piano*.

The point here is not to survey and assess the literature of 'future shock', and my references to it in the book list are quite superficial; but to open up the question of the next level of adaptivity, the metalanguage of learning how to learn and act; which of course (in Stafford Beer's terms) will in the end require a meta-meta-language of learning how to learn how to . . . and so forth.

Information and Energy

The argument follows naturally from those of Chapter 16 and Chapter 17, but is not so easy to sustain as that about the fashion of 'future shock', since it must proceed simultaneously on two levels; the facts of what is being done, the pattern of what might be done, to evolve a working system of adaptivity. Perhaps it can be put like this.

The books tell us that a system which is to be adaptive and ultra-stable must be rich in information, in the sense that it has many alternative channels for messages, many ganglia or exchange points, much redundancy – using that word technically, to the effect that it can pass the same message in many different forms. Some energy is needed, to carry messages and to gain a grip on the environment. But a massing of energy without information cannot be purposeful (in Beer's sense); and in principle a hierarchical pattern of information channels is less adaptive than a network pattern. But massed energy can readily wipe out information.

This metaphor would say – 'centralized world government would be a better instrument for slowing the rate of change than for adaptation to change arising outside its control.' World government is not in prospect; there is at least a chance that centralization in Peking, Moscow, Brussels, Washington may slow the rate of technological change by the ponderous character of their movement. But much (not all) of the spurt in technology has arisen out of their competition, and each of them (except perhaps Moscow) is committed in principle to the policy of decentralization to 'self-organizing systems', each of them innovatory and competitive within boundaries which each will continuously seek to erode.

It is scarcely possible for the rate of change to continue to grow exponentially, unless it changes its character, since we are clearly approaching some limit in relation to the bulkiness of projects and the time that intervenes from first sketch on the drawing-board to operational effectiveness. Perhaps by now all top people know the catch-phrase 'If it works it's obsolete.'[5]

But a change in character is possible and perhaps is foreshadowed. The huge production lines, chemical plants, oil tankers and refineries have been the basis of quantity and cheapness: but in rich countries much of the wealth gained has been deployed towards consumption industries; on the one hand towards small things in electronics, in drugs, in plastics, on the other hand to what John O'Neill calls 'the skin trades'.[6] He takes hair-dressing ironically as an example: but the range of personal service trades (above all in health and education) is growing all the time, and can be regarded as characteristic of 'post-industrial' society. Some of these (as in education) may themselves conduce directly to adaptation; others (such as swift and cheap communications) extend the scope of the information network available to the world.

Certainly world networks proliferate, and it is now commonplace that in swift moving areas of science the pace is set by quite small worldwide groups of men and women in personal contact, and that they communicate electronically or by travel (now quite cheap in relation to any big research programme – better to speak on the phone or nip over to Brookhaven or CERN for a day rather than to waste the time of a cyclotron or big computer), and by the pre-print about work in progress, which is beginning to displace the scientific article in these disciplines. Indeed, the big conferences, the big journals, begin to be fronts for the working groups, ritual rather than instrumental occasions.

Among these many networks there are now some specifically oriented towards adaptivity. Indeed, they proliferate, and it

5. Stafford Beer puts it neatly into Latin: *Absolutum Obsoletum*: the dedication of his book *Brain of the Firm* (Penguin Books; 1972).

6. *Sociology as a Skin Trade* (Heinemann; 1972).

would require serious research to enumerate them and assess their value.

The Institutions of Adaptivity

There was a hopeful notion after World War I that Institutes of International Relations might serve as organs of foresight in relation to the League of Nations and the continuing structure of Great Power politics. Nothing really came of this, except for the development of a new branch of academic study: after World War II the comparable movement was towards Institutes of Strategic Studies on the one hand, on the other hand Institutes of Peace Research and of Conflict Research. These also have their sages, their literature, their examination questions; and perhaps provide better channels of communication, in that their range is wider and more varied, and they have some slight connection with organs of power; on the one side, with movements of agitation, on the other with the more intelligent of the soldiers.

'Pugwash' and the *Bulletin of the Atomic Scientists* arose independently out of Hiroshima and the nuclear arms race, and set new standards for the social concern of science in a corporate sense, not simply as a moral stand by individuals. And Rand played its part in a movement towards 'future studies' in general, a movement which in Europe owed much to Bertrand de Jouvenel and his SEDEIS.[7] The British Social Science Research Council under its first two chairmen, Michael Young and Andrew Shonfield, was actively interested; had from the outset (1965) a Committee on the Next Thirty Years; sponsored in 1967 a joint meeting with the Royal Society; and split almost fifty-fifty on the question of endowing a British Institute of 'future studies' in some form, as part of the international network which was then emerging. The debate was between those who were concerned primarily with disciplines and those concerned primarily with (let's face the word) manipulation of the future; and it was a good debate, evenly balanced between carefully considered arguments, with no Left-Right axis that I could discern.

The decision went against the proposed Institute; and perhaps the moment for that sort of action has now passed. But it is not

7. Société d'Études et de Documentation Économiques, Industrielles et Sociales.

easy, without such a focus, to find out just how the pattern is developing. The Society for General Systems Research has been arguing about systems and futures since it was founded in 1954 by the late Ludwig von Bertalanffy and others; it has gathered influence but largely in the USA. The Society for Long Range Planning seems to be primarily British and primarily concerned with industrial research and its prospects. Then there is the Club of Rome, and the MIT Group headed by Dr Jay Forrester; and a polarization into the school of growth and the school of equilibrium, points of view which begin to be associated with able and persuasive individuals.[8]

There are other signs of movement. It is perhaps an optimistic commonplace that the collection of economic statistics over a long period has at last reached such a point of sophistication that economic 'steersmen' can plot their course on the basis of economic indicators, and that the cybernetic dimension thus added to the capitalist system has enabled it to keep its oscillations within bounds since 1945. There are other possible explanations; and the course of social change is not quite analogous to economic change, in that it has no observed cyclical character and deals in longer perspectives than those needed for economic management. But, granted these reservations, nevertheless one must respect the movement towards the establishment of reliable and comparable social indicators for the world and its states. We have a fairly long run of population statistics, but their accuracy is limited except in developed countries, and (even there) their predictive value is not very high.[9] Otherwise, there was almost nothing before World War II; now the study of social and political indicators has become yet another new discipline, or sub-discipline, with important bearings on the development of health, nutrition and food supplies, as well as for social services in general.

Undoubtedly, much has been due to the leadership given by

8. For instance, E. J. Mishan: *The Costs of Economic Growth* (1967): Wilfred Beckerman: 'Economic Growth and Welfare', *Minerva* (1973) p. 495.: press reports of the recent Fawley Foundation lecture at Southampton University by Professor Dennis Gabor, FRS, and Nobel Laureate, who is an 'equilibrium' man.

9. A humiliating case is that of population projections for the UK at the year 2000: in 1964, the figure was 75m., in 1971 66.5m., in 1972 63.1m. (the present population is 55.7m.), *Population Projections No. 2, 1971–2011* (HMSO; 1972).

various bodies within the sphere of UNO. This is the kind of contribution to sensitivity within the self-organizing system of mankind which appears nowhere in the political commentaries on the success or failure of international organizations; and of course for each table of indicators there is a small worldwide group of those who produce and consume such tables, and who have an experienced sense of the limits of accuracy set by the process of collection.

'Social indicators' are therefore not a new thing: but they were perhaps first taken up as a movement in a volume edited for the American Academy of Arts and Sciences in 1966.[10] This was one of a series dealing with 'Technology, Space and Society' and seems to have been paid for by the National Aeronautics and Space Administration, as spin-off from the moon programme. But of course it was at least as closely related to the Great Society programme which followed the death of John Kennedy, and so was the sudden outbreak of PPB in the same period. Both, in different ways, were necessary to the logic of choice, for a government concerned to intervene in the management of social processes.

Similarly, there was in Britain a long build-up, a point of decision (when in 1967 a social statistician, Claus Moser, became head of the Central Statistical Office in place of Sir Harry Campion, the economic statistician who had built it out of nothing in the course of a generation), and then a period of relatively slow reorganization. The first publication of the series *Social Trends* (December 1970) can serve as landmark.

Once again, new experience produced new demands; one can date from 1970 or a little earlier the emergence of graduate study, academic journals and textbook series in a field called Policy Sciences or Policy Studies.[11] As usual the USA were earliest in assembling the resources, money, students and teachers, and (also 'as usual') the instinctive reaction elsewhere was that a new band-wagon is rolling – let's see how it rolls before we jump on. The logic of the move is coherent. New techniques need new professionals and also men capable of handling administrative

10. R. A. Bauer, ed., (MIT Press; 1966).

11. See for instance Yehezkel Dror, 'The Challenge of Policy Sciences', in *Policy Studies Journal*, 1 (1972), p. 4.

jobs which require the management of techniques and professionals; and such jobs ought to appear in the process of orienting American society towards a longer future. Funds for this would be a proper call on the funds of a big programme of social intervention at the end of the Vietnam War, which everyone foresaw confidently. But it seems that Nixon after his re-election has set his face against it.

One aspect of these developments is that books sell, and make the reputation of peripatetic sages, such as Herman Kahn, J. Buckminster Fuller, Marshall McLuhan. Perhaps one should mention specially the late Rachel Carson, the first to make ecology readable and saleable, who died tragically not long after the success of *Silent Spring*, first published in 1962.[12] It is rather a sad parody of human intelligence that more energy has gone into the campaign against fluoride than into any other; and that this has been the only one to attract research into the style and mechanics of the campaign.[13]

The intellectual world is largely a money market. How is research to be financed? how are results to be diffused? The resources are governments, foundations, books, the press. In that context it would be unreal not to enlist the manipulators of money as a potential resource. Students of politics have heard of the commodity markets, are quite innocent about the world money market and the financing of small enterprise within a national state or across its frontiers. The impression given by the City pages is that it is easy to raise and gamble with very large sums, but hard to raise small amounts of risk capital, which were the essential solvents in the first technological revolution. And yet it does not seem that the pop groups, the small hairdressers, the *boutiques* have failed to raise the entry fee (though winners are few); and a legend has grown about the facility with which small flexible enterprises – management consultants, advertising men, research groups, highly specialized producers – can flourish in the wake of big producers. It may be true that the system still has reserves of flexibility for those who know the tricks.

12. Penguin Books; 1965.

13. J. A. Brand, 'The politics of fluoridation: a community conflict'. *Political Studies*, 19 (1971), p. 430 and references given there.

Polarization Towards Power

One thing to regret is that few of these organizations and reputations are truly worldwide. Some of the East European states have been actively interested, but not the USSR; China has not yet shown its hand; few of the poor countries except India have had resources to contribute. What this has meant in practice is that most of these enterprises have depended on American names and on American money. In part this has come about because of the greatness and manoeuvrability of American resources, partly because concerned Americans believe that their country has been, and should be, the leader in the role of adaptive society, an exemplar of flexible structure which can absorb much stress without flying apart.[14] But there is always the bogey (and sometimes the reality) of 'CIA money'; and there is the risk that these enterprises may be seen as 'rich men's clubs', trying to stop activities (such as fertilizers and pesticides) which the poor need if they are to live. Hence of course the tendency to build debate about ecology and the environment into the confrontation between rich and poor.

In fact, the institutions of adaptivity are threatened by the institutions of power, as soon as they begin to be important for action. The biggest trial so far has been that of control over nuclear tests in the atmosphere; pollution was drastically reduced in the 1960s largely because the international science lobby was well-organized and vocal – in a situation where power-bargaining was possible. There is still great doubt whether opinion alone can control French testing in the Pacific, Chinese testing in Central Asia.

The other big and dangerous case is that of the international arms trade, which is now almost entirely in the hands of governments, though there is spill-over through corrupt private channels; enough for assassins and high-jackers, not enough for a regular war. This is an area rich in double-talk, as is that of international traffic in drugs and pharmaceuticals. On the face of it, to decentralize control of arms is to decentralize power and

14. I wish I had been able to use more fully the huge book by Amita Etzioni *The Active Society: A Theory of Societal and Political Processes*, (Collier-Macmillan; 1968).

violence; by selling arms the industrial nations weaken their own relative power and increase the risks of escalating explosions. But (they will argue) the arms are really quite useless without ammunition, spare parts, and technical advisers; and (besides) these may serve to balance dangerous situations, as in the help given by the USSR to Cuba, Egypt and Hanoi, the UK to Nigeria, the Indians to Bangladesh.

This is not an argument to pursue here; the point made is that institutions of adaptivity are continually threatened by institutions of violence. The former are strong in the richness of information; the latter are strong because they can destroy information, and can harness men's unthinking energy rather than their capacity for forethought.

It is however relevant to repeat a scrap of Sophocles, a chorus injected at a turning-point in the tragedy of Antigone, who died in defence of eternal law as she perceived it. 'There is nothing in the world more extraordinary than man. He sails the sea even in winter storms, he forces the earth to give harvests year after year, he can trap birds, beasts and fishes – a very clever fellow; and he can kill the mountain lion, he can tame horses and bulls.'

> And he has taught himself speech and wind-swift thought and the temperament of a city-dweller . . . he contrives for everything, and he is not without resources for whatever the future may bring. From death only will he find no escape.[15]

This was written some thirty years after the *Prometheus*, and seems to reflect its language. But Sophocles' man needs no Prometheus to teach him. He can teach himself and destroy himself.

In the end, said Heraclitus, 'the thunderbolt steers all things'.[16]

> The news of the day, meanwhile, was being written in a ribbon of light on a building to Billy's back. The window reflected the news. It was about power and sports and anger and death. So it goes.[17]

Well, 'so it goes'.

15. Sophocles, *Antigone*, ll. 332–364, my own paraphrase and translation.
16. Fragment 28, trans. W. H. S. Jones in Loeb edition (Heinemann; 1931).
17. Kurt Vonnegut: *Slaughterhouse Five* (Cape edn), p. 173.

BOOK LIST

Primarily, this is a list of books referred to in the text. It is not a bibliography, but a reader should be able to build, from the books listed, the bibliographies relevant to particular topics. At one stage, I tried to divide the List itself by topics, for the convenience of readers; but there was so much overlap and repetition between sections that I gave it up, confirmed by this evidence in the belief that the concepts of power, violence and decision do indeed interlock.

As an exception, I have included, as part of the evidence for Chapter 18, a number of books on man and environment which illustrate the wave of publication in that field in 1971 and 1972. Probably some of these are trivial and repetitive.

Adelphi Paper No. 82, *Civil Violence and the International System: Part I: The Scope of Civil Violence* (International Institute of Strategic Studies; December 1971).

No. 83, *Civil Violence and the International System: Part II: Violence and International Security* (IISS; December 1971).

Adkins, A. W. H., *Merit and Responsibility. A Study in Greek Values* (OUP; 1960).

Moral Values and Political Behaviour in Ancient Greece: From Homer to Fifth Century (London, Chatto & Windus; 1972).

Aldiss, Brian W., *Greybeard* (Panther Books; 1968).

'Confluence' in Judith Merril, ed., *The Best of Sci-Fi 12* (Mayflower Books; 1970).

'Danger: Religion!', in *The Inner Landscape* (Corgi Books; 1970).

Aldous, Tony, *Battle for the Environment* (Fontana Books; 1972).

Allaby, Michael, *Who Will Eat?* (Tom Stacey; 1972).

Allison, Graham T., *Essence of Decision: Explaining the Cuban Missile Crisis* (Little Brown; 1971).

Althusser, L., *For Marx* (trans. B. Brewster. Penguin Books; 1969).

Alvarez, A., *The Savage God: a study of suicide* (Penguin Books; 1974).

Ambler, Eric, *Judgment on Deltchev* (Hodder & Stoughton; 1951).

Andréas-Salomé, Lou, *Frédéric Nietzsche* (1932; Reprint Gordon & Breach, 1970).

Andreski, Stanislav, *Military Organization and Society* (second edn with postscripts. Routledge & Kegan Paul; 1968).

Arendt, Hannah, *On Violence* (Penguin Books; 1970).

Argyle, Michael, *The Psychology of Interpersonal Behaviour* (Penguin Books; 1967).
Social Interaction (Methuen; 1970).

Armengaud, André, *Population in Europe, 1700–1914* (Fontana Books; 1970).

Arnold, D. O., ed., *The Sociology of Subcultures* (Berkeley, Glendessary Press; 1970).

Aron, Raymond, *La Révolution Introuvable* (Paris, Fayard; 1968).

Arrow, Kenneth J., *Social Choice and Individual Values* (New York, Wiley, second edn; 1963).

Arvill, Robert, *Man and Environment* (Penguin Books; 1967).

Ashby, W. R., *Design for a Brain* (Chapman & Hall, second edn; 1960).
An Introduction to Cybernetics (Methuen; 1966).

Ayres, Robert U. *Technological Forecasting and Long-Range Planning* (New York, McGraw-Hill; 1969).

Ayrton, Michael, *The Rudiments of Paradise* (Secker & Warburg; 1971).

Bachrach, P., and Baratz, M. S., 'Two Faces of Power', *American Political Science Review* (1962) pp. 947–52).
Power and Poverty: theory and practice (OUP; 1970).

Bagehot, W., *Lombard Street* (London; 1873).

Bailey, F. G., *Stratagems and Spoils* (Blackwell; 1969).

Bailey, Stephen K., and Samuel, Howard D., *Congress at Work* (Douglas Saunders in association with MacGibbon and Kee; 1953).

Baker, Paul T., and Weiner, J. S., ed., *The Biology of Human Adaptability* (OUP; 1966).

Banfield, E. C., *Political Influence: A New Theory of Urban Politics* (New York, Free Press; 1961).

Barnard, C. I., *The Functions of the Executive* (Harvard UP; 1938).

Barnett, S. A., 'Biological myths', *New Society*, 12 April, 1973, pp. 68–9.

Barrett, William, *Irrational Man: A Study in Existential Philosophy* (New York, Doubleday; 1958).

Barth, F., *Political Leadership among the Swat Pathans* (London University, Athlone Press; 1959).

Barthes, Roland, *Mythologies* (Paris, Editions du Seuil, 1957; sel. and trans. Annette Lavers, Cape; 1972).

Bauer, Raymond A., ed., *Social Indicators* (MIT Press; 1966).

Bayley, D. H., and Mendelsohn, Harold, *Minorities and the Police: confrontation in America* (New York, Free Press; 1968).

Beauvoir, Simone de, *The Marquis de Sade* (In French, *Faut-il brûler Sade*, 1951: English translation Annette Michelson and Paul Dinnage; Calder & Bryans; 1962).

Beckerman, Wilfred: *British Association for the Advancement of Science*, Annual Meeting, 1970. Paper included in 'Conflicts in Policy Objectives: papers presented to Section F (Economics)' ed. by Nicholas Kaldor, (Blackwell; 1971).

(a shorter version is –
'Why We Need Economic Growth', *Lloyds Bank Review*, October 1971, pp. 1–15.)

Bedau, H. A., ed., *Civil Disobedience: Theory and Practice* (New York, Pegasus; 1969).

Beer, Stafford, *Decision and Control: The meaning of Operational Research and Management Cybernetics* (Wiley; 1966).

Brian of the Firm: The Managerial Cybernetics of Organisation (Penguin Books; 1972).

Bell, Daniel, *Towards the Year 2000* (New York, Houghton Mifflin; 1968).

Bell, Quentin, *Virginia Woolf: a biography* (Hogarth Press; 1972).

Bellamy, Edward, *Looking Backward, 2000–1887* (1887).

Beloff, Max, *Public Order and Popular Disturbances 1660–1714* (1938; Cass; 1963).

Benewick, R., and Smith, T., eds., *Direct Action and Democratic Politics*, Allen & Unwin, 1972, Acton Society Study No. 1).

Bentham, Jeremy, 'The Constitutional Code' in J. Bowring (ed.), *The Works of Jeremy Bentham* Vol. 9, (Edinburgh, Tait; 1843).

Bentley, A. F., *The Process of Government* (1908; reissued Bloomington, Indiana, Principia Press; 1949).

Bernstein, Basil, *Class, Codes, and Control: Vol. I. Theoretical Studies towards a Sociology of Language* (Routledge & Kegan Paul; 1971).

Bernstein, Edward, *Evolutionary Socialism: a criticism and affirmation* (1899; trans. E. C. Harvey, New York, Schocken Books; 1961).

Berrien, F. K., *General and Social Systems* (Rutgers UP; 1968).

Bertalanffy, L. von, *Problems of Life* (Watts; 1952).

General Systems Theory (Penguin University Books; 1973).

Bienen, Henry, *Violence and Social Change: A Review of Current Literature* (Chicago UP; 1968).

Birmingham, Walter, *Economics: An Introduction* (Allen & Unwin, second edn; 1972).

Black, Duncan, *The Theory of Committees and Elections* (Cambridge UP; 1958).

Black, Perry, ed., *Physiological Correlates of Emotion* (New York, Academic Press; 1970).

Blackburn, Robin, ed., *Ideology in Social Science* (Fontana Books; 1972).

Blackwood, Caroline, article in *The Listener*, 3 June 1971, p. 697.

Blatchford, Robert, *Merrie England* (London; 1894).

Blau, P. M., *Exchange and Power in Social Life* (New York, Wiley; 1964).

Blumer, Herbert, *Symbolic Interactionism: Perspective and Method* (New Jersey, Prentice-Hall; 1969).

Boaden, Noel, *Urban Policy-Making: Influences on County Boroughs in England and Wales* (Cambridge UP; 1971).

Botvinnik, M. M., *Computers, chess and long-range planning* (1969; trans. A. Brown, Longman; 1971).

Boudon, R., *The Uses of Structuralism* (French edn, 1968; trans. Michalina Vaughan, Heinemann; 1971).

Boulding, Kenneth, *A Primer of Social Dynamics: History as Dialectics and Development* (New Yrok, Free Press; 1970).

Bradley, A. C., *Ethical Studies*, Essay V (1876; OUP, second edn, 1927).

Brand, J. A., 'The politics of fluoridation: a community conflict', *Political Studies*, 19 (1971), p. 430.

Bray, J., *Decision in Government* (Gollancz; 1970).

Braybrooke, D., and Lindblom, C. E., *A Strategy of Decision: Policy Evaluation as a Social Process* (Glencoe, Free Press; 1963).

Bridgwater, Patrick, *Nietzsche in Anglosaxony: A Study of Nietzsche's impact on English and American literature* (Leicester UP; 1972).

Bright, James R., ed., *Technological Forecasting for Industry and Government* (New Jersey, Prentice-Hall; 1968).

BBC Audience Research Department, *Violence on Television: Programme Content and Viewer Perception* (BBC; 1972).

British Museum, *The Succession of Life Through Geological Time* (HMSO, sixth edn; 1964).

Bronowski, J., *William Blake and the Age of Revolution* (1944; Routledge and Kegan Paul; 1972).

Buchanan, J. M., and Tullock, G., *The Calculus of Consent: Logical Foundations of Constitutional Democracy* (Michigan UP; 1962).

Burgess, Anthony, *A Clockwork Orange* (Penguin Books; 1972).

'Clockwork Marmalade' in *The Listener*, 17 February 1972, p. 197–9.

Burnet, Mary, *The Mass Media in a Violent World* (UNESCO Reports and Papers on Mass Communication, No. 63, 1971:

reporting a UNESCO symposium held in June/July 1970).
Burnham, James, *The Machiavellians: defenders of freedom* (Putnam; 1943).
Butler, William F., and Kavesh, Robert A. (eds.), *How Business Economists Forecast* (New Jersey, Prentice-Hall; 1966).
Calvert, Peter, *A Study of Revolution* (OUP; 1970).
Revolution (Macmillan; 1970).
Campbell, Angus, Converse, Philip E., Miller, Warren E., and Stokes, Donald E., *The American Voter* (New York, John Wiley & Sons; 1960).
Camus, Albert, *L'Homme Révolté* (published in France 1951; English translation as *The Rebel* by A. Bower, Penguin Books; 1971).
Canetti, E., *Crowds and Power* (1960; trans. Carol Stewart; Gollancz; 1962).
Cantril, H., with Helen Gaudet and H. Herzog, *The Invasion from Mars* (Princeton UP; 1947).
Carr, E. H., *The Bolshevik Revolution, 1917–1923* (Penguin Books; 1966).
Carson, Rachel L., *Silent Spring* (Penguin Books; 1965).
Carswell, E. A., and Rommetveit, R., ed., *Social Contexts of Messages* (Academic Press; 1971).
Cassirer, Ernst, *The Myth of the State* (Yale UP; 1946).
Castles, F. G., Murray, D. J., and Potter, D. C., ed., *Decisions, Organizations and Society* (Penguin Books in association with the Open University Press; 1971).
Caute, David, *The Left in Europe since 1789* (Weidenfeld & Nicolson; 1966).
Cecil, Robert, *The Myth of the Master Race: Alfred Rosenberg and Nazi Ideology* (Batsford; 1972).
Chadwick, John, *The Decipherment of Linear B* (Cambridge UP, second edn; 1967).
Chapman, Brian, *The Police State* (Pall Mall; 1970).
Chapman, David, 'Some types of party competition and their function in social choice' in B. Lieberman (ed), *Social Choice* (Gordon & Breach; 1971).
Christensen, A., *Politics and Crowd-Morality: A study in the Philosophy of Politics* (Williams and Norgate; 1915).
Clausewitz, Karl von, *Clausewitz on War*, ed. Anatol Rapoport (Penguin Books; 1968).
Cohn-Bendit, G. and D., *Obsolete Communism: The Left-Wing Alternative* (trans. A. Pomerans. Penguin Books; 1969).

Cole, J. Preston, *The Problematic Self in Kierkegaard and Freud* (Yale UP; 1972).

Coleman, J. S., 'Foundations for a theory of collective decisions' in B. Lieberman, ed., *Social Choice* (Gordon & Breach; 1971).

Coleridge, H. N., ed., *The Literary Remains of Samuel Taylor Coleridge* (William Pickering; 1835) Vol. 2.

Collcutt, R. H., *The First Twenty Years of Operational Research* (London, BISRA; 1965).

Conant, R. W., and Levin, Molly A., ed., *Problems in Research on Community Violence* (New York, Praeger; 1969).

Conway, Martin, *The Crowd in Peace and War* (New York, Longmans; 1915).

Cooper, D. G., ed., *The Dialectics of Liberation* (Penguin Books; 1968).
The Death of the Family (Penguin Books; 1971).

Cornford, F. M., *Thucydides Mythistoricus* (Arnold; 1907).
Microcosmographia Academica (Bowes & Bowes; 1908).
The Unwritten Philosophy, and other essays (Cambridge UP; 1950).

Corning, Peter A., and Corning, Constance Hellyer, 'Toward a general theory of violent aggression', *Social Science Information*, 11 (3/4), pp. 7–35, 1972.

Coser, L. A., *The Functions of Social Conflict* (Routledge & Kegan Paul; 1956).
Continuities in the Study of Social Conflict (New York, Free Press; 1967).

Cowling, Maurice, *1867: Disraeli and Gladstone and revolution: the passing of the second reform Bill* (Cambridge UP; 1967).

Cox Commission on Disturbances in the Provinces, November 1955 to March 1956 (Crown Agents for the Government of Sierra Leone; 1956).

Crosby; Theo: *How to play the Environment Game* (Penguin Books, 1973).

Crozier, B., *The Rebels: a study of Post-War Insurrections* (Chatto & Windus; 1960).
'The Study of Conflict', *Conflict Studies*, No. 7 (1970).

Crozier, Michel, *Le Phénomène Bureaucratique* (Paris, Le Seuil; 1963).

Curry-Lindahl, Kai, *Conservation for Survival* (Gollancz; 1973).

Darling, Frank Fraser, *Wilderness and Plenty* (Pan Books; 1973).

Darvall, F. O., *Popular Disturbances and Public Order in Regency England* (OUP; 1934).

Dasmann, R. B., *Planet in Peril?: Man and the Biosphere Today* (Penguin Books; 1972).

Davis, B. W., 'Waterpower and Wilderness', *Public Administration (Australia)* Vol. 31 (1972), p. 21.

Davis, J., *Political Violence in Latin America* (International Institute of Strategic Studies, Adelphi Paper No. 85; 1972).

Davis, Kingsley, 'The Myth of Functional Analysis as a Special Method in Sociology and Anthropology', *American Sociological Review*, Vol. 24, No. 6 (1959), pp. 757–72.

Dedijer, V., *The Road to Sarajevo* (MacGibbon and Kee; 1967).

Department of Education and Science, *Report of the Committee on Football*, Chairman; D. N. Chester (HMSO; May 1968).

Department of the Environment, *Sinews for Survival; A Report on the Management of Natural Resourses* (London HMSO, 1972).

Derrick, Christopher, *The Delicate Creation: Towards a theology of the environment* (Stacey; 1973).

Deutsch, K. W., *Politics and Government: How People Decide their Fate* (Boston, Houghton Mifflin; 1970).

Devons, Ely, *Planning in Practice: Essays in Aircraft Planning in War-time* (Cambridge UP; 1950).

Papers on Planning and Economic Management (Manchester UP; 1970).

Dillistone, F. W., *Traditional Symbols and the Contemporary World* (Epworth; 1972).

Dodd, C. H., *The Interpretation of the Fourth Gospel* (Cambridge UP; 1953).

Dodds, E. R., ed., *Euripides, Bacchae* (Oxford, Clarendon, 1944; second edn, 1960).

The Greeks and the Irrational (California UP, 1951).

Dodge, D. L., and Martin, W. T., *Social Stress and Chronic Illness: mortality patterns in industrial society* (Notre Dame UP; 1972).

Douglas, Jack D., *The Social Meanings of Suicide* (Princeton UP; 1970).

Douglas, Mary, *Purity and Danger* (Routledge & Kegan Paul; 1966).

Dow, Sterling, and Chadwick, John, *The Linear Scripts and the Tablets as Historical Documents* (Cambridge UP; 1971).

Downs, A., *An Economic Theory of Democracy* (New York, Harper, Row; 1957).

Inside Bureaucracy (Boston, Little Brown; 1967).

Dror, Yehezkel, *Ventures in Policy Sciences* (New York, American Elsevier; 1971).

'The Challenge of Policy Sciences', *Policy Studies Journal*, 1 (1972), p. 4.

'Administrative Aids to High-level Decision-Making', UNO, *Public Administration Newsletter* (No. 45, May 1972), p. 4.

Droz, Jacques, *Le Romantisme Politique en Allemagne* (Paris, Colin; 1963).

Duncan, Hugh Dalziel, *Language and Literature in Society* (1953. New York, The Bedminster Press; 1961).

Dunn, John, *Modern Revolutions: an introduction to the analysis of a political phenomenon* (Cambridge UP; 1972).

Dunne, Finlay Peter, *Mr Dooley in Peace and in War* (London, Grant Richards; 1899).

Dupuy, R. J., ed., *Politique de Nietzsche* (Paris, Colin; 1969).

Easton, David, *The Political System* (New York, Knopf; 1953).

A Framework for Political Analysis (New Jersey, Prentice-Hall; 1965).

A Systems Analysis of Political Life (New York, Wiley; 1965).

ed., *Varieties of Political Theory* (New Jersey, Prentice-Hall; 1966).

Ecologist, The, *A Blueprint for Survival* (Penguin Books; 1972).

Edelman, Murray, *The Symbolic Uses of Politics* (Urbana, Illinois UP; 1964).

Edwards, Owain, Martin, Graham, and Scharf, Aaron, *Romanticism.* Units 33–34 of Age of Revolutions course (Bletchley, Open University Press; 1972).

Eibl-Eibesfeldt, Irenäus, *Love and Hate: On the natural history of basic behaviour patterns* (Methuen; 1971).

Éliade, Mircea, *The Myth of the Eternal Return.* Trans. W. R. Trusk (New York, Pantheon Books; 1956).

The Quest: History and Meaning in Religion (Chicago Univerity Press, 1969).

Ellis, Brian, *Basic Concepts of Measurement* (Cambridge UP; 1966).

Ellis, Elmer, *Mr Dooley's America: A Life of Finley Peter Dunne* (New York, Knopf; 1941).

Ellul, Jacques, *Contre Les Violents* (Paris, Le Centurion; 1972).

Emery, F. E., ed., *Systems Thinking* (Penguin Books; 1969).

Empson, W., *Seven Types of Ambiguity* (Chatto & Windus; 1930).

Enright, D. J., *Daughters of Earth* (Chatto & Windus; 1972).

'Epistémon', *Ces Idées qui ont ébranlé la France (Nanterre, Novembre 1967-Juin 1968): Comprendre les étudiants* (Paris, Fayard; 1968).

Erickson, John, 'Radiolocation and the air defence problem: the design and development of Soviet radar 1934–40', *Science Studies* 2 (1972), p. 241.

Etzioni, Amitai, *The Active Society: A Theory of Societal and Political Processes* (Collier-Macmillan; 1968).

Demonstration Democracy (Gordon and Breach; 1970).

Evans-Pritchard, E. E., *Nuer Religion* (Clarendon; 1956).

Ewald, William R., Jr, ed., *Environment for Man: The Next Fifty Years* (Indiana UP; 1967).
Falk, Richard A., *This Endangered Planet – Prospects and Proposals for Human Survival* (New York, Vintage Books; 1972).
Fanon, Frantz, *The Wretched of the Earth* (in French 1961; trans. Constance Farnington; Penguin Books; 1967).
Farmer, Philip José, 'The God Business' (1954) in *The Alley God* (Sphere Books; 1972).
Farquharson, R., *Theory of Voting* (Blackwell; 1969).
Farrington, B., *Science and Politics in the Ancient World* (Allen & Unwin; 1939).
Farris, John, *The Captors* (New York, Trident; 1969).
Feierabend, Ivo K., Feierabend, Rosalind L., and Gurr, Ted Robert, ed., *Anger, Violence, and Politics: Theories and Research* (New Jersey, Prentice-Hall; 1972).
Feierabend, L., *et al.*, 'Social Change and Political Violence', in Hugh D. Graham and Ted R. Gurr (eds.), *Violence in America* (New York, Signet; 1969).
Finer, S. E., *Pareto: Sociological Writings, selected and introduced by S. E. Finer* (trans. by Derick Mirfin. Pall Mall; 1966).
Fogelson, Robert M., 'Violence as Protest', in *Urban Riots, Violence and Social Change* (Proceedings of the Academy of Political Science. Columbia University; 1968).
Footman, David, *Red Prelude: a life of A. I. Zhelyabov* (The Cresset Press; 1944).
Forrester, J. W., *World Dynamics* (Cambridge, Mass., Wright Allen; 1971).
Foster, C. D., *Politics, Finance and the Role of Economics: An Essay on the Control of Public Enterprise* (Allen & Unwin; 1971).
Frankenberg, R., *Village on the Border* (Cohen & West; 1957).
Frazer, Sir J. G., *The Golden Bough: Vol. I, The Magic Art and the Evolution of Kings* (Macmillan, third edn; 1913).
Freedman, Jonathan L., and Doob, Anthony N., *Deviancy. The Psychology of Being Different* (Academic Press; 1968).
Freund, Paul A., ed., *Experimentation on Human Subjects* (Allen & Unwin; 1972).
Friedmann, F. G., *Youth and Society* (Macmillan; 1971).
Friend, J. K., and Jessop, W. N., *Local Government and Strategic Choice* (Tavistock; 1969).
Fuller, R. Buckminster, *Utopia or Oblivion* (Penguin Books; 1973).
Furst, Lillian R., *Romanticism* (Methuen; 1969).
George, P., *Dr Strangelove: or How I learned to stop worrying and love the Bomb* (Corgi Books; 1965).

Gerth, H. H., and Mills, C. Wright, *From Max Weber: Essays in Sociology* (Routledge & Kegan Paul; 1943).
Giddens, Anthony, *Politics and Sociology in the thought of Max Weber* (Macmillan; 1972).
Gluckman, Max, *Custom and Conflict in Africa* (Blackwell; 1955).
The Judicial Process among the Barotse of Northern Rhodesia (Manchester UP; 1955).
The Ideas in Barotse Jurisprudence (1965. extended reprint, Manchester UP; 1972).
Goldschmidt, Walter, *Comparative Functionalism* (California UP; 1966).
Goldsmith, M. J. F., 'Pressures within Pressures' in *Political Studies*, Vol. XIII, 1965, pp. 235–40.
Gosnell, H. F., *Machine Politics: Chicago Model* (Chicago UP; 1937).
Gouldner, A. W., *The Coming Crisis of Western Sociology* (Heinemann; 1971).
Grabo, Carl, *Prometheus Unbound: An Interpretation* (North Carolina UP; 1935).
Graham, Douglas, *Moral Learning and Development* (Batsford; 1972).
Graham, H. D., and Gurr, T. R., eds, *Violence in America, Historical and Comparative Perspective* (New York, Signet; 1969).
Graham, H. D., ed., *Violence: the Crisis of American Confidence* (Johns Hopkins UP; 1971).
Gray, J., and Cavendish, P., *Chinese Communism in Crisis: Maoism and the Cultural Revolution* (Pall Mall; 1968).
Greenwood, Colin, 'Controlling violent crime', *New Society*, 24 (31 May 1973), p. 491.
Firearms Control (Routledge & Kegan Paul; 1972).
Gregory, Roy, *The Price of Amenity: Five Studies in Conservation and Government* (Macmillan; 1971).
Grene, D., and Lattimore, R. (trans.), *Euripides, Vol. 5* (Chicago UP; 1959).
Gurr, T. R., *Why Men Rebel* (Princeton UP; 1970).
Gurr, T. R., and Ruttenberg, C., *The Conditions of Civil Violence: First Tests of a Causal Model* (Princeton, Centre of Int. Studies, Research Monograph No. 28, 1967).
Halloran, James, ed., *The Effects of Television* (Panther Books; 1970).
Hamburger, Joseph, *James Mill and the Art of Revolution* (New Haven, Yale UP; 1963).
Hammond, J. L. and Barbara, *The Town Labourer, 1760–1832: The New Civilisation* (Longmans; 1917).
Handler, Philip, ed., *Biology and the Future of Man* (OUP; 1970).

Harré, R., and Secord, P. F., *The Explanation of Social Behaviour* (Blackwell; 1972).
Harris, Nigel, *Competition and the Corporate Society: British Conservatives, The State, and Industry 1945–1964* (Methuen; 1972).
Hasluck, Margaret, 'The Albanian Blood Feud', in P. Bohannan (ed.), *Law and Warfare: Studies in the Anthropology of Conflict* (New York, Natural History Press; 1967).
Havens, M. C., Leiden, C., and Schmitt, K. M., *The Politics of Assassination* (Prentice Hall; 1971).
Hawkins, C. J., and Pearce, D. W., *Capital Investment Appraisal* (Macmillan; 1971).
Hawkins, G. S., *Stonehenge Decoded* (Souvenir Press; 1966).
Heinlein, Robert, 'His Bootstraps' in Kingsley Amis and R. Conquest (ed.), *Spectrum* (Gollancz; 1961).
Stranger in a Strange Land (1961; New English Library; 1971).
Glory Road (1963; New English Library; 1971).
The Moon is a Harsh Mistress (1960; New English Library; 1969).
Helmer, Olaf, ed., *Social Technology* (New York, Basic Books; 1966)
HMSO: *Population Projections No. 2, 1971–2011* (HMSO; 1972).
Hobsbawm, Eric, 'Terrorism', article in *The Listener*, 22 June 1972
Hofstadter, R., *Social Darwinism in American Thought 1860–1915* (1944. Rev. edn; 1955, Boston, Beacon Press, reprinted; 1967).
Hollingdale, R. J., ed., *Nietzsche: the Man and his Philosophy* (Routledge & Kegan Paul; 1965).
Homans, G. C., *Social Behaviour: Its Elementary Forms* (Routledge & Kegan Paul; 1961).
Home Office/Scottish Home & Health Dept., *Report of the Inquiry into Crowd Safety at Sports Grounds*, by The Rt. Hon. Lord Wheatley (London, HMSO, 1972, Cmnd. 4952).
Howard, Eliot, *Territory in Bird Life* (Murray; 1920).
Hudson, W. H., *A Crystal Age* (1887; London, Duckworth, second edn; 1913).
Hughes, J. J., *Cost-Benefit Aspects of Manpower Retraining* (HMSO; 1970).
Hughes, Ted, 'Mayday on Holderness', *Selected Poems, 1957–1967* (Faber; 1972).
Humphry, Derek, *Police Power and Black People* (Granada; 1972).
Huson, Paul, *The Devil's Picture Book* (Sphere Books; 1972).
Huxley, Aldous, *Brave New World* (Penguin Books; 1955).
Isard, Walter, *Ecologic-Economic Analysis for Regional Development* (Collier-Macmillan; 1972).

Israel, Joachim, and Tajfel, Henri, ed., *The Context of Social Psychology: A Critical Assessment* (Academic Press; 1972).
Janis, I. L., *Stress and Frustration* (New York, Harcourt Brace; 1971)
Jaspers, K., *Philosophy of Existence*, trans. R. F. Grabau (Pennsylvania UP; 1971).
Jencks, Charles, and Silver, Nathan, *Adhocism: The Case for Improvisation* (Secker and Warburg, 1973).
Jessop, Bob, *Social Order, Reform and Revolution* (Macmillan; 1972).
Jones, R. E., *The Functional Analysis of Politics: an introductory discussion* (Routledge & Kegan Paul, 1967).
Jouvenel, Bertrand de, ed., *Futuribles: Studies in Conjecture* (Geneva, Droz; 1963).
L'Art de la Conjecture (Monaco, Éditions du Rocher; 1964).
Kahn, Herman, *On Thermonuclear War* (Princeton UP; 1960).
On Escalation: metaphors and scenarios (Pall Mall; 1965).
Kahn, Herman, and Wiener, A. J., *The Year 2000* (Collier-Macmillan; 1968).
Kahn, Herman, and Bruce-Biggs, B., *Things to Come: thinking about the 70s and 80s* (Collier-Macmillan; 1972).
Kautsky, Karl, *Ethics and the materialist conception of history* (1906; trans. J. B. Askew; Chicago, Kerr, rev. edn; 1909).
Kassouf, Sheen, *Normative Decision Making* (Englewood Cliffs, Prentice-Hall; 1970).
Kee, Alistair, 'Christianity without religion', *The Listener*, 14 December 1972, p. 830.
Keller, Hans, on 'Billy Budd', article in *The Listener*, 28 September 1972, p. 419.
Kermode, Frank, *Romantic Image* (Routledge & Kegan Paul; 1957).
Kettle, Arnold, *William Blake* (Units 21–22 of Age of Revolutions course, Open University Press; 1972).
Kidd, B., *The Science of Power* (Methuen; 1918).
Kitson, Frank, *Low Intensity Operations* (Faber & Faber, 1971).
Kotarbinski, T., *Praxiology: An Introduction to the Science of Efficient Action* (in Polish 1965. Trans. Olgierd Wojtasiewicz, Pergamon; 1965).
Laing, R. D., *The Divided Self* (Tavistock; 1960).
The Self and Others (Tavistock; 1961; Penguin, second edn; 1969).
Laing, R. D., and Cooper, D. G., *Reason and Violence* (Tavistock; 1964) [with a foreword by J. P. Sartre].
The Politics of the Family, and Other Essays (Tavistock; 1971).
Landes, D. S., *The Unbound Prometheus: Technological change and*

industrial development in Western Europe from 1750 to the present (Cambridge UP; 1969).
Larner, John, *Culture and Society in Italy, 1290–1420* (Batsford; 1971).
Lasswell, H. D., *Psychopathology and Politics* (Glencoe, Free Press; 1930).
Politics: Who Gets What When How (1936. reprinted Glencoe, Free Press; 1951).
Lasswell, H. D., Leites, N., and Associates, *The Language of Politics* (New York, Stewart, 1949; MIT; 1965).
Lawick-Goodall, Jane van, *In the Shadow of Man* (Collins; 1971).
Lawrence, D. H., *Psychoanalysis and the Unconscious* (1923. Penguin Books; 1971).
Le Bon, G., *The Crowd: A Study of the Popular Mind* (1895; English Translation, Unwin; 1917).
Lee, J. M., *Social Leaders and Public Persons* (OUP; 1963).
Lee, Wayne, *Decision Theory and Human Behavior* (New York, Wiley; 1971).
Leicester, Colin, *Britain 2001 AD: Forecast of the U.K. economy at the turn of the century* (HMSO; 1972).
Lessnoff, Michael H., 'Functionalism and explanation in social science', *Sociological Review* 17 (New Series) 1969, p. 323.
Levi, Mario Attilio, *Political Power in the Ancient World* (in Italian 1955; trans. Jane Costello, Weidenfeld & Nicolson; 1965).
Lévi-Strauss, Claude, *The Savage Mind* (Weidenfeld & Nicolson; 1966).
Lewino, Walter, *L'Imagination au Pouvoir* (Paris, Losfeld; 1968).
Lewis, I. M., ed., *History and Social Anthropology* ASA Monograph 7, (Tavistock; 1968).
Lieberman, B., ed., *Social Choice* (Gordon & Breach; 1971).
Lipset, S. M., and Rokkan, Stein, ed., *Party Systems and Voter Alignments: Cross-National Perspectives* (New York, Free Press; 1967).
Lloyd, P. C., 'Conflict Theory and Yoruba Kingdoms', in I. M. Lewis (ed.), *History and Social Anthropology* (Tavistock; 1968).
Classes, crises and coups (MacGibbon & Kee; 1971).
Lloyd-Jones, Hugh, *The Justice of Zeus* (California UP; 1971).
Loftas, Tony, *The Last Resource, Man's Exploitation of the Oceans* (Penguin Books; 1973).
Lorenz, Konrad, *Studies in Animal and Human Behaviour*. 2 vols. (Methuen; 1970).
Lowe, Victor, *Understanding Whitehead* (Johns Hopkins UP; 1962).
Lowell, R., *Prometheus Bound* (Faber; 1970).

Lowes, J. L., *The Road to Xanadu: a study in the ways of the imagination* (Boston and New York, Houghton Mifflin; 1927).

Luttwak, Edward, *Coup d'Etat: a practical handbook* (Penguin Books; 1969).

Lutz, W., and Brent, Harry, ed., *On Revolution* (Cambridge, Mass., Winthrop; 1971).

Maass, A. and others, *Design of Water-Resource Systems* (Macmillan; 1962).

McArthur, A., and Long, K., *No Mean City* (1956; Corgi Books; 1964).

Macfarlane, L. J., *Political Disobedience* (Macmillan; 1971).

MacFarquhar, R., *The Hundred Flowers* (Stevens; 1960).

MacIntyre, Alasdair, *Against the Self-Images of the Age* (Duckworth; 1971).

Mackenzie, W. J. M., *Politics and Social Science* (Penguin Books; 1967).

'Models of collective decision-making' in *The Social Sciences: problems and orientations* (The Hague, Mouton, for UNESCO; 1968).

Mackenzie, W. J. M., and Grove, J. W., *Central Administration in Britain* (Longmans; 1957).

McLellan, D., trans. and ed., *Karl Marx: Early Texts* (Blackwell; 1971).

MacNaghten, Hugh (trans.), *The Poems of Catullus* (Cambridge UP; 1925).

Macpherson, C. B., *The Real World of Democracy* (OUP; 1966).

McRae, T. W., ed., *Management Information Systems* (Penguin Books; 1971).

Maddox, John, *The Domesday Syndrome* (Macmillan; 1972).

Mailer, N., *Miami and the Siege of Chicago* (Penguin Books; 1969).

Maine, Sir Henry, *Ancient Law* (1861. OUP World's Classics; 1931).

Malinowski, Bronislaw, *A Scientific Theory of Culture and Other Essays* (North Carolina UP; 1944).

Mao Tse-Tung, 'On Practice', *Selected Works*, Vol. I (Peking, FLP; 1965).

Maranda, Pierre, ed., *Mythology* (Penguin Books; 1972).

Mark, Sir Robert, 'The Containment of Social Violence', reported in *The Times*, 20 August, 1971.

Martino, Joseph P., *Technological Forecasting for Decision-making* (New York, American Elsevier; 1972).

Mather, F. C., *Public Order in the Age of the Chartists* (Manchester UP; 1959).

Matthews, G. V. T., *Bird Navigation* (Cambridge UP, second edn; 1968).

Mays, J. B., *Growing Up in the City: a study of juvenile delinquency in an urban neighbourhood* (Liverpool UP; 1954).

Mazrui, A. A., *Violence and Thought: Essays on Social Tensions in Africa* (Longman; 1969).

Medawar, P. B., *The Art of the Soluble* (Methuen; 1967).

Megargee, E. I., and Hokanson, J. E., eds., *The Dynamics of Aggression: Individual, Group and International Analyses* (New York, Harper & Row; 1970).

Mercer, David, 'A Suitable Case for Treatment', in *Three TV Comedies* (Calder & Boyars; 1966).

Merriam, C. E., *The American Party System: An introduction to the study of political parties in the United States* (New York, Macmillan; 1922).

Political Power: Its Composition and Incidence (NewYork, McGraw-Hill; 1934).

Meyerson, Martin, and Banfield, E. C., *Policy, Planning and the Public Interest: The Case of Public Housing in Chicago* (New York, Free Press; 1955).

Miller, Henry, Review of Thomas Szasz, *The Manufacture of Madness* (Routledge & Kegan Paul, 1971) in the *Listener*, 23 May 1972.

Miller, James G., 'Living Systems: Basic Concepts', *Behavioral Science*, Vol. 10, 1965, pp. 193–237.

Miller, S. M., 'Mirror Error', article in *New Society*, 13 July 1972, p. 86.

Millett, Kate, *Sexual Politics* (Abacus; 1972).

Ministry of Housing and Local Government, *Report of the Working Party on Crowd Behaviour at Football Matches*, Chairman: Sir John Lang (HMSO; 1969).

Mishan, E. J., *The Costs of Economic Growth* (Penguin Books; 1969).

Welfare Economics: an assessment (Amsterdam, North Holland Publishing Co.; 1969).

Cost-Benefit Analysis (Allen & Unwin; 1971).

'To Grow or not to Grow', *Encounter* 40 (1973), p. 9.

Monod, J., *Le hasard et la nécessité: essai sur la philosophie naturelle de la biologie moderne* (Paris, Éditions du Seuil; 1970).

Moore, B., 'Thoughts on Violence and Democracy', *Proceedings of the American Academy of Political Science*, 29 (1968).

Morin, E., Lefort, C., Coudray, J.-M., *Mai 1968: la Brèche* (Paris, Fayard; 1968).

Morris, Desmond, *The Naked Ape: a zoologist's study of the human animal* (Corgi Books; 1971).
Morris, William, *News from Nowhere: or an epoch of rest, being some chapters from a Utopian romance* (1890. Routledge; 1970).
Moss, R., *Urban Guerrilla* (International Institute of Strategic Studies, Adelphi Paper No. 79; 1971).
Moynihan, Daniel P., *Maximum Feasible Misunderstanding. Community Action in the War on Poverty* (New York, Free Press; 1970).
Multi-Level Planning and Decision-Making (Papers for sixth meeting of ECE Senior Economic Advisers – New York, UNO; 1970).
Murray, D. J. and others, *Patterns of Decision Making* (Block VIII, 'Decision making in Britain', Open University Press; 1972).
Murray, G., trans., *Euripides* (1902; Allen & Unwin, London, fourth edn; 1908).
Murray-Brown, Jeremy, *Kenyatta* (Allen & Unwin; 1972).
Musil, Robert, *Young Törless* (1906; trans. Eithne Wilkins and E. Kaiser; Panther Books; 1971).
Neumann, John von, *The Computer and the Brain* (Yale UP; 1958).
Nicholson, Michael, *Conflict Analysis* (English Universities Press; 1970).
Nietzsche, F., *La Naissance de la philosophie à l'époque de la tragédie grecque* (Geneviève Bianquis, trans. and ed., Paris, Gallimard; 1938).
The Genealogy of Morals and The Birth of Tragedy trans. Francis Golffing (New York, Doubleday Anchor Books; 1956).
Nursey-Bray, Paul, p. 154, 'Marxism and Existentialism in the thought of Frantz Fanon', *Political Studies*, 20; 1972.
Oakeshott, Michael, *Rationalism in Politics and Other Essays* (Methuen; 1962).
Olson, Mancur, Jr., *The Logic of Collective Action: Public Goods and the Theory of Groups* (Harvard UP; 1965).
O'Neill, John, *Sociology as a Skin Trade* (Heinemann; 1972).
OECD, *Brain and Behaviour* (Paris, OECD Science Policy Studies; 1972).
Palmer, Tony, 'Have you got Soul', in *The Observer* colour supplement, October 1972.
Palsson, H., and Richards, P., trans., *Hrolf Gautreksson* (Southside; 1972).
Parkinson, C. Northcote, *Parkinson's Law* (Murray; 1957).
Parry, Adam, 'Thucydides' Historical Perspective' in Adam Parry (ed.), *Yale Classical Studies*, XXII (Cambridge UP, 1972), p. 47.

Parsons, Talcott, *The Structure of Social Action: a study in social theory with special reference to a group of recent European writers* (1937; Glencoe, Ill., Free Press, second edn; 1949).
Pattanaik, P. K., *Voting and Collective Choice* (Cambridge UP; 1971).
Pearce, D. W., *Cost-Benefit Analysis* (Macmillan; 1971).
Pearson, John, *The Profession of Violence* (Weidenfeld & Nicolson; 1972).
Peston, M., *Public Goods and the Public Sector* (Macmillan; 1972).
Pinter, Harold, *The Caretaker* (Methuen; 1966).
Podlecki, Anthony J., *The Political Background of Aeschylean Tragedy* (Ann Arbor, Michigan UP; 1966).
Pool, I. de Sola, and Abelson, R., 'The Simulmatics Project', in H. Guetzkow, *Simulation in Social Science* (Englewood Cliffs, N.J., Prentice-Hall; 1962), pp. 70–81.
Popper, Sir Karl, *Objective Knowledge, An Evolutionary Approach* (OUP; 1972).
The Poverty of Historicism (Routledge & Kegan Paul; 1957).
Pörn, Ingmar, *The Logic of Power* (Blackwell; 1970).
Porter, J., *The Vertical Mosaic: an analysis of social class and power in Canada* (Toronto UP; 1965).
Posner, C., ed., *Reflections on the Revolution in France: 1968* (Penguin Books; 1970).
Post, Laurens van der, *The Lost World of the Kalahari* (Hogarth Press; 1958).
The Heart of the Hunter (Hogarth Press; 1961).
Praz, Mario, *The Romantic Agony* trans. Angus Davidson; OUP; 1933).
On Neoclassicism (trans. Angus Davidson; Thames & Hudson; 1969).
Prest, A. R., and Turvey, R., 'Cost-benefit analysis: A Survey', *Surveys of Economic Theory*, Vol. 3, (Macmillan; 1966).
Rabushka, A., and Shepsle, K. A., *Politics in Plural Societies: a theory of democratic instability* (Columbus, Ohio, Merrill; 1972).
Radcliffe-Brown, A. R., *Structure and Function in Primitive Society* (Cohen and West; 1952).
Raggio, Olga, 'The Myth of Prometheus; Its survival and metamorphoses up to the 18th century', *Journal of the Warburg and Courtauld Institutes* 21 (1958), p. 44.
Ramsay, William, and Anderson, Claude, *Managing the Environment: An Economic Primer* (Macmillan; 1972).
Rawls, John, *A Theory of Justice* (OUP; 1972).

Report From Iron Mountain on the Possibility and Desirability of Peace. With introductory material by Leonard C. Lewin (Penguin Books; 1968).

Riker, W. H., *The Theory of Political Coalitions* (Yale UP; 1962).

Robbe-Grillet, A., *Projet Pour Une Revolution A New York* (Paris, Éditions de Minuit; 1970).

Robbins, Lionel, *An Essay on the Nature and Significance of Economic Science* (Macmillan, second edn; 1935).

Roberts, Adam, *The strategy of civilian defence: non-violent resistance to aggression* (Faber; 1967).

ed., *Civilian Resistance as a National Defense: Non-Violent Action against Aggression* (Penguin Books; 1969).

Roberts, Adam, Carter, April, and Hoggett, David, ed., *Non-Violent Action: a selected bibliography* (Housmans, rev. and enl. edn; 1970).

Roberts, J. M., *The Mythology of Secret Societies* (Secker & Warburg; 1972).

Robertson, Roland, and Taylor, Laurie, *Deviance, Crime and Socio-Legal Control: Comparative Perspectives* (M. Robertson; 1973).

Robinson, Richard, *Definition* (OUP; 1954).

Ronay, Gabriel, *The Dracula Myth* (W. H. Allen; 1972).

Rose, C. R., *Governing without Consensus: an Irish Perspective* (Faber; 1971).

Royko, Mike, *Boss: Major Richard J. Daley of Chicago* (Paladin Books; 1972).

Rudé, George, *The Crowd in History: A Study of Popular Disturbances in France and England, 1730–1848* (New York, Wiley; 1964).

Russett, Cynthia, *The Concept of Equilibrium in American Social Thought* (Yale UP; 1966).

Salera, Virgil, *Multinational Business* (Houghton Mifflin; 1969).

Sartre, J. P., *Saint Genet: Comédien et Martyre* (1952; English translation B. Frechtman, *Saint Genet: Actor and Martyr;* W. H Allen; 1964).

Schaller, George, *The Mountain Gorilla: Ecology and Behavior* (Chicago UP; 1963).

Schapera, Isaac, *Government and Politics in Tribal Societies* (Watts; 1963).

Schelling, T. C., *The Strategy of Conflict* (Harvard UP, 1960).

Schneirla T. C., *Army Ants: A Study in Social Organization* (Freeman; 1971).

Schultze, C. L., *The Politics and Economics of Public Spending* (Washington DC, The Brookings Institution; 1968).

Scientific American, *Energy and Power, Scientific American* book (Hart Davis; 1971).
Seale, Patrick, and McConville, Maureen, *French Revolution, 1968* (Penguin Books; 1968).
Séchan, Louis, *Le Mythe de Prométhée* (Paris, Presses Universitaires de France; 1951).
Sen, A. K., *Collective Choice and Social Welfare* (San Francisco, Holden-Day; 1970).
Seton-Watson, R. W., *Disraeli, Gladstone and the Eastern Question* (Macmillan; 1935).
Shelston, A., ed., *Thomas Carlyle, Selected Writings* (Penguin Books; 1971).
Shonfield, A., and Shaw, Stella, eds., *Social Indicators and Social Policy* (Heinemann, for SSRC; 1972).
Silone, Ignazio, *L'Avventura d'un Povero Cristiano* (Milan, Mondadori 1968).
Simmel, Georg, *Conflict and the Web of Group Affiliations* (New York, Free Press paperback; 1964).
Simon, H. A., *Models of Man: Social and Rational* (New York, Wiley; 1957).
The Sciences of the Artificial (Cambridge, Mass., MIT Press; 1969).
Sisson, Charles, *The Spirit of British Administration* (1959; Faber, second edn; 1966).
Skinner, B. F., *Walden Two* (1948 Collier-Macmillan; 1962).
'Freedom and Dignity Revisited', in the *New York Times*, 11 August 1972.
Beyond Freedom and Dignity (Cape; 1972).
Skolnick, Jerome H., *The Politics of Protest* (New York 1951).
Sloan, S., *A Study in Political Violence. The Indonesian Experience* (Chicago, Rand McNally; 1971).
Small, C., *Ariel Like a Harpy: Shelley, Mary and Frankenstein* (Gollancz; 1972).
Smelser, N. J., *Theory of Collective Behavior* (Routledge & Kegan Paul; 1962).
Smith, B. L. R., *The Rand Corporation* (Cambridge, Mass.; Harvard UP; 1966).
Smith, Stevie, *Scorpion and Other Poems* (Longman; 1972).
Snow, C. P., *The Two Cultures and the Scientific Revolution* (Cambridge UP; 1959).
Science and Government (Harvard UP; 1960).
Solmsen, Friedrich, *Hesiod and Aeschylus* (Cornell UP; 1949).

Sorel, Georges, *Réflexions sur la violence* (1906; Paris, Rivière, eighth edn; 1936).

Spielberger, C. D., ed., *Anxiety and Behavior* (New York, Academic Press; 1966).

Anxiety: Current Trends in Theory and Research (New York, Academic Press; 1972).

Stanley, J. Lyndon, *The Making of Walden* (Chicago UP; 1957).

Stapledon, Olaf, *Last and First Men* (1930; reissued in Penguin Books; 1972).

Steering Sub-Committee, Report of House of Commons Expenditure Committee; H.C. 147 of 1971–2, 27 January 1972.

Steffens, Lincoln, *The Shame of the Cities* (New York, Heinemann; 1904).

Autobiography. (1931; Harcourt Brace; 1968).

Steinbach, R. A., *Pain, A Psycho-physiological Analysis* (New York, Academic Press, 1968).

Steiner, G., *Extra-Territorial: Papers on Literature and the Language Revolution* (Faber; 1972).

Steiner, John M., 'Power, Ideology and Political Crime', *International Journal of Criminology and Penology*, 1973 I, p. 5–14.

Stengel, Erwin, *Suicide and Attempted Suicide* (Penguin Books; 1972).

Stone, I. F., *The Killings at Kent State: How murder went unpunished* (New York, Vintage Books; 1971).

Stone, L., *The Causes of the English Revolution, 1529–1642* (Routledge; 1972).

Storey, David, *This Sporting Life* (Longman; 1960).

The Changing Room (Cape; 1972).

Storr, Anthony, *Human Aggression* (Penguin Books; 1968).

The Dynamics of Creation (Secker & Warburg; 1972).

Human Destructiveness (Sussex UP; 1972).

Strategic Survey, 1971, (International Institute of Strategic Studies, 1971), p. 67, 'Political Violence').

Strawson, P. F., and Pitcher, G., ed., *Wittgenstein, The Philosophical Investigations* (Macmillan; 1968).

Streeten, Paul, 'Cost-benefit and other problems of method'; reprinted from *The Political Economy of Environment* (The Hague, Mouton; 1972).

Stringer, J., 'Operational Research for "Multi-organizations"', *O.R. Quarterly*, Vol. 18, p. 105.

Swanson, D. W., Bohnert, P. J., and Smith, J. A., *The Paranoid* (Boston, Little Brown; 1970).

Szasz, Thomas, *The Manufacture of Madness* (Routledge & Kegan Paul; 1972).
Taylor, A. J. P., *Beaverbrook* (Hamish Hamilton; 1972).
Taylor, Charles Lewis, and Hudson, Michael C., *World Handbook of Political and Social Indicators* (Yale UP, second edn; 1972).
Taylor, G. Rattray, *Rethink* (Secker and Warburg; 1972).
Taylor, Laurie, *Deviance and Society* (Michael Joseph; 1971).
Taylor, R., *The Romantic Tradition in Germany: an Anthology* (Methuen; 1970).
Teyler, Timothy J., *Altered States of Awareness* (Freeman; 1972).
Thatcher, David S., *Nietzsche in England, 1890–1914* (OUP; 1972).
Thom, A., *Megalithic Sites in Britain* (OUP; 1967).
Megalithic Lunar Observatories (OUP; 1971).
Thompson, D'Arcy, *Growth and Form* (1917; Cambridge UP, abridged edn; 1961).
Thompson, J. E. S., *Maya Hieroglyphs without Tears* (British Museum; 1972).
Thompson, Richard F., *Physiological Psychology* (Freeman; 1971).
Thomson, George, *Aeschylus: Prometheus Bound* (Cambridge; 1932).
Aeschylus and Athens: A Study in the Social Origins of Drama (Lawrence & Wishart; 1941).
Thomson J. A. K., 'The Religious Background of the *Prometheus Vinctus*', *Harvard Studies in Classical Philology*, Vol. XXXI, 1920, (London, Oxford UP), pp. 1–37.
Tiger L., *Men in Groups* (Panther Books; 1971).
ed., 'Understanding Aggression'; *International Social Science Journal*, 23 (1971).
Tiger, L., and Fox, R., *The Imperial Animal* (Secker & Warburg, 1972).
Toch, Hans, *Violent Men, An Inquiry into the Psychology of Violence* (Penguin Books; 1972).
Toffler, Alvin, *Future Shock* (Pan Books; 1970).
Trevor-Roper, H. R., Article in *The Listener*, Vol. 89, January 1973, p. 101.
Tribus, Myron, and McIrvine, E. C., 'Energy and Information' in *Energy and Power* (Hart Davis; 1971).
Trotter, W., *Instincts of the Herd in Peace and War* (Benn; 1916).
Truman, D. B., *The Governmental Process* (New York, Knopf, 1951).
Tudor, Henry, *Political Myth* (Macmillan, 1972).
Tullock, Gordon, *The Politics of Bureaucracy* (Washington, DC, Public Affairs Press; 1965).
A Practical Guide for Ambitious Politicians (South Carolina UP; 1961).

Towards a Mathematics of Politics (Michigan UP; 1967).

Turvey, R., *Economic Analysis and Public Enterprise* (Allen & Unwin; 1971).

Public Enterprise (Penguin Books; 1968).

Twain, Mark, *The Adventures of Huckleberry Finn* (1834, Penguin Books; 1966).

UNESCO, International Symposium on Human Aggression, Brussels, Belgium, September 11–15 1972.

'Use and Conservation of the Biosphere', Proceedings of the Intergovernmental Conference of Experts on the Scientific Basis for Rational Use and Conservation of The Resources of the Biosphere (Paris, 4–13 September 1968) (UNESCO; 1970).

United Nations, Conference on the Human Environment (Stockholm, June 5–16, 1972): *Man's Home*: (1) The Art of Progress; (2) A Watch on the Arts; (3) A World of Cities; (4) Pollutants.

Vandvik (Eirik), *The Prometheus of Hesiod and Aeschylus* (Oslo, I Kommisjon, Hos Jacob Dybwad, 1943).

Vernon, Raymond, *Sovereignty at Bay. The Multinational Spread of US Enterprises* (Longman; 1971).

Von Der Mehden, Fred R., *Comparative Political Violence* (Englewood, Prentice-Hall; 1973).

Vonnegut, Kurt, *Player Piano* (Panther Books; 1969).

Cat's Cradle (Penguin Books; 1965).

The Sirens of Titan (Hodder & Stoughton, 1967).

Slaughterhouse-Five (Panther Books; 1970).

Vowles, David M., *The Psychobiology of Aggression* (Edinburgh UP; 1970).

Voznesensky, A. A., *Antiworlds: Poems by Andrei Voznesensky;* Patricia Blake and Max Hayward (eds.); trans. by W. H. Auden *et al.*, OUP; 1967).

Wagar, W. Warren, *Building The City of Man: Outlines of a World Civilization* (Freeman; 1972).

Waldo, Dwight, ed., *Temporal Dimensions of Development Administration* (Duke UP, for Comparative Administration Group, 1970).

Walker, N. D., and Others, *The Violent Offender: Reality or Illusion?* (Blackwell; 1970. Oxford University Penal Research Unit, Occasional Paper No. 1).

Walker Report, The, *Rights in Conflict* (New York, Bantam; 1968).

Wallas, Graham, *The Life of Francis Place, 1771–1854* (Allen & Unwin, rev. edn; 1918).

Wallraff, C. R., *Karl Jaspers: An Introduction to his Philosophy* (Princeton UP; 1970).

Walters, P. L. H., 'Farming politics in Cheshire: a study of the Cheshire County branch of the National Farmers' Union', Manchester University Ph.D. thesis; 1970.

Walton, John, 'Substance and Artefact: the Current Role of Research on Community Power Structure'; *American Journal of Sociology*, Vol. 21, 1966.

Ward, Barbara, and Dubos, Réne, *Only One Earth: The Care and maintenance of a small Planet* (Penguin Books; 1972).

Warner, Rex, trans., *Thucydides: The Peloponesian War* (Penguin Books; 1954).

Watson, James D., *The Double Helix: a personal account of the discovery of the structure of DNA* (Weidenfeld & Nicolson; 1968).

'The Double Helix Revisited', in *The Listener*, Vol. 88, 14 December 1972, p. 819.

Waugh, Evelyn, *Decline and Fall* (Penguin Books; 1937).

Weil, Simone, *Intimations of Christianity among the Ancient Greeks* (ed. and trans. E. C. Geissbuhler, Routledge & Kegan Paul; 1957) (based on *La Source Grecque*; published in 1952 by Librairie Gallimard – and *Les Intuitions Pré-Chrétiennes*; published in 1951 by Les Éditions de la Colombe).

Werner, J. S., *A Guide to the Human Adaptibility Proposals* (London, International Biological Programme, second edn; 1969).

West, D. J., *Murder followed by Suicide* (Heinemann; 1965).

Whitaker, Ian, 'Tribal Structure and National Politics in Albania, 1910–1950', in I. M. Lewis (ed.), *History and Social Anthropology* (Tavistock; 1968).

White, D. J., *Decision Theory* (Allen & Unwin; 1969).

Whyte, William Foote, *Street Corner Society: the social structure of an Italian slum* (1943; Chicago UP, second enlarged edn; 1955).

Wiener, N., *The Human Use of Human Beings* (Cambridge, Mass., Houghton Mifflin; 1950).

Williams, Basil, *The Whig Supremacy, 1714–1760* (OUP; 1939).

Williams, Roger, *Politics and Technology* (Macmillan; 1971).

Williamson, Rt Rev. Robin, 'Souvenirs of Ulster', in *The Listener*, 25 May 1972, pp. 678–9.

Wilson, B. R., ed., *Rationality* (Blackwell; 1970).

Wittgenstein, Ludwig, *Philosophical Investigations* (Blackwell; 1963).

Wollheim, R., *Freud* (Fontana-Collins; 1971).

'Ivan Illich', in *The Listener*, 16 December 1971.

'Democracy and Violence', in *The Listener*, 17 February 1972.

Woodcock, George, *Anarchism* (Penguin Books; 1963).

Herbert Read: The Stream and the Source (Faber; 1972).

Woodhead, A. G., *Thucydides on the Nature of Power* (Martin Classical Lectures Vol. 24; Harvard UP; 1970).

Wolfe, Tom, *Radical Chic or Mau-Mauing the Flak-Catchers* (New York; Bantam Books; 1972).

Wolin, Sheldon, 'Political Theory as a Vocation', *American Political Science Review*, 63 (1969), p. 1082.

World Council of Churches, Consultation on 'Violence, Nonviolence and the Struggle for Social Justice', Cardiff, 3–7 September 1972.

Wyndham, John (writing as 'John Beynon'), *Stowaway to Mars* (1935, Coronet Books; 1972).

Wyndham, John, 'Compassion Circuit', reprinted in Kingsley Amis and Robert Conquest (ed.), *Spectrum 4* (Pan Books; 1965).

Young, J. Z., *The Memory System of the Brain* (OUP; 1966).
An Introduction to the Study of Man (OUP; 1971).

Young, Michael, ed., *Forecasting and the Social Sciences* (Heinemann; 1968).

Zashin, E. M., *Civil Disobedience and Democracy* (New York, Free Press; 1972).

Zinn, Howard, *Disobedience and Democracy: Nine Fallacies on Law and Order* (New York, Random House; 1968).

INDEX